P9-DHA-984

DON'T MISS A MOMENT!

2005-2006 Season (ver. 24)

	Rehearse	1st Tech	1st Preview	Open
FRIDAY May 31	June 28	July 2		

Hamlet
Sponsored by Target
Final Performance on Vineland Place

Sunday, May 7, 2006 - 7pm

725 Vineland Place, Minneapolis
612-377-2224 or 1-877-447-8243
SHEILA LIVINGSTON

MAIN FLOOR

AISLE 7
ROW   N
SEAT   68

841511
50.00

000000H

RG6

BOATS

MEASURE

CAROL
Gisselman

KLING

ARLECCH

EDGARDO

TOUR

Jan 3   Jan 17

Jan 22   Mar 19

Nov
Dec
Nov
Nov 2
Feb 5
Feb 12

Forward Motion

Guthrie Theater
2000-2001 ANNUAL REPORT

The Guthrie Theater

Images, History, and Inside Stories

The Guthrie Theater

Images, History, and Inside Stories

by Peg Guilfoyle

Executive Editor | Sheila Livingston
Director of Community Relationships, Guthrie Theater

NODIN PRESS

Copyright © 2006 by Margaret Guilfoyle. All rights reserved.

Printed in China

No portion of this book may be reproduced in any form
without the written consent of Nodin Press, except for review purposes.

ISBN: 1-932472-39-8

09   08   07   06   05   6   5   4   3   2   1

Project Origination: Peg Guilfoyle and Sheila Livingston
Project Director: Peg Guilfoyle, Peg Projects, Inc.

Design by Holly Welch

® Guthrie Theater and "G" are registered trademarks of
the Guthrie Theater Foundation. Used by permission. All rights reserved.

Nodin Press is a division of Micawber's, Inc.
530 N. 3rd Street, Suite 120
Minneapolis, MN 55401

This book is dedicated to those who have shared their Guthrie stories over the years, weaving community as they went. Only a small fraction of stories are in these pages; there are enough to fill a library, or a green room, many times over.

Thanks, too, to the generous photographers: Michal Daniel, Mike Habermann, Joseph Giannetti, Mike Paul and Act Two Photography, T. Charles Erickson, Boyd Hagen, John L. Anderson, Marty Nordstrom, Gerald Brimacombe, Curt Anderson, Timothy Streeter, Carol Rosegg, George Byron Griffiths, Tim Rummelhoff, Donna Kelly. I regret that some photographers are unknown or unfound; the Guthrie archives are, well, uneven.

To Sheila Livingston, who loves these stories as much as I do. Ken did, too.

To Dennis Babcock, who believed in the project from the beginning, and made belief tangible through his support.

To Norton Stillman of Nodin Press, who took this book under his wing.

Thanks to the Guthrie, which issued repeated invitations to its community to participate in the book, provided lists of shows, directors and designers, and actors, and allowed access to its archives. To the intrepid Guthrie fact-checkers, especially Jacque Frazzini and Lee Borah. To Dennis Behl and his encyclopedic memory for Guthrie history and photos. Also to Joe Dowling, Tom Proehl, James Morrison, Melodie Bahan, John Miller-Stephany, Brooke Helgevold, and other Guthrie staff. To Barbara Brown, Jim Worthing, Judith Niemi, Nong Vue. To the running crew, the stage managers, and the 'shop guys,' who are the source of the very best backstage stories and the keepers of the tradition of craft, pride, and excellence.

And to my family, who lived with my long immersion in the research.

The writer Robert Louis Stevenson said, "Every book is, in an intimate sense, a circular letter to the friends of him who writes it."

Here it is, friends.

Peg Guilfoyle

The Guthrie Theater
Images, History, and Inside Stories

Foreword from Joe Dowling

The story of the Guthrie Theater to date is essentially the story of American Theater in the second part of the twentieth century. Opening in 1963 to a fanfare of publicity and excitement throughout the theatrical world, our theater pointed the way for others to follow. It fast became the flagship of the American resident theater movement. It was quickly and joyfully embraced by Minnesotans as a major contribution to the cultural and social life of our great state. Since its very first season, it has consistently produced work of the highest quality.

The foundation of the Guthrie was significantly different from the other pioneer theaters. While the other founders of resident theaters around the country were brave and resilient artists, they were young and untried outside their own areas. When Tyrone Guthrie and his colleagues decided to decentralize the American theater, they were already major figures throughout the world and brought a wealth of experience to the new enterprise. Inevitably, the fame of Tyrone Guthrie and his original company that included Hume Cronyn, Jessica Tandy, Zoe Caldwell and George Grizzard was such that the new institution was seen immediately as the hope of the whole movement. Joseph Wesley Zeigler in his definitive study of our movement, *Regional Theatre: The Revolutionary Stage,* describes the expectations clearly.

> Another more important possibility opened up with the emergence of The Guthrie Theater; the possibility that from the regional theater might come a National Theater for America. Before the Guthrie, there had been scant justification for such an idea. The Guthrie was the first regional theatre that looked as if it could conceivably develop into the realization of a long cherished dream. ...

It was a foolish hope and one that placed an impossible burden on the young "Minnesota miracle." While the Guthrie has evolved into a major national institution, it is clearly not a National Theater for America and, indeed, never aspired to that status. Given the geography and the diversity of culture in this country, a single American National Theater is not a realistic prospect or a desirable objective. The Guthrie Theater is now, as it has been since 1963, a theatre of its time and place. It has nurtured new talent, welcomed major figures from around the world and it has sent many actors, directors, designers and craftspersons into the mainstream of American Theater to spread the word of how special the Guthrie Theater is for both performers and audiences alike.

Now a new chapter is being written in this great story. As we move from the original home on Vineland Place to the new theater complex on the banks of the Mississippi River, we will create new theatrical excitement. We will develop a new generation of actors and audiences who will share the experience of live performance in our unique Thrust Stage, who will discover new adventurous productions in our Proscenium Theater and who will explore new techniques and forms in our Studio Theater. We will welcome many more students to the new Guthrie Learning Center and provide audiences with improved amenities to make their visit to us even more special than before. We will become a National Center for Theater Art and Theater Education.

This book, however, looks back as well as forward and helps to tell the Guthrie story in an immediate and lively way. Peg Guilfoyle has lovingly reached out to actors, stage managers, administrators and audiences who have shared the special times on Vineland Place and in the various spaces throughout the Twin Cities where the Guthrie has spread its wings. It is a wonderful testament to the humor and the fortitude of those who, night after night, both onstage and off, ensure that the audience are given a real sense how special the theater is. Some of the memories are of things gone wrong, some of magical moments where actor and audience connected in a way that is unique to live theater. All of the reminiscences are born of both love and respect; love for the craft that has sustained all of us who devote our lives to the theater and respect for the commitment of so many in our community who have made it possible for the Guthrie Theater to prosper and to grow.

Joe Dowling
Artistic Director
January, 2006

Amadeus, 2001-02 season.

Inside the
Guthrie

Open the door and come inside. We have some stories to tell you. These are the stories that Guthrie people tell each other, laughing or shaking their heads, about their time inside the stage door, in the shops and workrooms, under the bright lights onstage, or in the dim blue darkness of the backstage. Some are as fresh as today's performance, and some have been rattling around since 1960, when Sir Tyrone Guthrie and his associates landed in Minnesota to found a theater, and discovered an embracing community and a home. These tales are told over dinner and a bottle of wine wherever Guthrie folk gather – and by now, that could be anywhere on the globe. Two thousand actors, a thousand artists, five hundred or so community leaders, five thousand or more staff and artisans, unknown thousands of volunteers, and several million audience members complete the magic circle of story and listener. Once you've heard the fanfare, and settled back to see what there is to be seen, you are in the circle for good. You are part of the story.

People love to tell these tales, which spring from the passionate heart of the theater. It is a place endlessly boiling with artistic ambition, with idiosyncratic and opinionated people, right ready to do battle on behalf of their ideas. It's a crucible, and an enormous craft guild, both joyous and fierce. Great texts are the infrastructure, ideas form the currency. The next opening night is always coming, inevitable and relentless. Every person who walks through the door has something to prove. New stories are occurring every single day and hour.

The past is often present at the Guthrie, where the sense of tradition is everywhere. Guthrie people are keenly aware that they are the latest in a long line of artists and artisans to take the stage here, and of the inevitably ephemeral quality of the work they do. Every time a play closes, it is gone, along with all the work that created it. It will never return. Honoring the past with photo displays and artifacts is only a partial defense against disappearance. Most of the past is carried in the people and in the stories they tell about themselves, about each other, and about what the Guthrie Theater is.

This then is a collection of stories about the inside of the Guthrie Theater from its very beginnings, and from every section of its complicated and sometimes contentious community. They are revealing, stirring and sometimes comical (at least in retrospect). They might persuade the reader that every day in the theater is full of events, humor, artistic ambition and hard work. It is. You might gather that the theater is populated and surrounded by the creative, the opinionated, the dedicated, and those whose lives are full of dreams. Right again. The distinguished actor Hume Cronyn said in 1964, "We are members of a preposterous and sentimental profession." Well, yes. Come inside the Guthrie and listen to the offstage voices. We have some stories to tell you.

Opposite: *Medea*.
Stephen Yoakam, Brenda Wehle.
1990-91 season.

One of the ongoing themes at Guthrie dinner parties is that of the young person whose life was changed by the big theater. It happened to me in 1972. I was green, but not too green to have already been through my own theater disaster, as it seems nearly all young theater enthusiasts must. At Indiana University, some graduate students – how much older they seemed! – announced plans to start their own theater the following fall. Would I come and be their first stage manager? I could "go Equity." Whatever that was. On the day after graduation, I moved to Indianapolis. It turned out there wasn't any stage managing to be done over the summer. The theater had to be founded first, and by the time the fall opening came around, I was shaking hands at cocktail parties and writing promotion copy. The theater hired a more experienced stage manager, then a promotion person who actually knew something about promoting, and in January I was 'let go.'

The technical director, kindly, suggested the Guthrie to me, and me to the Guthrie. I had an idea it was in Milwaukee. I packed my car with everything I owned and started driving north.

I was hired as the most junior assistant in group sales, although I didn't really know any groups. I worked on a regional wall map; we pushed a pin into every city from which groups of senior citizens traveled to the theater. I learned to lurk in the dark at the back of the house during rehearsals, watching the stage managers operate and listening to Michael Langham's British accent. So exotic. I leaned against the wall at staff parties. It was not a great season. In the fall, the budget went south, my barely-above-penury position was cut, and I was again let go.

I lived the customary wandering theater life for seven years, working here, working there, like so many others. I came back to the Guthrie in 1980 as stage manager for a small production, rapidly followed by big ones, and stayed nearly ten years making plays with Liviu Ciulei, with Lucien Pintilie, Peter Sellars, Garland Wright and many more. I was a stage manager, then production stage manager and eventually production manager, the boss job for all the producing departments of the theater. That work formed my personal aesthetic and taught me everything I know about standards. I hardly ever came out of the basement on Vineland Place, even to get married and have my first child, who came to work with me at age three weeks. With my second, I left the staff but kept the contact, writing regularly for the theater, seeing most shows, and over time gaining the longer view that daily production work absolutely eliminates.

I lunched regularly with Sheila Livingston, my former fellow-traveler in senior citizen sales, who over time held nearly every position on the Guthrie staff. She knew almost everyone, and I knew the rest of them. We ate, we laughed, we repeated stories we'd seen or heard. Eventually we realized that the stories we told were largely unknown and that, however brief, acerbic, or even scatological, they held truth about the Guthrie and about the people who make it up. This book was born.

It is hard to decide on my favorite Guthrie story. It might be the night during the run of *Who's Afraid of Virginia Woolf?* when Patrick Stewart was on stage. Stewart has what you might call a strong following, based on his years on television as a Star Trek captain; the theater invested in a new security system before his arrival in Minneapolis. As the story goes, one evening the doorbell rang at the stage door, and the night man pushed a button to activate the camera. On the little screen was a Klingon warrior in full regalia, demanding to see "Captain Picard." In the Klingon language. Through an interpreter (presumably Minnesotan, or at least earthling). There's another version of this story, in which the Klingon and interpreter come to the box office to buy tickets.

Or a wedding I attended on stage in 1988, on an off night from *Richard III.* The stage crew chief and his bride rose from the trap room below the stage aboard a gigantic Shakespearean throne, under ominous stage light with show music filling the house, with maybe 75 Guthrie folk and family sitting right down front.

I remember an enormous gospel choir standing up from the mass of onstage risers during the first preview of *The Gospel at Colonus,* following conductor J.D. Steele, swaying left, swaying right, opening their mouths to sing and leaving the stunned audience with their hair standing on end from the power of the music.

There is a story told in the box office about a woman who was a Guthrie subscriber with her entire family, for years. When she died, her family kept the seat and filled it with a dozen red roses for the rest of the season.

In a long and hilarious conversation with some impossibly inventive scene shop artisans, I was told a mischievous story about placing some leftover scrap steel – they always had plenty around – in the old upstairs lobby between the Guthrie and the rather formal Walker Art Center on Vineland Place, and fabricating a perfect Walker-looking modern-art-identifying plaque for it. It stood there in splendor for several weeks before the hoax was discovered.

I've heard a report from a visitor to the London apartment of then-elderly Tanya Moiseiwitsch, the astonishing and seminal designer who, with Guthrie, designed the thrust stage in 1963. Among the memorabilia of her lifetime in the theater, a Minnesota Twins cap, sitting atop a bottle of Scotch.

As the theater's production manager, I was often stunned by the detailed perfection the shops created. For a beautifully-set period dinner table for *The House of Bernada Alba* in 1987, the propmaster researched exactly how dinner tables were set in rural Spain in 1900, fabricated what was needed, and provided the actors with an exquisitely complete, correct and right world in which to play a crucial scene. There isn't even a photograph of that; I looked.

My favorite memory, though, probably, is the sunny fall afternoon in 2003 when ground was broken for the new theater complex by the Mississippi River. The young actors from the theater's partnership program with the University of Minnesota, working for their Bachelors of Fine Arts under the wing of the Guthrie, stood on risers with the river behind them and the wind blowing their hair, lifting their chins and singing their hearts out, from Stephen Sondheim's *Merrily We Roll Along*. Each one was greatly talented. Each one was thinking inside 'look at me! Look at me!' "Feel the flow," they sang.

> Hear what's happening:
> We're what's happening.
> Don't you know?
> We're the movers and we're the shapers.
> We're the names in tomorrow's papers.
>
> It's our time, breathe it in:
> Worlds to change and worlds to win.
> Our turn coming through,
> Me and you, pal,
> Me and you!

Among the singers was Santino Fontana; two years later, he was cast to play Hamlet in the closing production at the old Guthrie on Vineland Place. It was his time.

Also in 2003, the actor Hume Cronyn, then nearing age 92, returned to the Guthrie where he first captivated audiences as *The Miser* in 1963. Seated onstage with artistic director Joe Dowling, Cronyn regaled the audience with tales both touching and ribald, and finally rose to deliver a speech from *Henry VI, Part 3*. All frailty fell away. He rose, crossed down left (with the lights dimming and following him), and held the audience spellbound with just words and actor power.

In those snippets, and in the stories that follow, lie the heart of the Guthrie Theater.

Any theater is a kind of rabbit warren, full of busy-ness, or a kind of factory where everything is one-of-a-kind, and handmade, and has only a brief purpose.

All around and behind and above and below the actor you see is a hive full of people creating the illusory world which the actor inhabits for the audience. Ushers close the doors, and close out the outer world, slipping last-minute patrons into their seats as the house lights dim. Other actors are poised in the dark, waiting for their entrances, or pulling on their costumes in their dressing rooms. The crew, dressed in black clothing to make them disappear, are ready at their stations on stage, in the fly spaces above looking down, or below in the trap room. Wardrobe folk are preparing for quick changes and maybe ironing a frill or throwing in a quick load of laundry. In the booth behind and above the audience, behind dark glass, the light and sound board operators are poised over the 'go' buttons on their computerized consoles. Follow spot operators have climbed into their constricted quarters, just big enough for them, a stool, and their big lighting instruments. Hidden musicians, surrounded by cups of coffee, pick up their instruments and turn their attention to the score. The stage manager takes a look at the opening sequence of cues that will orchestrate this complicated dance, pauses, and speaks softly into the headset. "Standby, house to half," she says. "House to half: Go." A collective breath is taken. The play begins, perhaps with a single voice or with a rush of entrances or a clap of thunder. The theater buckles down and goes to work; we are carried away.

There are many theaters, in Minnesota and elsewhere, but few can match the size, longevity and ambition of the Guthrie. Leading world artists of the time planted it in 1963 as an "oak tree," completely skipping the acorn stage. It was eagerly embraced by a community and state, and became the fortunate beneficiary of their constant and increasing attention, support, and pride through the decades – a magnet for the most artistically ambitious and a place with resources to permit them freedom to create.

It is, too, a place with decades of history, which creates its own kind of stability and force. There has been time for Minnesotans who came to the Guthrie as young students to grow up, have families, and bring their children back to meet Shakespeare. Some of those who attended student matinees are now teachers who bring their classes to the theater. The children of some of the original trustees have become the theater's community leaders. Young actors have transitioned from ingénue to leads to character work; the children of actors made their debut on the thrust stage, and have returned full-grown. Young artisans and staff people came to the Guthrie to learn from the best, and went on to lead other theaters across the country. The Guthrie is, in every season, a place where someone is thrilled to be; it is always someone's Golden Age.

To look over the list of productions the Guthrie has presented since 1963 – well over five hundred and going upward with every new season – is to go on a long and absorbing tour through the very best literature the theater can offer. You could read your way through human history, ranging freely through the centuries, dipping into the minds of playwrights and the human characters they've created. Except that literature and theater are not the same thing. Plays are meant to be made by people, and watched by people. Each of the five hundred, for each of the thirty or forty performances, was created by actors, directors, designers, artisans, crew folk, for that audience only, for that moment only. It is the theater people that make the art.

The work is ruthlessly difficult. It is hand-made, and heavily dependent on both art and craft. At every step, from the writing of the words to the making of the prop to the delivering of the speech in a pool of light, the work is touched and formed by human hands and choices. Every moment on the stage is created by a thousand decisions. From the darkened seats, we see the ideas of the playwright and his time, however antique, the contemporary intelligence of the director and designers, the skill of the artisans, and the craft and spirit of the actors, all join together. In the air between the speaker and the listener, a brief and brilliant life is kindled.

And sometimes it does not catch. Any of those thousand decisions can make it go wrong. Art is elusive, and can be notoriously indifferent to the resources brought to bear on its creation. It is an alchemy, and subject to disappearance at whim. Theater people who are in it for the long haul, whether they are professionals or audience members, teach themselves to love some aspect of the work, become aficionados of costumes, or a particular actor, or a particular writer or director. Look, look at that splendid gown, that shaft of light, that young actor, that stirring monologue. There is always and always something interesting to watch in the fantastic interplay on stage, when the thousands of ideas are compressed into a few hours and turned outward toward the seats for your pleasure. And that way your time is well and enjoyably spent in the hours or seasons or years while you watch for the moment when all effort disappears, the house is held spellbound, and the actors themselves, transcended, are touched with gold. You never know when the moment will come and, if you aren't paying attention, it may elude you entirely. It may come in a familiar text, or a play you've never heard of, or one you really had thought you'd skip. Watch, though. Be ready. In the nature of all things theatrical and alive, once it is gone, it is gone. It will never return.

Except in the memory, in the stories that are told. There are many such moments in the stories that follow.

The theater, and the Guthrie Theater, is a house for art and for the audience. Without the audience, someone told me in the backstage, we'd just be having a dinner party with interesting clothes and a lot of particularly witty conversation. Without that presence, the months and seasons and years of planning and craft and rehearsals would be for nothing at all. Theater can't be presented for itself. Your presence is requested; your presence is required.

> The first time I directed at the Guthrie Theater, I had never seen a production there and so I arrived at the first preview and there's this moment. You're sitting there and everyone's talking before the play starts and the audience is reading their programs and talking to their friends, and there's this moment where all of the doors around the theater close. And I'd never experienced a moment like that in my life. The sound, the blocking-out of the rest of the world. Everyone who had been looking at each other turned and looked straight at the stage and, literally, the stage glowed. In my mind. With the energy of people looking at it. And the actor who made the first entrance was also new to the space. She walked out that night and she said to me later 'I never experienced anything like that. I stumbled over their energy. I walked out and fell over it.' [Director Garland Wright]

That is what the audience, rustling, chatting, brings in to the theater.

What makes the hours of the play especially bright? It may be the hazard and impossibility of trying to make Art for every performance – the work of the actors and the brilliant engine of people that back up the work you see in the lights. It's partly, or perhaps entirely, about the brilliant energy of the performers reaching out to, and mixing with, the potential energy of the audience, bringing in with them their days and their lives, and releasing them when the lights go down. For the audience, that exchange may be unconscious. For at least some actors, it is a tool deliberately employed. Audiences watch actors. Actors watch audiences, too.

> We come in the backstage, through the stagedoor and we go through the maze of the place, and we come out and collect our piece of cheese at the other end. We don't see the audience. We don't. The light's in our eyes, we can't see. And so it could easily become kind of a little rote kind of a horrible thing. So what I do is, if I'm working with some people in the afternoon, I think about their faces in my head before I go on. I picture those people. Or I find a peek hole where I find one person in the house and say, that person's never seen this before and I'm going to keep them in my mind as I play it. And it helps me keep that energy up.

> You're constantly analyzing the audience. We play differently in the afternoon for the kids than we do for the adult audiences. And in almost every show, we know where the first laugh is. If an audience laughs at that, we know that they're listening and we've got a start. And then we can tell the direction it goes in. And that gives us a barometer for about nine or ten more moments in the play.

> If we lose the barometer, we know how we have to adjust to get it back. Anytime you can get laughs, it's so much easier to get the serious moments in there. And we can tell whether perhaps our performance is becoming too melodramatic or too funny, too pandering. We can tell pretty quickly. Are we leading the audience or are they leading us? So, when an audience laughs at something that we feel it's too much or we've gone too far, it's a slap in the face. There are little adjustments we make constantly through the play. It's like making a piece of clay pottery every night, and each one is different. [Actor Peter Michael Goetz]

Sometimes – more often than might be thought – the work on the stage reaches out and shapes someone's life in a direct way. Robert Booker was a student in 1972; he grew up to be the head of the Minnesota State Arts Board.

> When the Guthrie's *Of Mice and Men* tour came to Sioux Falls we high school kids were allowed to help unload the truck. Now this seems like grunt work for most, but for a young guy interested in theater, this was the Big Time. I can still remember rolling the dusty prop trunks off the truck and helping unload the flats on to the stage of the Sioux Falls Community Playhouse, an old Orpheum Theater. That night as I sat in the front row of the theater, I saw the Guthrie magic for the first time. There were the flats I'd helped unload. Let me repeat, the ones I helped unload. And there was the play with the great Guthrie actors and all of the wonder of live professional theater. I can remember it all so clearly even today.

When I left the South Dakota Arts Council to seek my fortune in Minnesota, I was given the prop rake from *Mice and Men*, which had been a gift to the council from the company after that tour. Today the rake proudly holds my bathrobe. I think of the theater and how it changed my life every morning.

And of course, the other kind of day can live in the memory, too.

> I was at a matinee (filled with noisy students) of some Restoration play, and had somehow secured a seat right alongside one of the voms. I remember Jeff Chandler taking this heroic pose, turned like a Watteau painting, ready to exit, and distinctly muttering above the crackle of candy wrappers and buzz of teenagers: "Goddamned kids" and then racing down the vom. [Screenwriter and one-time actor Ken LaZebnik]

So what kind of life is it, has it always been, backstage at the Guthrie? Humor (often of the in-the-trenches variety) and irony are mainstays of backstage culture in every exchange and endeavor, except the one most central to Guthrie life. The work itself – the pursuit of the artform – is taken with utter seriousness. The absolute importance of getting it right for the audience – right being defined as the playwright's intention and the director's vision filtered through the lens of company, shops, and crew – is axiomatic. That is the work of the Guthrie, and may be its most deeply embedded tradition.

It is a hard life, with long hours and high pressure. It is a rhythmic life, with intense work periods that lead inevitably to an opening night, and a closing. It is a ritualized life, marked with regular celebrations and ceremonies. It is intensely collegial and even intimate, with more than a fair share of romances, both brief and prolonged, and a full schedule of hellos and goodbyes, weddings, births and funerals. It has some of the characteristics of a family, framed closely in many of the characteristics of a business. The audience must be found for the work to go on, and office work is leavened by the occasional surprise appearance.

> I was working in my office one day, at a time when my office opened up into an area we used to call the Dram, where there were coffee and pop machines. Well, you forget in your office that sometimes when the theater is in mid-rehearsal or mid-show, the actors have big long breaks. Some are offstage for quite a long period of time and sometimes they come upstairs and they'll wander around the building. So you can be sitting at your desk and have a guy in a big poufy purple costume go by, carrying a soda and eating a candy bar. Even after all this time, it still throws me off a little bit because I'm so in awe of what they do. I worry. I think, if you talk regular words during the show, won't you forget what you're supposed to say in the play? It throws me to see the actors talk to me when they're listening to an intercom, waiting for their line to go back on. Wearing their purple poufy costumes. [Long-time staffer Trisha Kirk]

The Guthrie culture is a life based on classic texts, important ideas, and scholarship, although it is not a kind of scholarship that would necessarily be recognized in a classroom. When you study a play to present it, and then do forty performances, you carry those texts inside you as a kind of gift. You know the words, the work of the words, and the intention. This is true for actors, of course, and directors and designers. It also happens to others.

> One of the really cool things about this job is that every new show is like going back to school, in the best possible way. Along with everybody in the cast and company, we get a wonderful education on a whole new world, for every play we do. We get to spend a quality amount of time, and a quantity amount of time sitting around a table discussing the texts, tearing it apart, figuring out exactly what these people mean. The context, the milieu, the place these characters are in the world, the history of the time period. For a new play, we sometimes have the playwright right there. We have a world class dramaturg who can tell you about any aspect of the world of the play, where it fits in history and society. It's quite a remarkable opportunity, a remarkable experience.

> We do forty shows, or fifty, or thirty, for the run of the play and then we move on to the next one. We are exposed to a constantly-changing workplace. For me, that's one of the reasons why this job is like no other. If you don't like the show you're working on, maybe you'll like the next one, or the next. [Stage manager Chris Code]

> I often wonder as a stage manager when I'm up in the booth and watching the audience, I wonder if they really get it as much as I get it? Because I've been studying it for six weeks or so. And when I see the audience get it, I realize that six weeks was really worth it. That's why we take that much time to study and work on these plays; because we want to relay all that to the audience in three hours. [Stage manager Jenny Batten]

It is endlessly inventive; a life of constant problem-solving, as many of the stories in this book attest. At the Guthrie, it is a life of craft and quality; no one could impose the standards the Guthrie craftspeople seek to meet. For them, it is a matter of pride and tradition. They are keenly aware of what has been accomplished in the past, rigorous to uphold the standards in their time and pass them to the younger artisans coming up.

It is a life full of what might be called high-profile personalities. Many are included here. Some are not. I've left out all enraged actors who fling their costumes on the floor and stomp on them, and those who are predatory in the after-hours bar. I've left out the ghosts. And the sex in the flyspace. I've largely left out the petty, the demanding, the unreasonable, and the just plain incomprehensible. Those things are brief flashes against the long arc of the work.

And since 1963, it has been work ongoing. Administrations have come and gone. Artistic directors have made their marks and moved on. Perhaps two thousand actors have trod the boards; around five hundred community leaders have served as trustees.

And in all of those seasons, the rhythm of backstage life, with its humor, its incident, its cast of unseen characters, has been steady. Every day, the staff comes to work to make the theater possible. Eight times a week, and more, the company gathers, the pre-sets are made and checked, and the lights go down.

With full intention, and by glorious chance, through all the artistic directors and the collective strength of craft and ambition of the workfolk, the Guthrie has lived every moment to its fullest possible extent since 1963. No day is a quiet one. All days contain the lively, the idiosyncratic, the artistically ambitious. Out of the clash of ideas comes the work. An attentive ear can hear beneath the daily boiling the distant tread of the audience who will arrive on opening night. And every night at the half-hour call, the mechanism takes a breath and opens the doors to the house. Here comes the audience to complete the work.

One audience member wrote:

> A tiny moment best sums up my feelings about the Guthrie. As the actor came onstage to begin the most famous soliloquy from *Hamlet,* I could feel the audience rustle in anticipation of "To be or not to be." I heard a man about three rows behind me whisper, "Here it comes." That is my life at the Guthrie, waiting in my seat as the lights go down – holding my breath.

Peg Guilfoyle

Opposite: *You Can't Take it With You.*
Julie Briskman, Charles Janasz.
1997-98 season.

Clockwise
from upper left:

In the lobbies, 1965.

Poster, 1968.

St. Paul season posters,
1968 and 1969.

Advertising, 1963.

Opening night
tickets, 1963.

Steering Committee,
ca. 1962.

Brochure, 1963.

Volunteer report, 1966.

Lee Richardson gets
help with mask, *The
House of Atreus,* 1967.

Pulling tickets, ca. 1963.

Opening night
outfits, 1969.

Dedication
invitation, 1963.

725 Vineland Place,
ca. 1963.

Hume Cronyn
and Zoe Caldwell,
The Miser, 1963.

The Guthrie Theater

The Guthrie Theater opened on May 7, 1963 with a production of *Hamlet* directed by Sir Tyrone Guthrie, the theater's founder, who at that time was widely-regarded as the foremost director in the English-speaking theater.

The idea of the theater began in 1959 during a series of conversations among Guthrie and two colleagues – Oliver Rea and Peter Zeisler – who were disenchanted with Broadway. They wanted to create a theater with a resident acting company that would perform the classics in rotating repertory – several plays seen at the same time – with the highest professional standards.

The Guthrie became a prototype for an important new kind of theater, contrasting with the commercial environment of Broadway. There, the high costs associated with mounting a production, even in 1959, increasingly mandated that shows must be immediately successful at high ticket prices. The Broadway atmosphere was not conducive to producing the great works of literature, to cultivating the artists' talents, or to nourishing the audience over time.

The idea of a major resident theater was introduced to the American public in a small paragraph on the drama page of *The New York Times* on September 30, 1959, which invited cities to indicate interest in Tyrone Guthrie's idea. Seven cities responded: Waltham, MA, Cleveland, Chicago, Detroit, Milwaukee, San Francisco and Minneapolis. From Minnesota, Dr. Frank Whiting of the University of Minnesota wrote a response letter in, he said, "a moment of brashness and daring."

It has often been said that the Guthrie founders planted an oak tree, not an acorn, in Minnesota. Attracting the theater, raising the funds, erecting the building, selling tickets for the first season – it was a massive community effort.

John Cowles, Jr., then the Associate Editor of the *Minneapolis Star* and *Tribune* newspapers, was among the first community leaders to support the unusual and somewhat grandiose idea of bringing Tyrone Guthrie and a classical repertory theater to their city. The story of the 'conversation on the train' is part of Guthrie legend.

I got involved with the Guthrie by sheer chance. Sage and I had gone to Des Moines on the night before a big football game between the University of Minnesota and the University of Iowa, in the fall of 1959. We were attending a party at my cousin's house, and among the guests were Betty and Oliver Rea. I fell into conversation with them. I discovered what he was up to, which was traveling around the country beginning to look for places to locate a new away-from-Broadway resident theatre company. I liked them and I wanted to talk further about that, so I said "Let's try to sit together on the train from Des

STAGE UNIT SLATED OUTSIDE OF CITY

Guthrie Among Planners of Permanent Company That Would Perform Classics

By LOUIS CALTA

Concerned over the centralization of the legitimate theatre in New York and the general lack of opportunities for burgeoning professional actors, three prominent show people have taken steps to remedy these conditions.

The group, composed of Oliver Rea, produce...

lively and intelli... believe that such ... be fully successf... only if its works ... identified with the... city where it plays...

Too many citi... said, were being r... more and more... status where their... have very little co... portunity to origina... cultural ideas."

Broadway Dep...

"Mr. Guthrie," Mr... on, "has given me t... of his life. He doesn... work on Broadway b... climate has become v... because it no longer ... where one can really ... as an artist."

For himself, Mr...

The New York Times, September 30, 1959

Opposite: Tyrone Guthrie in the unfinished theater, 1962, at 725 Vineland Place in Minneapolis, across Hennepin Avenue from Loring Park.

Moines to Iowa City tomorrow morning, on our way to the football game."

Oliver and I spent most of that trip – I suppose it was about an hour and a half – talking about this project of his, and when we parted, I said "Why don't you look at Minneapolis?" He said "As a matter of fact, we are. We've gotten a letter from Frank Whiting at the University of Minnesota urging us to come." I said they should let me know when they came to Minneapolis and I gave Oliver my card, and so on.

Well, Oliver came, and we did connect. I had a couple of lunches for him and at one point, maybe even Guthrie himself, later on that fall. But I kind of had to stand aside while Frank Whiting tried to sell the trio on coming to the University of Minnesota.

After Frank gave up and Guthrie had turned him down, I said "well, let me keep going and see if I can't find a place for you that will be a better location." I was punching around, looking for some kind of framework in which to locate this thing, and finally I went to Harvey Arnason. He was part-time Art History Department at the University and part-time running the Walker Art Center in those days, in the old Moorish building. This was 1959 or perhaps early 1960. In hindsight things moved amazingly quickly.

I was keenly aware of the fact that while we had a pretty good symphony orchestra and a pretty good full-line museum in the Institute, we had no theatre to speak of. We had occasional road shows, which played in an awful hall called the Lyceum, and Don Stolz's Old Log. That was theatre. Oh, there might have been a few other groups scattered around, but really, that was about it. It seemed to me to be a big gap in the cultural offerings of this area. Just by sheer chance, Guthrie's book *A Life in the Theatre* came out in that Christmas season of 1959. I read it and was really quite entranced by all of that. I thought, this is really a first class guy we're backing here. That was reinforced when he was knighted by the Queen, which happened during our fundraising phase. That was perfect. I think it doubled attendance at the Women's Club, for example … it was Sir Tyrone and Lady Guthrie!

Also, he had no front. He wasn't interested in trying to make a good impression by how he dressed or namedropping or any of that. He was beyond feeling the need to impress anybody. He was very disciplined, though, when it came to his public appearances on behalf of the theater, really very good and attentive. The only thing he wouldn't do, which convention would otherwise require, was wear socks. He just never wore socks. Hated 'em, even with tuxedos and so on. He just wouldn't wear them.

Opposite: Tyrone Guthrie and company begin *Hamlet* rehearsals, 1963.

Our aim with the Minnesota Theater Company is to present a series of the greatest plays as well as we can. Whether the result is uplifting, purifying, corrupting, entertaining – or boring – depends only partly upon us. We'll do our best to interpret the plays. But what the public makes of our efforts … well, that's your business. The theater after all is a two-way traffic between the audience and the stage. … [Sir Tyrone Guthrie]

Tyrone Guthrie
Artistic Director 1963 – 65

In 1960, a steering committee that had been formed to attract Dr. Guthrie and his new theater to the Twin Cities obtained a commitment from the T.B. Walker Foundation to provide the land behind the Walker Art Center for a building and to contribute $400,000 for construction. The Walker itself was located in a rather Moorish-looking building on Vineland Place, across Hennepin Avenue from Loring Park.

The steering committee itself agreed to raise at least $900,000 from the community. Its members were H. Harvard Arnason, Pierce Butler III, John Cowles, Jr., Roger Kennedy, Otto Silha, Philip von Blon, Frank Whiting and Louis Zelle.

> A little further along in the proceedings of enticing the Guthrie to come here, John Cowles arranged to take a group of us to New York on the *Minneapolis Star* airplane to have lunch at the Century Club with the trio. The group was made up of the original steering committee and a few others. At that time, the thought of going to New York for the day was unheard of and excitement was high. Clearly the trio was impressed by the delegation, quite probably because of the youth of the group. We later heard that this contrasted with the Detroit entry, which was leather bound letters from the fancy folk of Grosse Point. [Louis Zelle]

> John Cowles, Jr. and others made a fine presentation, but as we left the meeting, we passed the Milwaukee delegation waiting in the lobby to present what we feared might be an even more effective bid. [Dr. Frank Whiting]

The triumvirate: Peter Zeisler, Tyrone Guthrie and Oliver Rea.

Tyrone Guthrie considering sites for the new theatre:

> Minne or Milly? Which shall it be?

Minneapolis won the day, and in 1962 the fledgling organization distributed a "long-playing" record aimed at potential ticket buyers. Dr. Guthrie's recorded voice was cultured, energetic, and very British. The message was charming and frank. He avoided any tinge of being, as he said, "dreadfully uplifting."

> A book only lives when taken from a shelf and read, so we build public libraries where the great works of literature are available for all. Likewise, we build galleries and museums in which important works of art can be enjoyed. Great music is just a mysterious splatter of dots on lined paper until a musician translates it into expressive sound. So we organize professional orchestras and build concert halls.
>
> Then there's drama. The great plays of our civilization can only live, can only entertain us, move us and inspire us when they are performed with high competence in satisfactory surroundings. But we haven't yet in most parts of the English speaking world, undertaken the creation of professional theater

Guthrie Will Locate His Repertory Theater in City

By BARBARA FLANAGAN
Minneapolis Star Staff Writer

Dr. Tyrone Guthrie and his activities will be built adjacent to the Walker Art center, it ter. with funds raised by a public campaign. The T. B. theater was being announced early Walker foundation voted $400,000 for the theater this afternoon at a press con-

ference in Walker Art center building at their annual meeting May 17.

The theater for Guthrie's choice of Minneapolis followed months of discussion between a group of Minnesota men interested in the theater and Guthrie's associates, Oliver Rea and Peter Ziesler of New York.

Both Detroit, Mich., and Milwaukee, Wis., were interested in building a theater for Guthrie, but the Irish-born director had indicated a preference for Minneapolis.

In an agreement with the Walker foundation's resolution, Guthrie and his associates will direct and manage a non-profit repertory theater company with 20 weeks of performances a year.

The acting group will be organized as a non-profit Minnesota corporation and will co-operate with the University of Minnesota theater.

It was his friendship with Dr. Frank Whiting, director of the University theater

Guthrie and Rea came to Minneapolis while touring the United States last fall looking for a theater site. They originally wanted to locate on the campus, but funds were unavailable for the project.

Whiting and Guthrie agreed at that time, however, that if the theater were in Minnesota, the University theater troupe would benefit by working with the professional company.

Although no date has been set to start the theater building, the fund committee headed by John Cowles, Jr., Minneapolis, has a year to raise $900,000.

Guthrie is famous for making the Shakespeare festival at Stratford, Canada, a success. In London he was associated with the Old Vic theater company for many years.

His most recent theatre success is the current Broad

companies which will do for drama the sort of things which libraries, art galleries and concert halls do for the sister arts.

The theater is still regarded by many as a rather morally dubious activity, and by many more as a form of entertainment, which if it's any good, will pay its own way. But no one expects picture galleries, museums, libraries or orchestras to pay their way. We believe that the theater at its best is no less indispensable to the health of the community than any of the other arts. And that the arts are as indispensable to a healthy community as its hospitals, universities, or churches.

Of course there are those who look upon classic theater as Culture, with a very capital C, as some kind of dreadfully uplifting experience. But that's not our view. We believe that the theater's business is to entertain, yet that entertainment needn't always be frivolous, nor on the other hand need frivolity exclude a serious, and yes, elevating, aim.

In his book *A New Theatre*, 1964, Guthrie talks about his first visit to the Twin Cities. The wise hosts brought him out in the fall, and drove him around the sparkling lakes framed by red and gold trees.

> But the river itself was what most charmed and amazed us. It had not yet frozen over and was flowing with a lively sparkle through winding gorges. … Eventually the Twin Cities will realize that their river can be, and ought to be, a wonderful and life-giving amenity without losing any of its utility.

Ralph Rapson, a prominent Minneapolis architect, designed the Guthrie Theater, and considers the opportunity of working with Sir Tyrone "a singular and wonderful experience." Rapson believed firmly in the thrust stage, but when it came to the color of the seats, architect and director had their differences. He talked about the experience in a 1988 interview for public television.

> Well, the working relationship with Sir Tyrone Guthrie and all his people at best may be described as traumatic. It seemed as though we were always fighting about something, then we'd come back the next day as though nothing had ever happened. I found him to be an exciting, invigorating, dynamic, arrogant, obnoxious bastard. He was always surrounded by this great entourage of people, and they'd wait until the great man made it clear what his feeling was about the design and then they'd all pounce on the Midwest architect. [Rapson]

> Guthrie and Moiseiwitsch were adamant that they should be of one color. I think it was a dark blue … which actually was the same color as the seats in Stratford, Ontario. And Ralph said they should be multi-colored. [Guthrie's partner Oliver Rea]

Every time I would see Guthrie he would say well, how are we doing on the seats, the coloring and so on, and I remember giving him almost every possible excuse I could think of. I think when they finally came they started uncrating the seats a couple of weeks before the theater opened and I was afraid the poor man was about to die or something! [Rapson]

There's a story of Guthrie and Rea meeting with prominent locals in a Rochester, Minnesota, living room in 1961 and beginning his pitch about why no city could consider itself truly civilized without a classical theater.

Suddenly, Rea was startled to hear Guthrie say that American plays like Arthur Miller's *Death of a Salesman* would be possible choices for the first season. Until then, Guthrie had been adamant about an all-classical, European repertory, and afterwards Rea asked Guthrie about the shift.

"Well dear boy, this quite charming gentleman came up to me and said *Death of a Salesman* was his favorite play and would we ever consider doing it. And I decided maybe we could do American plays of potential classic stature on occasion. Don't you think that would be all right?"

Thus was the theater's philosophy formed. Brad Morison, who told the story, said "We were flying by the seats of our pants more than anyone ever knew." (Morison was Audience Development Director from 1963-1968.)

From the very beginning, the somewhat improbable new venture rode on a wave of volunteer enthusiasm. In the 1963 souvenir program, Morison wrote about a memorable meeting, arranged for the volunteer group, the Stagehands. Stage and screen star Robert Preston, of *Music Man* fame, was the guest speaker; the theme was selling subscriptions for the new theater.

It was seven below zero. The wind that Sunday afternoon in January 1963 howled across Loring Park and whistled through the cracks of the as yet unfinished Guthrie Theatre.

Music Man Robert Preston stood huddled in an overcoat in one of the entrance ramps peering out at the 700 Stagehands who sat shivering on the cold cement for the season ticket drive kickoff meeting. "Incredible turnout," he whispered.

His cue came. "Seventy-six Trombones" blared out from the loudspeakers and Preston bounced out to the rostrum.

"I'm here this afternoon," he told the crowd, "representing the many theatre people all over the world who consider your project the most exciting thing that's happened in theatre in a long, long time. We want you to know that, and we want you to know that many of us are just begging for a chance to work in a theatre like this with a man like Dr. Guthrie."

He spun out his reasons, introduced some members of the Minnesota Theatre Company, then lowered his voice for a final remark: "From now on you're the most important people to this theatre. Because you're the ones who have to make the theatre and this ticket drive go."

And they did.

By mid-February, the Stagehands sold more than 14,000 season subscription tickets, setting a national record for noncommercial theater subscriptions. The Stagehands had 600 members, and blanketed an area within a 100-mile radius of the Cities.

It was an extraordinary opportunity for people like myself, who loved going to the theater, to be part of the adventure. Guthrie knew from the beginning that he could count on educators, artists, community leaders and corporations to make the theater thrive but I think that the army of everyday citizens were a surprise. I was at the Southdale Mall with the beautiful Flying G logo prominently displayed on our booth when someone asked what cereal we were giving away. She thought the G could only mean General Mills. It was an endless round of coffee parties, mailings, phone calls and planning meetings. We were tireless, we were excited, we knew we could help make it happen, and we did! [Sheila Livingston]

Every grand campaign has a few moments that become iconic over the years. This one canonized a certain Sunday school class in Mankato.

Lou Gelfand opened the door to his office and laughed all over again. It was still something of a shock to see his desk in the middle of a 30 x 50 foot art gallery full of pottery and jade. But that's where the administrator of the new non-profit Tyrone Guthrie Theatre Foundation had his headquarters.

Gelfand's job was to coordinate the monumental fund-raisng efforts being made by the finance committee: arrange appearances for Rea and Guthrie; make as many speeches himself as possible; recruit volunteers; get things organized; open the mail. He sat down to perform the latter task.

Things seemed to be going well. The T.B. Walker Foundation grant had given the drive real momentum. Nobody was actually turning down requests for money, and contributions were coming from all over the Midwest – from businessmen, housewives, professional men, corporations, clubs, and school benefits. Yet they were little more than half-way to the goal of $2,300,000, and things were getting tougher. Gelfand wondered if they'd ever actually make it to the end of the road.

The next letter he picked up jingled. He slit the end. Out fell $6.37 with a short note from a Sunday-school class in the town of Mankato, Minnesota. An enormous smile spread across his face. Somehow there didn't really seem to be too much to worry about.

That 'widow's mite' of $6.37 was one of nearly 8,000 contributions that built the Guthrie Theatre. [Brad Morison and Kay Fliehr, 1968]

Stagehand enthusiasm in a mimeographed newsletter.

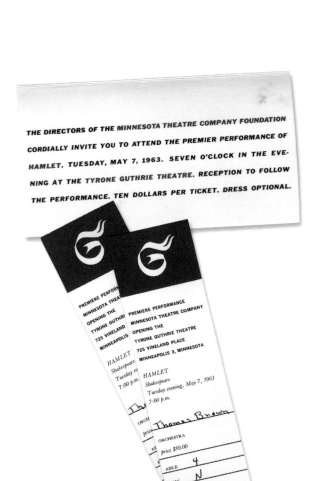

Designer Tanya Moiseiwitsch
working on, and wearing, stage armor.

Tanya Moiseiwitsch was Tyrone Guthrie's close collaborator on scenic and costume design, and on the design of the Guthrie stage, which was a radical departure from the customary proscenium, or picture-frame, stage. The "thrust" stage, surrounded on three sides by the audience, had been built by the same team at the Stratford Festival in Canada; the Minneapolis stage was the second thrust by Guthrie and Moiseiwitsch. It was the signature feature of the new theater.

Sir Tyrone and Lady Judy made quite a social stir in 1960s Minneapolis.

> Tony and Judy Guthrie were quite devout and attended St. Mark's regularly when they were in town. One Sunday a local elderly lady who considered herself a grande dame sat in front of them, and at a quiet time during the service she turned around and said , "Oh, Sir Tyrone, I don't believe we've met, I am Mrs. ____." Tony looked at her and said in a loud voice, "Silence, woman, this is the house of God." The entire congregation was delighted. [Louis Zelle]

The opening of the Guthrie focused the spotlight of national attention on the Twin Cities of Minneapolis and St. Paul, attracting out-of-town drama critics, according to *Newsweek,* "as thick as the smelt running in the northern streams." Stories and articles about the Theatre appeared in 1963 in almost every daily newspaper in the U.S. and Canada, and many sent correspondents to review the plays. Internationally, newspapers in Glasgow, Kenya, Copenhagen, Stockholm, London, Sydney and France carried stories. "The year's most exciting theatrical event," said the Washington *Post. Newsweek* called it "conceivably, the most important theatrical opening of the generation," and "the most pleasurable theater-going experience in the United States."

"The Tyrone Guthrie Theatre is a cause for celebration," said *The New York Times,* and "There is here something of the mood of a Stockholm or an Oslo … a mixture of sophistication and brawny love of the outdoors in the state of 14,000 lakes. … Affluence, a high educational level and civic leadership, combined with the spirit of a small town in the midst of a metropolis, have set the stage for Sir Tyrone Guthrie's triumphant entrance."

Tyrone Guthrie was famous in his profession, and outside it, and his new Guthrie Theater was a very big splash. Actors of all kinds wanted in, as Ken Ruta remembers:

> Well, I couldn't get a reading for the Guthrie Theater. I couldn't get it. I sent letters, but I didn't have an agent, and I read in *The New York Times* that they were in the final days. And somehow, out of blue, they called me. It was up in some hotel. In one room was the secretary and then you'd go into the other

room and talk to them for the interview, and then the actors would come out and tell the secretary, "Well, I am to book a time for an audition."

Well, I went into that room and babbled. For some reason, I'd brought all these pictures of me in beards and Guthrie would say, "Oooh, very good make-up! Very nice!" And I kept telling him how much I loved him: I was just babbling. And he said, "Well, perhaps we'll work together someday." And he didn't tell me to come back.

I remember walking out into that hall, and thinking I'm going to jump down the elevator shaft. And then, Guthrie's head pops out of the door, "Oh! Forgot to tell you! Come back tomorrow, and bring something … loud."

Ruta was cast as the Ghost (at the tender age of 26) and the 2nd Gravedigger in *Hamlet,* in the company with Jessica Tandy, Hume Cronyn, George Grizzard, Zoe Caldwell and others. He remembers trying to take his curtain call.

There used to be that window up there on the old stage. And Guthrie thought it would be so wonderful for the Ghost to be up there watching the whole thing, during the bows. Opening night, I'm climbing up the ladder and there's someone up there already; it was a photographer from *Life* magazine. I kept saying, "It's my curtain call! It's my curtain call!" but he just kept saying, "Get the hell out of the way!" and shooting pictures. So I never got to take my curtain call.

Lady Judith Guthrie gazes out front on opening night. What was called the 'greensward' was, at least on this occasion, covered with automobiles.

A theater is an enormous and complex machine to put together for the first time, and must function both behind the scenes and in the front, for the audience. One day, someone thought of music in the lobby.

Late one afternoon, I received a call from Douglas Campbell. The theater was thinking of having some trumpeters play a fanfare before each performance and could I possibly 'dash off an idea by tomorrow morning?' That night I wrote the fanfare, called for three trumpet players and a field drum player and asked them all to come over to my house for a late night rehearsal. The next morning I lined them up in the lobby and had them perform for Tyrone Guthrie and Douglas Campbell, and I was hired as the Guthrie's first musical director. Looking back, I think it was because I was fast, efficient, and showed up on time! [Herb Pilhofer]

Dick Whitbeck, who was on the staff for sixteen years starting in 1968, started playing fanfares in the lobby on four-foot trumpets.

We usually just carried the trumpets at our sides, but we did have to ask people to move so the sound wouldn't be right in their faces; it was a pretty robust sound. We played them over the stairwells, so people couldn't bump into the horns and knock our teeth out.

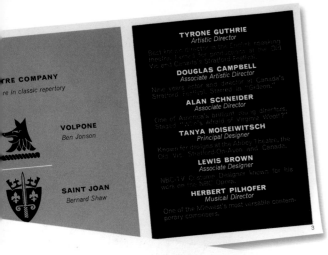

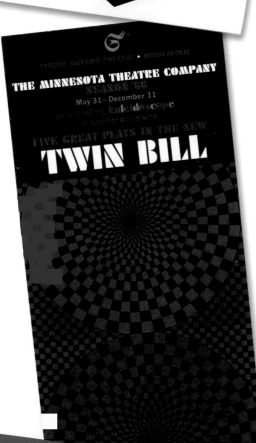

"Guthrie hates orchestra pits," said Oliver Rea, "but he likes to use music. He wanted a place where the musicians could be heard but not seen." The solution was a pit located up near the ceiling on the stage right side. Herb Pilhofer remembers calling it "the birdcage."

> During *Hamlet*, the production had special permission from the Fire Marshal to have 'total blackness' in the house during part of the grave scene. The whole house was pitch black with only a faint blue streak of light radiating from the opening of the stage floor/grave, which was at the center of the thrust. That is, until one of my adventurous trumpet players decided that during his break he would explore the theater a bit. He wandered into the dark basement area and flipped on every available light switch "to have a look around." A huge stream of light, an explosion of light, burst out of the grave opening. Tyrone Guthrie almost killed us all.

In the spring of 1964, the actor Hume Cronyn was in a dressing room in Boston, rehearsing a play for John Gielgud, and thinking of his previous season in Minneapolis, where he and his wife Jessica Tandy had anchored the 1963 company.

From Boston, he wrote:

> And what goes on in the rehearsal room of the Tyrone Guthrie Theatre? Tony's fingers will be snapping like fire-crackers. He will be pointing out that such a word has a final "D" or "T" and correcting pronunciations in French as well as English. The words 'cadenza', 'arpeggio', 'con brio', or 'ralentando' will be heard frequently, puzzling such musical clods as I. Through it all he will range back and forth across the platforms like a restive moose, infecting the company with a marvelous enthusiasm and revealing miracles – to say nothing of a touch of bare ankle above his sneakers. I wish I were there.

Dissension is integral to creative effort, or so people like to remind themselves while they are arguing. Here Brad Morison and Kay Fliehr reported staff consultation on designing a brochure for the 1965 season. One suspects that the actual discussions might have been more frank.

> Dear boy, we must not say our theatre is breathtaking. Let the people say it. [Tyrone Guthrie]

> What we need is more pizzazz in our printed stuff and promotion. More show biz. [Oliver Rea]

> I absolutely despised those purple and green colors we used on last year's brochure. [Tanya Moiseiwitsch]

Now we're getting somewhere. The orange and magenta in the Op art design are more memorable – like the purple and green in 1964. [Oliver Rea]

Take out that 'autumn adventure in theatre.' I just don't want it used. [Peter Zeisler]

I guess we have to tell people what the plays are about, but why do we have to use so many adjectives? [Douglas Campbell]

I'd like to have a brochure with a plain white cover and small type in the lower right-hand corner that said "Minnesota Theatre Company – 1965 season." [Oliver Rea]

Your 1965 brochure is terrible. It looks like the annual report for a bank. Or a funeral parlor. [Danny Newman]

Dear girl, we don't have to tell people what the plays are about. Just tell them the names and the fact that we're doing them. [Tyrone Guthrie]

The final summation came from a beleaguered art director, who can be imagined sitting in the middle of the room: "The trouble with the theater is that everyone there is an artist."

From the very beginning, busses pulled up on Vineland Place and students poured into the Guthrie, beginning a torrent of young people who would attend in succeeding years. Special series of student matinees sold out; in September 1964, the theater appointed its first Educational Advisory Council. In early 1965, a shortened version of *Macbeth* toured to high schools and played to 20,000 students.

Support for the founding of the theater had come from across the state of Minnesota, and touring outside the Cities started early at the Guthrie. A "combination touring company and traveling seminar" was sent out to colleges in the fall of 1964. *The Platform Now and Then* was written by John Lewin and James Lineberger; eight actors, including Paul Ballantyne and Robert Pastene, traveled.

One Guthrie-going couple found a particular way to study scripts before taking their seats on Vineland place:

For the first four or five years we attended the Guthrie, we would meet a weekend before the performance with three other couples, assign parts and read through the play we were about to see. It really enhanced the performance for us.

One highlight for us was *Richard III* (1965) with Hume Cronyn as Richard. The back of his throne was toward the section we were sitting in.

Hume Cronyn as *Richard III*.

Cronyn would lean around the edge of the throne and deliver his asides directly to us – eyeball to eyeball – unforgettable! [Lorens and Phyllis Brynesta]

Guthrie's stagings of the classics on both sides of the Atlantic had made him famous; he was said to bring out the very best in actors.

And that admonition. He'd say, "astonish me in the morning, dear boy," and of course you'd be wracking your brains trying to astonish the great man. And you couldn't, you couldn't.

It didn't matter what was happening. The roof could be falling in and he'd look at you and say, "rise above it, dear boy, rise above it." As a philosophy in life, it's absolutely magnificent. Rise above it, whatever the hell it is. It's not just, 'oh, I got better as an actor.' It's 'oh, you helped me define a philosophy.' That's extraordinary. [Charles Keating]

A letter received January 23, 1965, from a stalwart member of the board of the Duluth chapter of the Stagehands:

Dear Kay,

Here is the bill for expenses for the past two months that you asked me to send you.

Bus to Mpls for Mrs. Helling	$1.55
Telephone calls to Superior, Wisc	$1.00
Bus to Eveleth and return	$ .85
Yoho Photography (film repair)	$6.00
Tow truck hauling out of drift during film delivery	$2.00
Total	$11.40

I showed the film to 3,500 children and 712 adults in the last two months. Some of these expenses may be above and beyond the call of the Guthrie.

My husband said he was willing to pay for the new fender inasmuch as I had already dented it before I went into the snowdrift, but he balked at paying for the tow charges.

We really came out of the experience quite well. Johnny's toe, which was frost-bitten when he walked for the tow truck, is back to normal size.

I had planned to come to Minneapolis next week, but I chipped my front tooth on the steering wheel when I skidded into the drift and won't be through with the dentist until week after next. So I'll plan to see you then.

Cordially,
Biz Spencer

Opposite: *The Three Sisters*, 1963.

Douglas Campbell
Artistic Director 1966 – 67

The well-known classical actor and director Douglas Campbell became Artistic Director in 1966. Campbell had been Tyrone Guthrie's protégé in Minnesota since 1963, directing four plays on the mainstage and regularly performing leading roles, and had directed at the Stratford Festival Company in Canada. Campbell was Guthrie's choice to lead his namesake theater.

We think we have a point of view about our audiences: It is not enough merely to entertain those people who are already accredited and converted "attenders" of the theatre. We must play each season a repertoire of great variety which will strike some kind of happy medium between plays for that audience and plays which will attract to the theater another and new audience not yet used to the theatrical mystique. [Douglas Campbell]

In October 1966, Guthrie-goers could hardly get into the theater. A *Minneapolis Star* writer remarked that looking toward Parade Stadium, "where there is now nothing but earthmoving equipment and twisted land, in three years there will be Interstate Hwy 94, direct to downtown St. Paul."

View from the Guthrie to the Basilica of Saint Mary, 1965.

It was very difficult getting to and even finding the Guthrie. We were getting lots of phone calls about this. To help alleviate this problem we bought a huge Goodyear-type balloon, put a big red Flying G on it and flew it over the Guthrie as a landmark for people to use to locate us. [Don Schoenbaum, later the Managing Director.]

We would 'launch' it about 90 minutes before the performance as a beacon for those seeking culture. I recall standing in the lobby before the show one rather gusty night when, like in a Superman episode gone terribly wrong, everyone approaching the theater was looking up and pointing, and then I saw the blimp dive bombing Vineland Place. I raced to the roof of the theater with an usher or two to wrestle the beast back to its dock. [House manager Dan Berg]

STAGEHANDS —

Annette Garceau has asked if we can again help with the wolf pelts for the House of Atreus. It is urgent and immediate. Perhaps on your ushering days you could arrive at 9:30 and help again after seating and between intermissions – or plan on entire days when possible starting now. Report below stage by soft props. Thank you. Call Pat Rahders 825-0407 with questions.

* * * * * * * * * TA3

Annette Garceau, a co-founder of the costume shop, called for help from the volunteer group, who logged 480 hours assisting with wolf pelts.

In 1967, David Feldshuh was a young actor at the Guthrie, on a McKnight fellowship, rehearsing *The House of Atreus*.

I was sitting on a sofa in a narrow hallway near the old stage door. Suddenly, to my right I spied the towering figure of Tyrone Guthrie striding down the narrow hallway in my direction. I stand, nearly blocking the passageway and with false confidence but determination introduce myself. "Dr. Guthrie, I'm David Feldshuh." "Oh, yes, Feldshuh," he says, looking down on me and speaking with that memorable British music in his voice. "Good to see you again." He said it with such conviction and shook my hand so firmly that for a moment I thought that perhaps I had met him although I didn't think I would have forgotten it. In any case, I felt like a welcomed co-worker and that the captain was glad I was on board. In the next few days, Guthrie took us into rehearsal.

In the big rehearsal hall, the remarkable actors of that era were seated in a giant circle. Guthrie was perched on a higher chair, if I remember correctly, a chair like a bar chair. I was watching in awe and silence, a very young, very green, and very beginning actor. Guthrie announced that he wanted everyone to think about a specific challenge: how to impress upon the audience that the Furies were descending with blood revenge onto future generations.

I took this assignment most seriously and thought about it a lot. I came up with an idea and found a moment to tell Dr. Guthrie about it. The next rehearsal was again in the big rehearsal room, and again everyone was there. Dr. Guthrie announced to all, "Feldshuh's had a marvelous idea …" and he went on to explain it. And he used it in the production.

I have lived with the memory of Dr. Guthrie's generous mention of "my idea" for over 25 years. And I often think of Dr. Guthrie because to this day if I'm rehearsing and a young student has an idea that I'm going to try, I stop rehearsal for a moment and with Guthrie's presence perched over my shoulder,

Some rehearsals for *Julius Caesar* took place outside, with the new Walker Art Center beginning to rise in the background. Twenty-eight extras for *Julius Caesar* were from Minneapolis North High School. Herb Pilhofer remembers going out to the old Metropolitan Stadium one balmy afternoon to direct and record 18,000 Minnesota Twins fans in shouting "Hail, Caesar!" for the production.

I announce the student's name and my belief that he or she has offered us "a marvelous idea." I like to think that Guthrie would be pleased to know that the theater he helped create is nurturing another generation.

A St. Paul season in the Crawford Livingston Theater was added in the winter of 1968-69 and experimental theater was presented at The Other Place on Harmon Place in Minneapolis, the first manifestation of the desire for other performing spaces that would eventually lead to the theater's move to a new location in 2006. The new locations brought new audiences and new styles.

"The St. Paul opening," it was reported, "was something of a social blast. A host of social and civic leaders reported." At The Other Place, by contrast, "no gowns, no tuxes, no champagne. … It seemed to be about 80 percent theater people."

In that same winter, the Guthrie traveled to New York and Los Angeles with *The House of Atreus* and *The Resistible Rise of Arturo Ui*. The plane, converted to carry both freight and passengers, held "3,550 cubic feet of platforms, props, costumes, set and technical gear, along with 35 actors, three stage managers, 16 dependents, two dogs, one cat, one cello and 11 production personnel," reported the *Minneapolis Star*.

~

Sir Tyrone Guthrie died at home in Ireland on May 15, 1971. Sir Alec Guinness gave the address in a service at St. Paul's, Covent Garden, the 'actors' church.' He said, in part:

> 'A great tree has fallen.' Those were the words used by an old family friend, on the rather Chekhovian Guthrie estate, when it became apparent that death had claimed Tony Guthrie. …
>
> He was, I suppose, our own, original, home-grown 'enfant terrible' of the theatre; galvanizing, delighting and shocking a whole generation of performers and spectators, long before more recent 'terrible children' were born or thought of. And he showed no signs, even at the age of seventy, of relinquishing his provocative activities. …
>
> But he was not only a great man of the theatre, he was great in himself. Extremely witty – sometimes devastatingly so; generous with money and time to a fault; interested in all men and loving most; I think the clue to his greatness lies in the fact that he was never 'all things to all men' but, on the contrary, always totally himself to all men. He never cut his cloth, or trimmed his sails, to suit other personalities, but gave wholly himself. A man of the greatest integrity. …
>
> He had great personal humility – and rather hoped for it in others. And riding above all else was his laughter – rich, ironic, kind and memorable.

~

Minneapolis Tribune Photo by Powell Krueger
MEMBERS OF FIRST-NIGHT AUDIENCE ARRIVED AT 'THE OTHER PLACE'
New repertory theater in Minneapolis opened Wednesday night

GUTHRIE GANG'S NEWEST

No Tuxes, Champagne—Just Fine Theater at Other Place

By ALLAN HOLBERT
Minneapolis Tribune
Staff Writer

That Guthrie gang just keeps opening new theater operations right and left.

A couple of weeks ago it was the new St. Paul season, sometimes known as Guthrie East. Wednesday night it was The Other Place, an experimental theater known in the trade as Guthrie West No. 2.

The Other Place was christened with the premier of John Lewin's "The Blood of an Englishman" and two other one-acters by Moliere, "The Flying Doctor" and "The Jealous Husband."

THE ST. PAUL opening was something of a social blast. Formally attired theater lovers squeezed "She Stoops to Conquer" between preplay cocktails and dinner and a postplay champagne party. A host of social and civic leaders attended.

The opening of The Other Place didn't have all that dazzle. No gowns, no tuxes, no champagne. There was a miniskirt here and there and some of the men wore mod-type sweaters and military jackets. You could have a cup of coffee if you threw some change into a plate marked T. O. P. A host of social and civic leaders did not attend.

It was, however, one of the toughest audiences a Twin Cities company ever will have to play for . . . or against. It seemed to be about 80 per cent theater people.

TAKE THE front row, for example. There was Lewin, that Minnesota Theatre Company jack-of-all-trades tensely watching the birth of his baby; Mr. and Mrs. Cy Walter (he runs the Firehouse Theater); and John Donahue, Roberta Carlson, Frank McGovern, Wendy Lehr and Ben Bohle, all of the Children's Theater Company of the Minneapolis Institute of Arts.

And scattered about in the near-capacity audience of about 280 were such other theatrical luminaries as Grace Keagy, Emery Battis and Bob Mitchell, all of the Minnesota Theatre Company; Barbara Morison of Theater in the Round, and Jim Scott of Brave New Workshop fame.

After the plays everyone stood around for a while in the chilly wood-paneled lobby areas of the old build-

1963 SEASON

Hamlet
William Shakespeare
Directed by Tyrone Guthrie
Set and costumes by Tanya Moiseiwitsch
Lighting by Richard Borgen
Music by Herbert Pilhofer

The Miser
Molière
Directed by Douglas Campbell
Set and costumes by Tanya Moiseiwitsch
Lighting by Richard Borgen
Music by Paul Fetler

The Three Sisters
Anton Chekhov
Directed by Tyrone Guthrie
Set and costumes by Tanya Moiseiwitsch
Lighting by Richard Borgen
Music by Herbert Pilhofer

Death of a Salesman
Arthur Miller
Directed by Douglas Campbell
Set by Randy Echols
Costumes by Carolyn Parker
Lighting by Richard Borgen

Hamlet.
George Grizzard, Jessica Tandy
and company.

45

1964 SEASON

Henry V
William Shakespeare
    Directed by Tyrone Guthrie
    Set and costumes by Lewis Brown
    Lighting by Richard Borgen
    Music by Herbert Pilhofer

Saint Joan
George Bernard Shaw
    Directed by Douglas Campbell
    Set and costumes by Tanya Moiseiwitsch
    Lighting by Richard Borgen
    Music by Dominick Argento

The Glass Menagerie
Tennessee Williams
    Directed by Alan Schneider
    Set and costumes by Lewis Brown
    Lighting by Richard Borgen
    Music by Herbert Pilhofer

Volpone
Ben Jonson
    Directed by Tyrone Guthrie
    Set and costumes by Tanya Moiseiwitsch
    Lighting by Richard Borgen
    Music by Dominick Argento

Henry V.
George Grizzard and company.

1965 SEASON

Richard III
William Shakespeare
   Directed by Tyrone Guthrie
   Set and costumes by Lewis Brown
   Lighting by Richard Borgen
   Music by Herbert Pilhofer

The Way of the World
William Congreve
   Directed by Douglas Campbell
   Set and costumes by Tanya Moiseiwitsch
   Lighting by Richard Borgen
   Music by Purcell/Pilhofer/Stokes

The Cherry Orchard
Anton Chekhov
   Directed by Tyrone Guthrie
   Set and costumes by Tanya Moiseiwitsch
   Lighting by Richard Borgen

The Caucasian Chalk Circle
Bertolt Brecht
   Directed by Edward Payson Call
   Set and costumes by Lewis Brown
   Lighting by Richard Borgen
   Music by Herbert Pilhofer

The Miser (revival)
Molière
   Directed by Edward Payson Call
   Set and costumes by Tanya Moiseiwitsch
   Lighting by Richard Borgen
   Music by Paul Fetler

The Way of the World.
Company.

1966 SEASON

The Skin of Our Teeth
Thornton Wilder
> Directed by Douglas Campbell
> Set and costumes by Carolyn Parker
> and Tanya Moiseiwitsch
> Lighting by Richard Borgen
> Music by Herbert Pilhofer

The Dance of Death
August Strindberg
> Directed by Douglas Campbell
> Set and costumes by Lewis Brown
> Lighting by Richard Borgen
> Music by Herbert Pilhofer

As You Like It
William Shakespeare
> Directed by Edward Payson Call
> Set and costumes by Tanya Moiseiwitsch
> Lighting by Richard Borgen
> Music by Paul Fetler

The Doctor's Dilemma
George Bernard Shaw
> Directed by Douglas Campbell
> Set by Dahl Delu
> Costumes by Lewis Brown
> Lighting by Richard Borgen

S.S. Glencairn
Eugene O'Neill
> Directed by Edward Payson Call
> and Douglas Campbell
> Set by Dahl Delu
> Costumes by Lewis Brown
> Lighting by Richard Borgen
> Music by Dominick Argento

The Skin of Our Teeth.
Lee Richardson, Nancy Wickwire
and company.

51

1967 SEASON

The Shoemaker's Holiday
Thomas Dekker
 Directed by Douglas Campbell
 and John Olon Scrymgeour
 Set and costumes by Dahl Delu
 Lighting by Richard Borgen
 Music by Dominick Argento

Thieves' Carnival
Jean Anouilh
 Translated by Lucienne Hill
 Directed by Stephen Porter
 Set and costumes by Carolyn Parker
 Lighting by Richard Borgen
 Music by Herbert Pilhofer

Harper's Ferry
Barrie Stavis
 Directed by Tyrone Guthrie
 Set and costumes by Lewis Brown
 Lighting by Richard Borgen

The House of Atreus
From the Oresteia by Aeschylus
 Adapted by John Lewin
 Directed by Tyrone Guthrie
 Set and costumes by Tanya Moiseiwitsch
 Lighting by Richard Borgen
 Music by Dominick Argento

The Visit
Friedrich Durrenmatt
 Adapted by Maurice Valency
 Directed by Mel Shapiro
 Set by Dan Snyder
 Lighting by S. Leonard Auerbach
 Music by Herbert Pilhofer

The House of Atreus.
Robert Pastene, Douglas Campbell, company.

1968 SEASON

Twelfth Night
William Shakespeare
- Directed by Robert Lanchester
- Set by Ben Edwards
- Costumes by Jane Greenwood
- Lighting by Jean Rosenthal
- Music by Conrad Susa

Serjeant Musgrave's Dance
John Arden
- Directed by Mel Shapiro
- Set and costumes by Karl Eigsti
- Lighting by S. Leonard Auerbach
- Music by Conrad Susa

The Master Builder
Henrik Ibsen
- Adapted by Emlyn Williams
- Directed by Stephen Porter
- Set by Ben Edwards
- Costumes by Jane Greenwood
- Lighting by S. Leonard Auerbach
- Music by Conrad Susa

The Resistible Rise of Arturo Ui
Bertolt Brecht
- Translated by George Tabori
- Directed by Edward Payson Call
- Set and costumes by Richard L. Hay
- Lighting by Richard Borgen
- Music by Herbert Pilhofer
- Film sequence by S. Leonard Auerbach

Merton of the Movies
Marc Connelly
and George S. Kaufman
- Directed by Mel Shapiro
- Set by Karl Eigsti
- Costumes by Fred Voelpel
- Lighting by S. Leonard Auerbach
- Music by Herbert Pilhofer
  and Arthur Kleiner

The House of Atreus (revival)
From the Oresteia by Aeschylus
- Adapted by John Lewin
- Directed by Tyrone Guthrie
- Set and costumes by Tanya Moiseiwitsch
- Masks by Carolyn Parker
- Lighting by Richard Borgen
- Music by Dominick Argento

At the Crawford Livingston Theater

She Stoops to Conquer
Oliver Goldsmith
- Directed by Douglas Campbell
- Set by Robert D. Mitchell
- Costumes by Carolyn Parker
- Lighting by Richard Borgen

Tango
Slawomir Mrozek
- Adapted by John Lewin
  with Tadeusz Gierymski
- Directed by Edward Payson Call
- Set by Robert D. Mitchell
- Costumes by Carolyn Parker
- Lighting by S. Leonard Auerbach

Enrico IV
Luigi Pirandello
- Translated by Eric Bentley
- Directed by Mel Shapiro
- Set by Robert D. Mitchell
- Costumes by Carolyn Parker
- Lighting by S. Leonard Auerbach

At The Other Place

Blood of an Englishman
John Lewin
The Jealous Husband and
The Flying Doctor
Molière
- Directed by William Greene

Little Murders
Jules Feiffer
- Directed by Lee Richardson

Red Cross
Sam Shepard
The Indian Wants the Bronx
Israel Horovitz
- Directed by Michael Pierce

The Man with the Flower in his Mouth
Luigi Pirandello
- Directed by Len Cariou

Quirk (improvisations)
- Directed by Omar Shapli

Halloween
Leonard Melfi
- Directed by Michael Pierce

Charlie
Slawomir Mrozek
- Directed by Mel Shapiro

Brecht on Brecht
Bertolt Brecht
- Directed by Robert Lanchester

On Tour

New York and Los Angeles
The House of Atreus and
The Resistible Rise of Arturo Ui

Serjeant Musgrave's Dance.
Paul Ballantyne, Charles Keating,
Emery Battis, Len Cariou.

55

1969 SEASON

Julius Caesar
William Shakespeare
   Directed by Edward Payson Call
   Set by Douglas Schmidt
   Costumes by Carrie Fishbein Robbins
   Lighting by Robert Scales
   Music by Herbert Pilhofer

The Beauty Part
S. J. Perelman
   Directed by Philip Minor
   Set and costumes by John Jensen
   Lighting by Robert Scales
   Music by Arthur Kleiner

The Homecoming
Harold Pinter
   Directed by Joseph Anthony
   Set by Douglas Schmidt
   Costumes by John Jensen
   Lighting by Robert Scales

Mourning Becomes Electra
Eugene O'Neill
   Directed by Mel Shapiro
   Set and costumes by Karl Eigsti
   Lighting by Robert Scales
   Music by David Karr

Uncle Vanya
Anton Chekhov
   Translated by Tyrone Guthrie
   and Leonid Kipnis
   Directed by Tyrone Guthrie
   Set and costumes by Tanya
   Moiseiwitsch
   Lighting by Robert Scales

<u>At the Crawford Livingston Theater</u>

The Alchemist
Ben Jonson
   Directed by Mel Shapiro
   Sets and costumes by John Jensen
   Lighting by Robert Scales
   Music by David Karr

Ardele
Jean Anouilh
   Translated by Lucienne Hill
   Directed by Edward Payson Call
   Set by John Jensen
   Costumes by Carolyn Parker

<u>At The Other Place</u>

The Measures Taken
Bertolt Brecht
   Directed by David Feldshuh

The Dutchman
Leroi Jones
A Slight Ache
Harold Pinter
   Directed by Dan Bly

Krapp's Last Tape
Samuel Beckett
   Directed by Dan Bly

The Hostage
Brendan Behan
   Directed by Dugald MacArthur

The Ghost Dancer
Fred Gaines
   Directed by Edward Payson Call

Julius Caesar.
Robert Pastene,
Charles Keating
and company.

57

Clockwise
from upper left:

Staff, 1978.

Exterior, Guthrie 2,
ca. 1976.

Guthrie 2 contact
sheet, 1976.

Picnic outside
scene shop, 1978.

Billboard, ca. 1976.

Press release, 1972.

Season schedule, 1973.

Costume rendering
by Desmond Heeley.

The rush line.

Backstage class.

Stage door man
Larry Howard with
Peter Michael Goetz.

Traffic on Vineland Place.

Variety show flyer,
ca. 1975.

Fran Bennett leads
pre-show warm-ups.

Staff football team,
ca. 1975.

**Guthrie
Variety
Show**

The Guthrie Benefit Variety Show is that very special evening of musical
family fun when both on- and offstage members of the company "let their h
down" in a most entertaining way. Some memorable highlights of last seas
Variety Show included a show-stopping song by Michele Shay, English music
hall routines by Jon Cranney and Denny Spence, Broadway show tunes by L
Carlou and a bizarre rhythm number by Michael Langham, Donald Schoenbaum
John Jensen. Proceeds benefit the Tyrone Guthrie Award Fund, established
provide study and travel grants for Guthrie Theater personnel. All seats
are $3.50 with tickets available only through the Guthrie Box Office. Ea
reservations are suggested for this delightful once-a-year entertainment
call 377-2224 or visit the Box Office today. One performance only!

7:30 Sun. Aug. 6

Involve yourself in a plot.

With a Guthrie Season Ticket.

1970s

Guthrie '73

The Guthrie Theater
Minneapolis/St. Paul
Fall Schedule

There is always a tension between the enclosed and sometimes self-absorbed world of the theater and the sweep of current events. Many theater artists spend their lives finding the proper balance between the art form and the world. Sometimes the world comes calling on its own.

It was November 15, 1969. The Guthrie was performing *Uncle Vanya* with Paul Ballantyne in the lead role, Lee Richardson as Astrov, Patricia Connolly as Elena and Helen Carey as Sonia. I attended the production with my father – and we were completely enthralled.

Right in the middle of Elena's monologue – alone on stage – a whistle was blown from the audience and about four people stood up and 'mimed' having machine guns in their hands. The four people pretended to spray the sold out audience with machine gun fire with their 'rat tat tat' sounds. Then one of the people ran up on stage and said, "We are interrupting you as you have interrupted the lives of the Vietnamese people," and then ran off. All this while, Patricia Connolly stood still, her long statuesque neck getting even longer with a simple dignity and stillness which I had never seen before or since. Then, Lee Richardson, who was about to come on stage to do the famous 'map scene,' ran on ready to tear apart whoever had disrupted the production. However, by the time he ran on stage, the intruders had left as quickly as they had interrupted, leaving Patricia Connolly standing there. She was waiting now for the audience to calm down – they were yelling 'hang them!' and literally throwing programs from the balcony.

Richardson left the stage and Connolly continued with her monologue. Richardson entered on cue and the play continued.

But something extraordinary had happened. Back then, every 15th of the month was "Moratorium Day," a day of unified protest against the Vietnam War. [Actor David Kwiat]

Communication with artists can be a challenge, as any manager can testify. This story may describe the ultimate challenge in communicating with a playwright. Donald Schoenbaum was the theater's managing director for 21 influential years.

I was able to get the rights to the only play by Aleksandr Solzhenitsyn ever produced. The play was smuggled out of the Soviet Union a page at a time, like his other work, to his representative in Switzerland and then translated by two British writers. The title was one that audiences would have a hard time

Three cavaliers from *Cyrano de Bergerac* attend Aquatennial Queen candidates in the lobby. 1971. Ron Glass, David Feldshuh, Peter Michael Goetz.

understanding. I negotiated back and forth between Minneapolis, London, Geneva and then to the labor camp Solzhenitsyn was in, but we were never able to agree on another title. We ended up calling it *A Play* by Aleksandr Solzhenitsyn.

During his years at the Guthrie, the legendarily tough Schoenbaum managed, led and, during several artistic director transitions, even chose the plays for the Guthrie seasons. "I chose the plays for the 1970 season," he recalls. "The season opened with three plays in three days, playing in repertory, with a fully racially-integrated company, immediately following the civil race riots that were going on in Minneapolis and throughout the country. I was particularly proud of that."

Michael Langham, a friend and respected colleague of Tyrone Guthrie, came to the Guthrie after 12 years as Artistic Director of Canada's Stratford Festival Theatre and a distinguished career in England directing for the Royal Shakespeare Company and the National Theatre of Great Britain. His choice was celebrated, and his arrival much anticipated.

As society grows more and more dazzled and numbed by the brilliance of modern technology, it is my belief that a counter action must be induced – not only to save our sanity but our souls. This must place a premium on human contact and revive in us the life-giving assurance that we belong to more than our tiny moment of time, that we are part of the whole human experience – all laughter, all tears, and that we would be wise to take account of this if we are to have anything of lasting value to pass on to those who follow us. [Michael Langham]

There is a story that between the time that Michael Langham accepted the position of Artistic Director and the time of his arrival, the shaky financial situation at the Guthrie deteriorated. In the weeks leading up to the opening of *Cyrano de Bergerac*, members of the board personally guaranteed a loan to pay the Guthrie payroll, because there was not enough cash to cover it. If the opening had not gone well, and the box office had not gotten off to a good start, the theater would have closed the next day.

The 1971 season opened to great acclaim. "The great grey Guthrie," said critic Mike Steele, "has given way to a vigorous artistic vision."

Inside the theater, pressure was intense during rehearsals for the double opening of *Cyrano de Bergerac* and *The Taming of the Shrew*, both directed by Langham. Actor David Feldshuh:

"Press on" was a phrase I heard often in Michael Langham's rehearsals, rehearsals that as a young actor and director I would watch with awe. I was

Opposite: Michael Langham and designer Desmond Heeley.

Michael Langham
Artistic Director 1971 – 77

thrilled just to hear the voices and be near the skill. I felt sure the Guthrie was the center of the universe.

In *Cyrano* I played Valvert, the swordsman. I remember, however, a particular rehearsal in which all was not well. Michael was sick that day with a kind of stomach flu. Though looking a bit weak and weary, he insisted we "press on." He sat in the big rehearsal hall in a simple chair with a small bucket to his right and rehearsal began. It wasn't long before Paul Hecht (with his rich and evocative voice) completed one of the Cyrano's most soaring speeches. Michael promptly and seeming on cue turned in his seat, gracefully leaned forward from the waist, and vomited into the bucket. Paul: "Was it that bad?" Laughter. Michael: "Press on." Rehearsal continued. The message was clear if unintended: you didn't miss rehearsal unless you were dead. There was another message, as well. Nothing was going to stop us from creating something extraordinary. This was a vital message because *Cyrano* came at a time of financial crisis for the Guthrie.

At the final performance of *Cyrano* I felt that we had regained the trust and affection of our audience. It was completely sold out. Michael was asked what to do about all the people standing outside wanting to see the show. After a decision that was no doubt as illegal as it was wonderfully symbolic, all the people were let in. I can still see the audience that night. They were everywhere: standing at the back, crouched near the stage, seated in the aisles. The Phoenix had risen. The Guthrie had survived.

Bush Fellows appear on the Nicollet Mall before their departure on the *Fables Here and Then* tour. Steve Ryan, Ivar Brogger, Lance Davis, Tovah Feldshuh, Katherine Ferrand.

Fables Here and Then played a nine-week tour with 52 performances in 43 communities. Louis Zelle, in the 1971 President's Report, called it "one of the most successful and enthusiastically received events of the Guthrie's year. Its young actors, largely on fellowships from the University of Minnesota, were thrilled to play the mainstage on their return from tour." The tour staff still remembers driving out to Devil's Lake, North Dakota, to cook a Thanksgiving feast for the company in a motel basement kitchen.

66,000 people saw the much-lauded 1972 tour of *Of Mice and Men,* the first mainstage production to tour regionally, with Peter Michael Goetz as Lenny.

Peter Michael Goetz.

There never was an actor like Peter Michael Goetz out in the community. He was gracious, he was charming, he was just genuinely interested in these people. We asked him to do everything. For *Of Mice and Men,* we asked him to do puppy-judging contests. In every town we needed a puppy – that's the puppy that's going to get 'killed' in the play. We would advertise weeks in advance: 'bring your puppies on Tuesday afternoon at 3 and one puppy will be cast in the play.' We'd get the photographers there. In each town, Peter would have puppies to choose from. He would look at each puppy and hold them up and cuddle them. "Oh," he would say, "this is a good puppy. This is a fabulous puppy." Then he would pick one, flashbulbs would pop, and every town would have a story about its own puppy. [Carolyn Bye, tour manager]

A walk through the Guthrie backstage can be full of surprises and sometimes shocks.

I worked in a small office across from the door that led down to the set-building areas. I often would roam around to see what I could learn that might be of interest to the Guthrie donors or to our Board members, for whom I was responsible. One day, as Michael Langham's *Oedipus* was in rehearsal, I went down to the cavernous set area. That day, it was quite empty. As I opened the door, I saw at the far corner the actor Len Cariou standing with Michael. Len's hands went up to his eyes and, suddenly, horrifying amounts of blood gushed and spurted from his eyes. I let out a scream that resonated nicely in the vast empty room. Michael looked over at me and said something like, "well, that was effective." They were, of course, trying out propman Jimmy Bakkom's invention which would allow Len/Oedipus to put out his eyes with a brooch. [Pamela Paciotti Michaelis].

Len Cariou as Oedipus.

Collaboration is the very definition of the theater, but strong direction is an absolute necessity.

Michael told me that my job as Jocasta in *Oedipus the King* was to frighten everybody. I made my first entrance at rehearsal and he said, 'Why are you behaving like a West Hollywood matron?' I'm sure it was true; but it wasn't very helpful. The next day I collared him in his office. He listened very sweetly and said, 'I think I can help you with the dread queen.' The next time I came on, he made the chorus take two steps back and make a sharp intake of breath – and my job was done. [Patricia Connolly]

And sometimes even the god-like stage managers simply cannot control everything about a show. From the booth above and behind the stage, one has a superb view of the performance, the effects ... and the problems.

In *Oedipus*, there was a huge earthquake effect. There were timpani drums in the 'clouds' above the stage, shotgun explosions reverberating in metal drums in the washrooms off the upper lobby, an enormous and complex score and lots of fog from a full complement of fog machines concealed under the various outcroppings of the steel set. Also an enormous and complex score from the orchestra, concealed in a black velvet cocoon upstage of the set. Throughout, the acting ensemble of Thebans writhed and moaned and screamed. It was a challenge and a delight to a stage manager.

Oedipus the King. Company.

But one day – I cued the various components and it gloriously built to a loud, frighteningly physical, awfully beautiful, unforgettable climax. Then I gradually cued the earthquake to subside. Quiet was supposed to take over. Calm should finally prevail, Jocasta and her little daughters should enter and the show should continue. Stop the gunshots, stop the fog, stop the timpani, fade out the sound, stop the fog. Oh, my God, turn off the fog!

I shouted into the headset. All you could hear onstage was the unrelenting hiss of the fog machines; all you could see was a rising thick cloud starting to climb past the bang boards and overtake the audience. The writhing Thebans had disappeared completely. All I could hear was the calm voice over the headset: "It's stuck on, the button is stuck on." All the stagehands, now free from their earthquake duties, dove under the black velvet and into the orchestral cocoon. They began unplugging an enormous number of electrical connections in their quest for the one plug to the fog machines. I helplessly watched the fog roll in over the bottom third of the audience.

Then, obeying the old adage, "the show must go on," Jocasta and her two little ones made their entrance. The girls were engulfed immediately but Jocasta, who had hiked up to the topmost promontory of the set, was visible from her shoulders up. She raised her arms heavenward and, staring straight at me, uttered her first line: "This, too, will pass, but not without help from the gods." At that very moment, the plug was found, the power was disconnected and the fog began to dissipate. [Charlotte Green]

Sally Wingert.

Actor Sally Wingert began her work at the Guthrie in 1985, playing leads and coquettes, barmaids, character women and the occasional murderous female, to many a standing ovation. But before she was an actress, she was a Minnesota high school student:

The Guthrie literally is the reason that I'm a stage actor! In ninth grade, we moved here from Duluth. It was the season that Michael Langham did *Oedipus,* and my school offered a student matinee, and I went.

I had always been a ham, but much more in the lip-synching-to-Eydie-Gorme-during-the-Ed-Sullivan-show mode than anything serious. But performing had always interested me. I went to this play. I had no idea what it was going to be about, not a clue. I never had read any Greek plays, and I was feeling like the whole thing was going to be a great lark, getting out of school. I had no idea it was going to change my life. None.

I was up in the balcony, pretty much center balcony a little house right. And this play began and Langham opened it with the sacrifice of a child in the downstage right corner, with what looked like a beating heart.

I don't think I blinked. I was absolutely spellbound, in the best way. They took this curtain call at the end and instead of breaking the mood, because it's such a majestic piece, there was this sonorous sort of bell that came on and these actors, with more dignity than anybody I'd ever seen, came and took positions on stage and just sort of stood there, and accepted this wave of applause.

It was then (and this is not just my little theatrical re-imagining of my life) I remember vividly saying that is what I want to do. That, right there, on that stage – I want to be there.

It is the work of the theater to present a complete and self-contained world for the audience to watch. But sometimes, big things are happening right in front of your eyes. Actor Bernard Behrens spent five seasons at the Guthrie "of very hard work, most of which I felt was the best I had done over the previous twenty years." He played Estragon in *Waiting for Godot,* with Larry Gates as Vladimir.

I remember very fondly that Larry Gates had trouble retaining his lines, and whenever he 'dried up' he would raise and spread his arms, call out "Gogo," race across the stage to embrace me (which the two were constantly doing throughout the performance) and whisper in my ear, "What the hell do I say now?" I would give him his line and the scene would then move forward until his next dry. On the opening night of that production, I came on first, struggled to remove my boots without success, and just fell on the floor saying my line "Nothing to be done." Larry then entered; he was supposed to run about for a few seconds and then say "I'm beginning to come to that opinion." Well, after I had said my line there was silence except for the pitter patter of his feet running about all over the place. I realized that he had dried, and suddenly he shouted, "Gogo," raced over, knelt beside me, kissed my cheek and whispered "I can't remember my first (expletive!) line." I gave it to him. He whispered, "Thank you," got up, went back to his position, said the line, and *Waiting for Godot* finally got underway.

Waiting for Godot.
Bernard Behrens, Larry Gates.

In 1973, the Irish actress Pauline Flanagan came to the Guthrie for the first time; she returned in every decade thereafter. She was cast as Jocasta in the revival of *Oedipus the King* ("That's no little chore, you know. She does go on a bit, doesn't she?") and in the title role of *Juno and the Paycock.*

The Guthrie was a bit scary at first because you think you're going to get lost. You think, I'm going to be ready for an entrance and I won't be able to find it; you have one of those awful nightmarish dreams of getting lost in the innards. I had played in a lot of these kind of theaters before, but somehow this one seemed to be very very big and very sprawling. The fact that the dressing rooms were not on the same level and you had to go up and down an elevator – I didn't like that at all to start with.

Doing *Juno* here was such a joy; I'll never forget that as long as I live. Tomás Macanna came out from the Abbey and he knew all the things that we didn't have to talk about. Like making tea – how one makes real tea in Ireland and what you need on the set. We were doing the dress rehearsal and the costume designer, who was not Irish, handed me an umbrella as I'm ready to

The School for Scandal with
Jack Barkla's "masterpiece" paintings.
Kenneth Welsh, Oliver Cliff, Larry Gates.

INTER-OFFICE MEMO
TO: PROP DEPARTMENT
FROM: MICHAEL LANGHAM
SUBJECT: POSTAL CONGESTION IN NAVARRE

1. Letter from the King to Berowne, outlining the ground rules of the commune.

2. Letter from Armado to the King, regarding Costard's incontinence.

3. Formal diplomatic letter from the King of France to the King of Navarre. (As its contents are questioned, other letters between the two realms are flourished, examined, discarded.)

4. Don Armado's letter -- partly composed before our eyes -- to Jaquenetta. (This is given to Costard to deliver.)

5. A "sealed-up counsel" from Berowne to Rosaline. (This is also given to Costard to deliver.)

...up -- ... goddess on the ground" -- ...with an accompanying jewel. from Berowne to Rosaline,

Fourteen letters in all, and of vastly different character. Some challenge to the inventiveness of the prop department.

go out. And I said, I don't think she'd have an umbrella, you know. They're very poor and their shawl was the raincoat, the coat, the umbrella, everything. And he said, I would like you to carry it, so I said all right. So I brought it out and Tomás yelled from the house, 'What's that you're carrying, Pauline?' I said, 'it's an umbrella' and he said, 'Throw that into the wings, will you?'

Stephen Kanee, later a professor of theater at the University of Minnesota, has to work a bit to enumerate his various jobs at the Guthrie during the seventies. "I was a Bush Fellow, an assistant stage manager (the only thing I got out of that was I learned to crochet), an understudy, an actor (once only!), a guest director, an associate director, an associate artistic director, and an acting artistic director." He collaborated many times with scenic designer Jack Barkla:

> Jack Barkla is an extraordinarily gifted artist and human being. He had designed *The School for Scandal* and there was a scene that takes place in a library or attic. There were supposed to be a lot of things gathering dust and Michael thought it would be great if there were a lot of huge paintings from the period lying about, like Gainsboroughs and Constables. So I walked into the rehearsal room one day and there were a series of canvases set up against the wall. And there's Jack working like a dervish, sort of throwing paint on these things. I looked at the ones he'd completed, and from five feet away, they looked like a mess. From fifteen feet away, they looked like a painting. And from thirty feet away, they looked like a Constable or a Gainsborough. I clocked him; he was making those paintings in twenty minutes each. I have never seen anything like that in my life, and he was capable of this kind of magic time and time again.

In production, everything flows from the text and director. In this wonderful note, Langham lists for the often-beleaguered prop department all the special letters he'll need for *Love's Labor's Lost*. Each would be specially written, constructed, and aged; many would be made in multiples to cover the run of the show. Note the closing sentence, a wry understatement.

In January 1976, the Guthrie opened an alternative performance space in an historic building on the West Bank, one of a series of additional spaces over the years. In the first season at Guthrie 2 (later the Southern Theater), all seven plays were regional premieres and five were world premieres. But before the plays could be mounted, the theater had to be renovated.

Guthrie 2 was an attempt by the mainstage to create a space where they could do smaller, more experimental works that could not be done at the Guthrie itself. I'm not sure they knew quite how experimental they would be.

The Guthrie 2 space had been a theater before, but not in recent memory; it was a shambles when the first of the company arrived to begin work. The program cover for the season shows it in its starting glory – a big empty room filled with rubble, holes in the walls, and a crumbling plaster proscenium which was the only evidence of the former theatre. The proscenium was never repaired or used as such – the space was always intended as a flexible black box – but for one show we hung a partial red velour curtain in it and built a two-thirds size replica of the arch and curtain jutting out from it at a 45 degree angle. This created a wonderful optical illusion as the actors appeared to grow and shrink as they moved from one area to another.

The building was in what was already a thriving theater district – next door to Dudley Riggs' Café Espresso, around the corner from Theatre in the Round, a couple of blocks from the Firehouse [later Mixed Blood]. Dudley loved having us next door and I owe my coffee habit to this day to the regular free coffee breaks he gifted us with.

I was one of the first staff to arrive to start turning the rubble into a usable space. This was 1976. Except for the directors and actors and a tiny handful at the top, everybody on the company phone list is listed as apprentice, intern, or volunteer, and nobody could explain the difference. We all had our specialties and many of us evolved into titled positions – I was the assistant technical director by the second show, because I could draft. But money wasn't a factor. In the indelicate words of a mainstage administrator to a friend of mine in the Dram Shop one night, "We're going to do this one with freebies." [Mark Freij, technician, Guthrie 2]

Guthrie 2 posters, designed for use on telephone poles.

For several years, the Guthrie had experimented with the idea of being open during the winter holidays. The 1972 offering was *Fables Here and Then*, back from its successful fall tour. 1973 was a story theater version of *A Christmas Carol*. 1974 was *The Miracle Man*, an "original ragtime musical" loosely based on Moliere's *The Doctor in Spite of Himself*. In December 1975, the Guthrie presented its first production of Barbara Field's adaptation of *A Christmas Carol*. It began a tradition for several generations of Minnesota families; children who attended in the seventies grew up to bring their own children to the Guthrie, and to live theater. Sheila Livingston remembers the beginning.

For me, the story of *A Christmas Carol* dates back to November 1970. I was a volunteer then, and Michael Langham, who was to become artistic director in 1971, was guest director for *A Play* by Aleksandr Solzhenitsyn. It was a beautiful but grim and dark play about life in a Stalinist labor camp.

My family was having Thanksgiving dinner when the phone rang. The crisp English voice said "Michael Langham here." I was frozen in space – my feelings about artistic directors and artists were a mixture of hero worship and pure fear. While I was an avid theatergoer, I had no confidence in my knowledge of theater.

He went on, "I am very upset. There are only 350 people in the theater tonight. It's not fair to the actors – what are you doing about it?" I was literally trembling but managed to utter, "It's Thanksgiving, you know, and most everyone is at home with their families." "It won't do," he said, and hung up. Shortly thereafter he left to return to London but the memory of that call stayed with me as I tried to do something about it.

Michael did become artistic director in 1971 and during the next couple of years the theater flourished and the season stretched out. We opened *The School for Scandal* in November 1974. One December morning, Michael summoned marketing director Doug Eichten and myself to his office and said no one was coming to *The School for Scandal*. This time I was prepared.

"But Michael, why should people come in December to see a play they can see in January? Don't you think we should be doing a holiday play during that time?"

"Like what?" he said sharply.

"Like *A Christmas Carol*," I said with some confidence. On December 12, 1975, we opened our full-blown production of *A Christmas Carol*, adapted by Barbara Field. It was unbelievable – an unqualified artistic and box office hit; people began ordering tickets for the next year the moment it was announced.

Stephen Kanee directed the first *A Christmas Carol;* he recalls quickly accepting the invitation from Langham to direct, and then walking all over late-night Manhattan to find a copy so he could read the story.

There is a convention in the theater called the "fourth wall," an invisible barrier which separates the players from the audience. On occasion, someone crashes through. Actor Peter Michael Goetz has been telling this story since a late Wednesday afternoon in June 1975, just after this very eventful matinee.

I was playing in *Arsenic and Old Lace* in a scene with Barbara Bryne, somewhere in the first act. I think we may have had volunteer ushers at matinees, but in any case, two very old ladies had gotten away from the ushers. They made their first entrance at the top of the Alpine Slope, the long aisle, and they came down, well, just forever. One had a cane. Boompity-boomp. They were kind of talking and looking for their seats and they came all the way down to the gutter. Then they walked up the next aisle. From on stage, we'd see the door open and close and we'd think, well, they're gone. Then at the top of the next aisle, the door would open and boompity-boomp. Down to the gutter, and around, and then back up; the door would close. It took about a half-hour. Finally, they came right down and I was opening the window seat, and one woman came right up on stage and said to me, 'Can you help us find our seats?' Because obviously, no one else had!

Barbara was laughing so hard that she left me on stage. I tried to say "we'll see what we can do." We had to stop the play. It was incredible, incredible.

Barbara Bryne remembers another mishap, in Act III of the very same performance:

> Then, later in the same matinee, well! As Abby Brewster, I wore a fob watch on the top right hand side of my dress. They, as you know, have a little chain on them. Peter at one point asked me the time. "What time is it, Auntie?" I pulled out the watch on its chain and somehow, I don't know how, the chain of the fob watch caught on a drop earring I was wearing, and my head jerked to one side. Peter asked me for the time three times; every time he asked me, my head shot to one side. This sight was too much for Peter who ran up the staircase on the set and left me alone on stage. He came back, though. Needless to say, the next few minutes were also very tricky trying to control the giggles. I had to take the earring off finally, which solved the problem!

Actor Ken Ruta tells this story about the Guthrie's gravel-voiced character actor Oliver Cliff, who played in *Mother Courage and Her Children*, a rather long production which placed the company in the aisles as observers with the audience:

> I wasn't in it, thank God, but I was in the building. The show was going on towards its end, like three-and-a-half hours later. I was sitting in the dressing room and I could hear Ollie's voice over the blower from the house. There was a man, an audience member, asleep in the front row, and Ollie reached over and shook him, and said, in that voice, "It's all right, honey, it's almost over."

The fabrication shops at the Guthrie – for scenery, props, costumes, wigs – are their own fiefdoms, with their own traditions and their own brands of humor. Many of the artisans have been part of the Guthrie for years, and have found their own ways of managing the year-round tensions of building toward relentless opening nights. They are capable of nearly anything, and everything they do is done with style.

> When I was there, the boys in the shop became inadvertent social coordinators for the building. In those days we had the greatest work schedule ever. We would work 7 to 4, and then Friday was 7 to 11 in the morning. Then the driver would go up to the Lowry Hill Liquor Store, come back with a case of beer and a bag of peanuts, and we'd all sit there and drink a beer and eat some peanuts and then head out.
>
> We were always trying to raise a little money to do things like buy a tape player so we could listen to music in the shop or something. For a while we speared aluminum cans in the dumpster and saved those and recycled them, until we'd get a little money together. Then we hit the mother lode. Tom Serrill and I decided that actors didn't want to just drink sodas or pop when

Oliver Cliff.

they were working. They wanted bottled water. Bottled water was just coming in, and we thought it would be great if we had some. So I called up the Coca-Cola company and said, "This is Jim Worthing from the Guthrie Theater. We've come across a need for one of those old vending machines," and the guy said, "Oh, is it going to be on stage? Will people see it?" And I said, "Well, you never know."

They gave us a working vending machine, a beautiful little thing. Randy Arnold built us a rack to hold the bottles and a coin mechanism that took two quarters. And before you know it, we're making money.

It was a great service to all the people and we made maybe fifteen hundred bucks a year, and a party fund like no other. Every time there was an opening night, we would have lunch for the entire building, in the shop. We'd go to Kramarczuk's and buy Bratwursts or Polish or something. These parties would have themes. There was get-back-to-summer party in the middle of the winter, and everybody would dress in their shorts and t-shirts and sunglasses. Or Underwear-on-the-Outside Day. We rented a dunk tank one time; we tried to get one person from every department to sit in that dunk tank during the party.

Underwear-on-the-Outside day didn't go very well. We had two or three participants in the shop and the people from upstairs came down and looked at us funny, so we ran with Hat Day. We had a box of hats, and we'd put a hat on the bust of Tony Guthrie, and everybody would come and wear hats and there were prizes for different categories. [Jim Worthing]

Hat Day is still going on at the Guthrie. Underwear-on-the-Outside Day has never been revived.

The Guthrie Board of Directors, all community leaders and all volunteers, have provided powerful continuity and countless hours of service since the theater's founding. Usually, their work is behind-the-scenes. In February, 1978, Andy Andrews found himself in the very middle of the maelstrom.

I get a call. Don Schoenbaum [the Managing Director] has had a heart attack and is in the hospital. We were right in the middle of negotiating contracts for the new season. Actor contracts, purchase orders, designers, everything. I basically walked out of my law firm and was sitting in Don Schoenbaum's chair for three weeks. Jon Cranney [then the Production Manager] was an incredible help. And we sort of ran the show. I was signing checks, doing budgets. I gave people vacation time. Negotiating the contracts was the scariest thing I had ever done in my life. Here I thought I was this pretty fancy lawyer and I had to call up and negotiate a contract for some lead that we wanted. I think our maximum at that point was $350 or $400 a week. I called this guy up on the phone, some tough New York agent, and I introduced myself. I said, "Our top contract here is $350/week." He said, "That's unacceptable." I said, "That's fine. I'm prepared to do $400/week and that's all." And all of a sudden, I was talking into an empty phone. That was it. That was the end of negotiations! Negotiating with agents was a real lesson.

I had never realized how much went into the theater. Half the time I spent meeting with department heads and everyone had employment issues, purchasing issues, budgeting issues, trying to plan, playwrights sending in material ... it was unbelievable. I can't imagine any CEO who could have a more stressful job. And the talents that are involved in that position! Everything from labor negotiations to being able to read a play and figure it out, and to the idea of trying to cost out a production! I remember dealing with the wigmaker who needed what seemed to me an incredible amount of money. I said 'what?!' But the complexity of budgeting, ordering, negotiating, and appeasing and working with the artistic director. Michael would come in and say, "I have to have this" and I would look at the numbers and say, "Well, maybe not!"

I knew it was pretty complicated, but I had no idea the day-to-day operations were that involved. Everybody ought to do that for a while. I had visions of the theater opening and we didn't have any cast, because of these negotiations! I thought I'm going to have to go out there with the board members and be in the play.

A 1976 season billboard.

Alvin Epstein was the first American to lead the Guthrie as Artistic Director. A prominent and fine actor, he had been involved for many years with the Yale Repertory Theatre. As associate artistic director there, his work with Bertolt Brecht/Kurt Weill plays, and with Shakespearean productions involving music, established him as a major force in the American music theater. Epstein arrived in the Twin Cities in September 1977 fresh from a directors' tour of Russian theater; in the following eighteen months, he brought Russian director Anatoly Efros to the Guthrie for remarkable productions of *Marriage* and *Monsieur de Moliere*.

*M*y feeling is that the stage is a place to celebrate life. One way or another, everything that happens in theater should be a celebration, be it an affirmation of our experience or a protest against it. [Alvin Epstein]

Over the years, the Guthrie has welcomed artists from all over the world into the work. Translators have abounded, but Russian Anatoly Efros may have been the first Guthrie guest director who used an interpreter to speak to actors in rehearsal. Barbara Field was the Guthrie Literary Manager. She adapted *Marriage*, and took notes:

Opposite: Alvin Epstein (left) directs
The Pretenders. From left: Stephen Lang,
Cara Duff-McCormick, Ken Ruta.

Before the first meeting of Efros and his Guthrie cast and staff, there is an air of excitement and apprehension. None of us knows what to expect from him or, indeed, what will be expected from us. Much nodding of heads, forced smiling, to compensate for our inability to welcome him with words. Language differences, by the third week, begin to melt away for all concerned. The first week, Efros looked at the interpreter as he spoke, and she then turned to the actors with the translation. By the second week, he was speaking to the actors directly, as the translation poured forth, attended almost subconsciously. By the third week, we often grasp his meaning before the translation starts. Efros had one English word, which he picked up on the first day, stopstopstop. The same day we learned several Russian ones, *plooche* (bad), *gloope* (silly) and *skoochne* (boring). Later on, we learn the word for "good," and hear it with greater frequency.

By the end of the third week, during a social evening with the cast, Efros pays the Guthrie actors an enormous compliment. "Except for the small matter of language, you are like my actors in Moscow. I am very pleased." We are all pleased. We invite ourselves to visit him in Moscow.

The speed with which Efros has gotten the actors on their feet and playing "full out," holding nothing in reserve, is dizzying. During a rehearsal post-mortem, Peter Goetz says to Efros, "When you learn to fly a plane, they usually put you in a little room in a training cockpit, first. Then, after you've learned the mechanics, they put you in the real plane. But Mr. Efros, you have us flying in the real thing on the first day. It's a little scary – we keep grazing

Alvin Epstein
Artistic Director 1978 – 79

the trees, and there's a possibility we might crash any time." Efros grins. "You'll fly," he replies, "but even if you crash." He gestures. It's better to have started in the real plane.

Anatoly Efros was such a fascinating man. He came with an official Soviet translator who looked like one of the women from the James Bond movies, and later did admit she was KGB. But Jon Cranney, who was the production manager at the time, hired a very funny spunky American girl whose parents were Russian as his translator. She had the vocabulary because she'd worked at the Met. Eventually, she became the translator because the KGB woman only wanted to shop. Shopping was the subtext of the whole rehearsal period.

Anatoly Efros (left) and his interpreter (foreground) communicating with the cast of *Marriage*. Randall Duk Kim, Jake Dengel, and Jon Cranney.

Emily Mann, later the Artistic Director at Princeton's McCarter Theatre, was the first woman to direct on the mainstage at the Guthrie. She still recalls the challenges.

Everyone forgets what a gate of fire women had to go through in the seventies to do any real work that was taken seriously as directors in the American theater. There had to be an institutional shift at the Guthrie and I think that shift did take place. I think I was always undergoing a test. Not only was I the first female director at the Guthrie, but also the first resident director. I'd fought to get that position, but I remember that they wouldn't give me a desk and phone. I remember this: "Yeah, you can work here, but you should be paying us for the privilege."

Particularly proud scenery and prop shop artisans pose by a trick table built for the final moment of *Marriage*. On an entirely empty stage, by radio control, all the bottles popped their corks and champagne spewed out. This table under stage light on page 97.

I was told once I shouldn't show my legs around the theater. There are so many stories of not being taken seriously; there was still that attitude at the theater. I remember being asked if I wanted to be a director or an actress. When I said a director, the response was, "Well, you know, all the women directors I know are either hysterical or dykes. Which are you?" And I thought, well, it's going to be a push. It's going to be a push.

I remember at Guthrie 2 early on getting a lot of rough notes, not only on the play but how I had to change the way I dressed and the way I was; I became very angry and began to cry. Here was the response: "Directors who cry end up as housewives. Do you want to be a housewife or do you want to be a director?" I remember just being in a silent rage, saying "leave me alone" and stalking back into rehearsal. Really, I was so intimidated that a surge of adrenaline went through me. I said, "If you allow yourself to back down here, your life is over." It got me into such a towering rage that it intimidated all my intimidation. I was a very angry young lady because of events like that, but it fueled me and gave me the energy to keep fighting.

I think the decision to give me *The Glass Menagerie* was an artistic decision and not a feminist decision, and that was the way I preferred it. And yet, it was very distressing that the lead on the review was, "Mann first woman to direct on the Guthrie mainstage."

The occasional brutalities form you as much as the moments of brilliance and ambition. At the Guthrie I think I saw what theater at its highest level could be, artistically. I learned it from the shops, from the woman who did soft props. How perfectly wrought even the underwear was from the costume shop, and how much pride was taken in the craft of cutting and draping and millinery. I would make sure I went into the shop every day on my way to rehearsal, because I was just captivated by what they were doing. The stage managers, the designers, the acting company. It's a constant source of inspiration to me. It's lasted, basically, a lifetime – my professional lifetime to date.

When I run into Guthrie people around the country, there's a common language, a level of technical expertise and knowledge that is just assumed. Without even having to say so, you know the league you're in. A certain level of accomplishment and professionalism; things are just taken care of in the right way at the Guthrie. It sets a standard and it's the gold standard. One doesn't settle for less.

Teibele and Her Demon.
F. Murray Abraham, Laura Esterman.

When the prominent theater and film actor F. Murray Abraham came to town, the theater rented a home in south Minneapolis for the actor and his family.

Teibele pictured Jews from a small town in Poland in the 19th century, but our neighbors never even blinked; and believe me, we did not look like our neighbors. They would invite us to their homes along Minnehaha Creek and offer to babysit our kids; so many many kindnesses.

Actor John Spencer had a wide career in film and television, including playing the President's Chief of Staff on *The West Wing*. In the 1979 season, he came to the Guthrie:

I remember that I auditioned and auditioned and auditioned, and I remember the audition being fierce. I had to do monologues and read from the plays and do improvisations and physical work and, well, it was like getting into drama school. I was very impressed and grateful that I got accepted because to me, the Guthrie was like the granddaddy of regional theater. That theater had such a sense of importance, like when the lights went down, you were really going to see something that was important. I remember that my agent said, "You're going away for a year?" But I thought this was something I just had to do.

Spencer was cast that season in *The Glass Menagerie,* in *Romeo and Juliet,* in *Monsieur de Moliere,* and for the *Menagerie* tour. *The Glass Menagerie* came up first and, early in rehearsals, Spencer stepped onto the stage for the first time. Immediately, he knew he had a problem.

> Suddenly, about ten days in, we're up on the stage doing it without set or costumes or anything. And I'll tell you a scary thing. I felt eaten by that stage; I felt devoured. I felt frightened like I had no arms or legs. That thrust stage, well, it is a mighty thrust.
>
> I had to break that fear for myself. So I guess it's not a secret anymore. I stayed late after rehearsal, hid in the dressing room, and spent the night alone on that stage. I remember I came up from the stage right vom, and there was only a single light on. I leaned up against the side and kind of did some yoga breathing. As I tell the story now, I can kind of see a picture of it, with just my little body sitting sort of lotus position on the stage, far up, stage left, so I could see the seats. It was empty and dark and very quiet.
>
> I did some lines; I did some moving around the stage. I managed to sleep a wink or two. Once the sun came up and people started coming in, I had to hide. As soon as they came in, I got out.
>
> It was a frightening experience, but it was an exorcism, too, of the fear I felt of that stage. I had to conquer it somehow. And, God knows, by the first audience for *The Glass Menagerie,* I had. I came out there and felt a wave of love. By that time, it was just fine.
>
> That was an important and wonderful season for me. A lot of roots began there for me. The Guthrie! I love that theater.

Near the very beginning of the 1979 season, Alvin Epstein resigned as Artistic Director. The newspaper reported that "the usual search committee" has been named. Actor Richard Russell Ramos was named artistic advisor, to see the season through. *Minneapolis Tribune* critic Mike Steele, a penetrating Guthrie observer, said that some "feel the job has become too complex for one man. There's been talk about two artistic directors, one to handle art, one to handle artistic administration. There's lots of talk about the fact that the Guthrie's ever-growing administrative staff (with batteries of market researchers, publicists, ad people, sales personnel, etc.) has simply become too large."

An interim season followed, while the search committee did its work. Guest directors included Stephen Kanee, former artistic director Michael Langham, and future artistic director Garland Wright. The theater mounted a full season and several tours.

John Spencer as the Gentleman Caller, *The Glass Menagerie.*

Actor Helen Carey performed in *Arms and the Man* and remembers two distinctly different events from that production. One took place in her dressing room, and the other onstage on a day of national celebration, when the acting company found a way to participate.

The first one involves Isaac Stern, who was on a tour across the country and came to see our production. When the play was over, I went back to my dressing room. It seemed only seconds before I heard a knock on my door and when I opened it, I said "Oh, my God!" And he said "No – Stern!" He sat down and stayed for twenty minutes; he said the play was like a piece of chamber music; he had intuited every single scene and nuance and instrument, which was just what Michael Langham had described in our first rehearsal. For a musician to hear our "music" in the theater was an achievement that you only dream about.

Also during that production, the Americans who had been held hostage in Iran were released. That night, before our performance, I asked the dresser to go downstairs and find a bolt of yellow ribbon. Everyone in the cast snipped a piece and we hid it in our costumes.

We had a double curtain call; we took a company bow and the lights went out. When they came back up, we had put on all these bows that we had hidden in our costumes. I'll never forget the sound in that house. The audience just went "ooohhhh." We were crying and they were crying. That was quite a day. The ether of this theater contains great theater, and it's cheek-by-jowl with life. It's all in the air, right out there on our stage.

Cathy Silvern interprets a performance of *Macbeth* in sign language for the hearing impaired. Silvern launched the Guthrie interpretive program in a single performance of *The Glass Menagerie* in October 1979.

Some performances on the Guthrie stage are really not meant to be seen at all.

I remember what was, no doubt, my most memorable performance on the Guthrie stage. Late at night after a long rehearsal of *A Christmas Carol*, the women left and the men were finishing showering in the first floor dressing rooms. An idea seemed to float spontaneously in the air. It was time for Shakespearean soliloquies in the buff. We walked into the darkened theatre wearing the costumes that God has given us. One by one we each walked onto the stage to perform to the silent, empty house (we hoped).

It may be hard to remember that the Guthrie stage in the early days of the theatre was a kind of sacred place. You didn't change its color, configuration or structure. It was a place for great and famous actors to stand. That night was perhaps an event of youthful silliness and rebellion. But I like to think it was really some young actors trying to soak up the magic of one of the earth's very special places. [David Feldshuh]

1970 SEASON

The Venetian Twins
Carlo Goldoni
Translated and adapted by
Robert David MacDonald
Directed by Robert David MacDonald
Set and costumes by Gordon Micunis
Lighting by Robert Scales
Music by Robert David MacDonald

Ceremonies in Dark Old Men
Lonne Elder III
Directed by Israel Hicks
Set by John Jensen
Costumes by Geraldine Cain
Lighting by Robert Scales

The Tempest
William Shakespeare
Directed by Philip Minor
Set and costumes by John Jensen
Lighting by Robert Scales
Music by John Gessner

A Man's A Man
Bertolt Brecht
Translated by Gerhard Nellhaus
Directed by John Hirsch
Set and costumes by Eoin Sprott
Lighting by Robert Scales
Music by Herbert Pilhofer
and David Karr

A Play
Aleksandr Solzhenitsyn
Adapted by Paul Avila Mayer
Translated by Nicholas Bethell
and David Berg
Directed by Michael Langham
Set and costumes by John Jensen
Lighting by Robert Scales
Music by David Karr/Maury Bernstein

At The Other Place

Silence and Landscape
Harold Pinter
Directed by Dan Bly

**Don Perlimplin's Love
for Belissa in His Garden**
Federico Garcia Lorca
Directed and translated by Philip Minor

Kumaliza
C.L. Burton
Directed by Israel Hicks

The Madness of Lady Bright
Lanford Wilson
Directed by Charles Keating

Stars and Stripes Forever
Fred Gaines
Directed by David Feldshuh

The Labyrinth
Fernando Arrabal
Directed by Milt Commons

Winners
Brian Friel
Directed by Dan Bly

Baal
Bertolt Brecht
Directed by David Feldshuh

**Encore
Food for Thought
A Mild Case of Death**
David Korr
Directed by Dan Bly

**Madam Popov
Wet Dream by God**
Gladden Schrock
Directed by Dan Bly

Ceremonies in
Dark Old Men.
Ed Bernard,
Maxwell Glanville,
Ron Glass,
Arnold Wilkerson.

81

1971 SEASON

Cyrano de Bergerac
Edmund Rostand
  Translated and adapted
  by Anthony Burgess
  Directed by Michael Langham
  Set and costumes by Desmond Heeley
  and John Jensen
  Lighting by Gil Wechsler
  Music by Anthony Burgess

The Taming of the Shrew
William Shakespeare
  Directed by Michael Langham
  Set and costumes by Desmond Heeley
  and John Jensen
  Lighting by Gil Wechsler
  Music by Stanley Silverman

A Touch of the Poet
Eugene O'Neill
  Directed by David Wheeler
  Set by John Jensen
  Costumes by Jack Edwards
  Lighting by Kerry Lafferty

Misalliance
George Bernard Shaw
  Directed by Edward Gilbert
  Set and costumes by Peter Wingate
  Lighting by Kerry Lafferty
  Music by Robert Samorotto

The Diary of A Scoundrel
Alexander Ostrovsky
  Translated by Rodney Ackland
  Directed by Michael Langham
  Set by John Jensen
  Costumes by Desmond Heeley
  Lighting by Gil Wechsler
  Music by Eric Stokes

Fables Here and Then
David Feldshuh and Guthrie actors
  Directed by David Feldshuh
  Set and costumes by Ron Hall
  Lighting by Robert Bye

<u>**On Tour**</u>

Fables Here and Then
David Feldshuh and Guthrie actors

Cyrano de Bergerac.
Paul Hecht, company.

1972-73 SEASON

A Midsummer Night's Dream
William Shakespeare
  Directed by John Hirsch
  Set by John Jensen
  Costumes by Carl Toms
  Lighting by Gil Wechsler
  Music: by John Duffy

Of Mice and Men
John Steinbeck
  Directed by Len Cariou
  Set and costumes by John Jensen
  Lighting by Gil Wechsler

The Relapse
Sir John Vanbrugh
  Directed by Michael Langham
  Set by John Jensen
  Costumes by Carl Toms
  Lighting by Gil Wechsler
  Music by Henry Mollicone

An Italian Straw Hat
Eugène Labiche and Marc Michel
  English version by David Feldshuh
  and David Ball
  Set by John Jensen
  Costumes by Hal George
  Lighting by John Jensen
  Music by Roberta Carlson

Oedipus the King
Sophocles
  Translated and adapted
  by Anthony Burgess
  Directed by Michael Langham
  Set and costumes by Desmond Heeley
  Lighting by Richard Borgen
  Music by Stanley Silverman

A Christmas Carol
Charles Dickens
  Adapted by David Feldshuh
  and David Ball
  Directed by David Feldshuh
  Set by James Bakkom
  Costumes by Jack Edwards

Cyrano
  A new musical version
  Directed by Michael Langham

On Tour

Of Mice and Men
John Steinbeck

Oedipus the King.
Len Cariou, Patricia Connolly, company.

85

Becket
Jean Anouilh
  Translated and adapted by Lucienne Hill
  Directed by David Feldshuh
  Set and costumes by Lewis Brown
  Lighting by Gilbert V. Hemsley, Jr.
  Music by Dick Whitbeck

Oedipus the King
Sophocles
  Translated and adapted by
  Anthony Burgess
  Directed by Michael Langham
  Set and costumes by Desmond Heeley
  Lighting by Richard Borgen
  Music by Stanley Silverman

The Government Inspector
Nikolai V. Gogol
  Translated by Leonid Ignatieff
  Adapted by Peter Raby
  Directed by Michael Langham
  Set by John Jensen
  Costumes by Tanya Moiseiwitsch
  Lighting by Gilbert V. Hemsley, Jr.
  Music by Raymond Pannell

Juno and the Paycock
Sean O'Casey
  Directed by Tomás MacAnna
  Set by Tomás MacAnna
  Costumes by Jack Edwards
  Lighting by Duane Schuler

I, Said the Fly
June Havoc
  Directed by Eric Christmas
  Set by John Döepp
  Costumes by Geraldine Cain
  Lighting by John Döepp and
  Gilbert V. Hemsley, Jr.
  Music by Dick Whitbeck

Waiting for Godot
Samuel Beckett
  Directed by Eugene Lion
  Set by Gregory Hill
  Costumes by Patricia Zipprodt
  Lighting by Richard William Tidwell
  Music by Dick Whitbeck

The Merchant of Venice
William Shakespeare
  Directed by Michael Langham
  Set by Eoin Sprott
  Costumes by Sam Kirkpatrick
  Lighting by Gilbert V. Hemsley, Jr.
  Music by John Cook

The Miracle Man
Adapted from Molière
  Book by Erik Brogger
  Directed by Joseph Rassulo
  Set by Eoin Sprott
  Costumes by Sam Kirkpatrick
  Lighting by Gilbert V. Hemsley, Jr.
  Music by John Cook and
  Roberta Carlson

On Tour

The Portable Pioneer and
Prairie Show
David Chambers and Mel Marvin
  Music by Mel Marvin
  Directed by David Chambers
  Set by James Bakkom
  Costumes by Bill Henry

King Lear
William Shakespeare
   Directed by Michael Langham
   Set by John Jensen
   Costumes by Desmond Heeley
   Lighting by Gilbert V. Hemsley, Jr.
   Music by Dick Whitbeck

Love's Labor's Lost
William Shakespeare
   Directed by Michael Langham
   Set by John Jensen
   Costumes by Desmond Heeley
   Lighting by Duane Schuler
   Music by John Cook

The Crucible
Arthur Miller
   Directed by Len Cariou
   Set and costumes by John Jensen
   Lighting by Robert Scales
   Music by Dick Whitbeck

Tartuffe
Molière
   Directed by Michael Bawtreet
   Set by Lowell Detweiler
   Costumes by Sam Kirkpatrick
   Lighting by Richard William Tidwell
   Music by Henry Mollicone

The School for Scandal
Richard Brinsley Sheridan
   Videotaped for PBS
   Theater in America series
   Directed by Michael Langham
   Set by Jack Barkla
   Costumes by Sam Kirkpatrick
   Lighting by Duane Schuler
   Music by Stanley Silverman
   and Dick Whitbeck

<u>On Tour</u>

Everyman
Anonymous
   Directed by Robert Benedetti
   Set by Bruce Cana Fox
   Costumes by Jack Edwards

Love's Labor's Lost.
Kenneth Welsh, Katherine Ferrand, Patricia Connolly,
Valery Daemke, Maureen Anderman.

1975-76 SEASON

Arsenic and Old Lace
Joseph Kesselring
   Directed by Thomas Gruenewald
   Set by Jack Barkla
   Costumes by Lewis Brown
   Lighting by Duane Schuler

The Caretaker
Harold Pinter
   Directed by Stephen Kanee
   Set by Jack Barkla
   Costumes by Lewis Brown
   Lighting by Duane Schuler

A Streetcar Named Desire
Tennessee Williams
   Directed by Ken Ruta
   Set by Jack Barkla
   Costumes by Lewis Brown
   Lighting by Duane Schuler
   Music by Dick Whitbeck

Loot
Joe Orton
   Directed by Tom Moore
   Set and costumes by John Jensen
   Lighting by Duane Schuler

**Mother Courage
and Her Children**
Bertolt Brecht
   Adapted by Robert Hellman
   Directed by Eugene Lion
   Set by Jack Barkla
   Costumes by Nancy Potts
   Lighting by Duane Schuler
   Music by Paul Dessau

Under Milk Wood
Dylan Thomas
   Directed by Kenneth Welsh
   Set by Robert T. Ellsworth
   Costumes by Jack Edwards
   and Robert T. Ellsworth

Private Lives
Noel Coward
   Directed by Michael Langham
   Set by Jack Barkla
   Costumes by Jack Edwards
   Lighting by Duane Schuler
   Music by Dick Whitbeck

A Christmas Carol
Charles Dickens
   Adapted by Barbara Field
   Directed by Stephen Kanee
   Set by Jack Barkla
   Costumes by Jack Edwards
   Lighting by Duane Schuler
   Music by Hiram Titus

Measure for Measure
William Shakespeare
   Directed by Michael Langham
   Set and costumes by Desmond Heeley
   Lighting by Duane Schuler

A Christmas Carol.
King Donovan, company.

1976-77 SEASON

The Matchmaker
Thornton Wilder
  Directed by Michael Langham
  Set and costumes by Desmond Heeley
  Lighting by Duane Schuler

Doctor Faustus
Christopher Marlowe
  Directed by Ken Ruta
  Set by Ralph Funicello
  Costumes by Robert Morgan
  Lighting by Duane Schuler
  Music by Dick Whitbeck

Cat on a Hot Tin Roof
Tennessee Williams
  Directed by Stephen Kanee
  Set by John Conklin
  Costumes by Jack Edwards
  Lighting by Duane Schuler

Rosencrantz and Guildenstern Are Dead
Tom Stoppard
  Directed by Stephen Kanee
  Set by John Conklin
  Costumes by John Conklin
  Lighting by Duane Schuler
  Music by Hiram Titus

An Enemy of the People
Henrik Ibsen
  Directed by Adrian Hall
  Set and costumes by Sam Kirkpatrick
  Lighting by Duane Schuler

The Winter's Tale
William Shakespeare
  Directed by Michael Langham
  Set and costumes by Desmond Heeley
  Lighting by Duane Schuler
  Music by Hiram Titus

A Christmas Carol
Charles Dickens
  Adapted by Barbara Field
  Directed by Stephen Kanee
  Set by Jack Barkla
  Costumes by Jack Edwards
  Lighting by Duane Schuler
  Music by Hiram Titus

The National Health
Peter Nichols
  Directed by Michael Langham
  Set and costumes by Sam Kirkpatrick
  Lighting by Duane Schuler
  Music by Dick Whitbeck and
  Matt Barber

Guthrie 2

The Collected Works of Billy the Kid
Michael Ondaatje
  Directed Eugene Lion

The Future Pit
Menzies McKillop
  Directed by David Feldshuh

Annulla Allen – Autobiography of a Survivor
Emily Mann and Annulla Allen
  Directed by Emily Mann

Triple bill:
Cold
Michael Casale
  Directed Emily Mann
Glutt
Gladden Schrock
  Directed by Stephen Kanee
Waterman
Frank B. Ford
  Directed by James Wallace

Ilk's Madhouse
  Adapted by Ken Campbell
  Directed by Ken Campbell

Up the Seminole
Keane Bonath
  Directed by Nicholas Kepros

Hello and Goodbye
Athol Fugard
  Directed by Mark Lamos

Open and Shut
Robert Hellman
  Directed by Eugene Lion

On Tour

A Party for Two
Written and performed
by Dominique Serrand and
Barbara Berlovitz

The Matchmaker.
Peter Michael Goetz,
Karen Landry,
Helen Carey,
John Pielmeier.
(Background)
Tony Mockus,
Barbara Bryne.

93

She Stoops to Conquer
Oliver Goldsmith
  Directed by Michael Langham
  Set by Ralph Funicello
  Costumes by Lewis Brown
  Lighting by Duane Schuler
  Music by Catherine MacDonald

A Moon for the Misbegotten
Eugene O'Neill
  Directed by Nick Havinga
  Set by John Conklin
  Costumes by Lewis Brown
  Lighting by Duane Schuler

La Ronde
Arthur Schnitzler
  Directed by Ken Ruta
  Set by Ralph Funicello
  Costumes by Lewis Brown
  Lighting by Duane Schuler
  Music by Dick Whitbeck

Catsplay
István Örkény
  Translated by Clara Gyorgyey
  Directed by Stephen Kanee
  Set by John Ferguson
  Costumes by Lewis Brown
  Lighting by Duane Schuler

The White Devil
John Webster
  Directed by Michael Blakemore
  Set by Patrick Robertson
  Costumes by Annena Stubbs
  Lighting by Duane Schuler
  Music by Dick Whitbeck

Design for Living
Noel Coward
  Directed by Michael Langham
  Set and costumes by Annena Stubbs
  Lighting by Duane Schuler
  Music by Dick Whitbeck

A Christmas Carol
Charles Dickens
  Adapted by Barbara Field
  Directed by Jon Cranney
  Set by Jack Barkla
  Costumes by Jack Edwards
  Lighting by Duane Schuler
  Music by Hiram Titus

Pantagleize
Michel de Ghelderode
  Adapted by Barbara Field
  Directed by Stephen Kanee
  Set by Jack Barkla
  Costumes by Jack Edwards
  Lighting by Duane Schuler
  Music by Hiram Titus

<u>Guthrie 2</u>

Ashes
David Rudkin
  Directed by Emily Mann

**Samuel Beckett: ...
Mouth on Fire, Not I,
Play, Krapp's Last Tape**
Samuel Beckett
  Directed by Henry Pillsbury

**The Conversion of
Aaron Weiss**
Mark Medoff
  Directed by J. Ranelli

Dear Liar
Jerome Kilty
  Directed by Mark Lamos

Dark Pony and **Reunion**
David Mamet
  Directed by Emily Mann

<u>On Tour</u>

A Moon for the Misbegotten
Eugene O'Neill

Clowns, Lovers & Kings
Developed by Tom Hegg
and Susan Dafoe

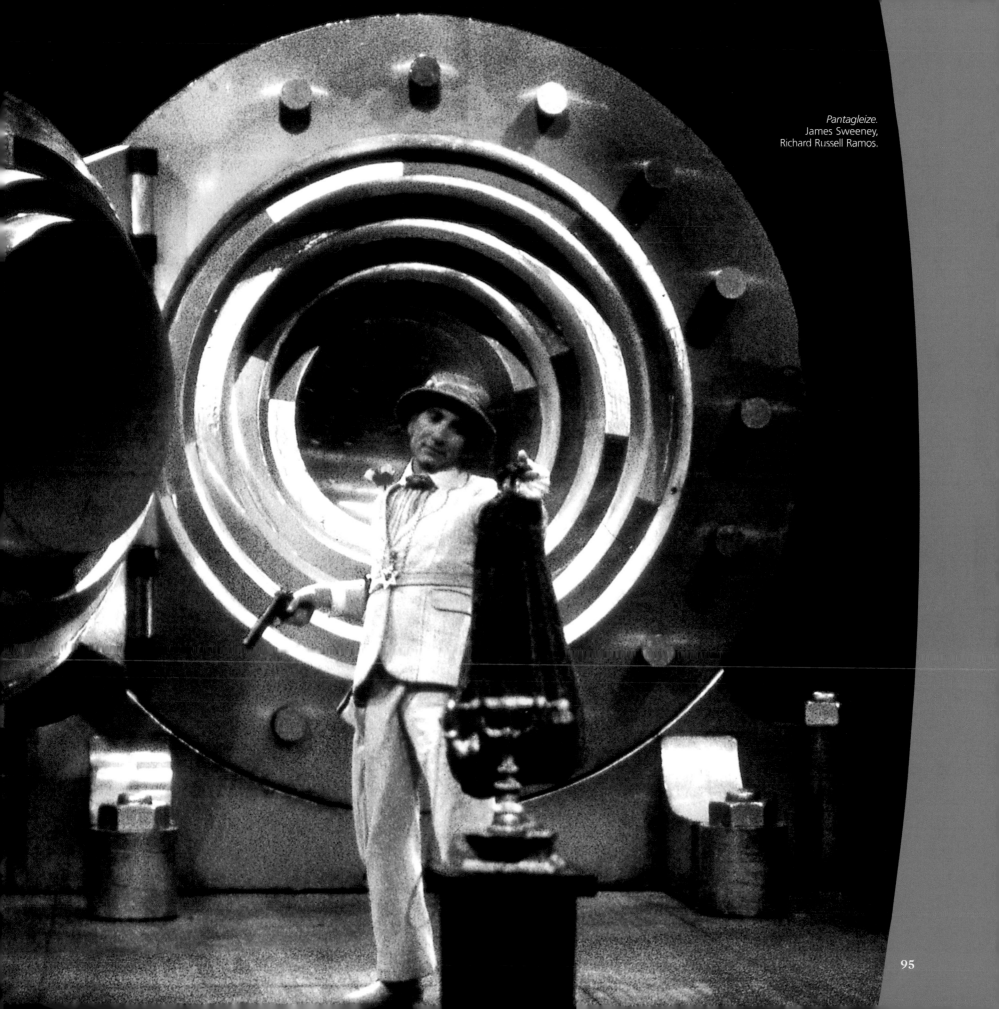

Pantagleize.
James Sweeney,
Richard Russell Ramos.

95

The Pretenders
Henrik Ibsen
  Adapted by Michael Feingold
  Directed by Alvin Epstein
  Set by David Lloyd Gropman
  Costumes by Dunya Ramicova
  Lighting by Duane Schuler
  Music by Dick Whitbeck

Teibele and Her Demon
Isaac Bashevis Singer and
Eve Friedman
  Directed by Stephen Kanee
  Set and costumes by Desmond Heeley
  Lighting by Duane Schuler
  Music by Richard Peaslee

Boy Meets Girl
Bella and Samuel Spewack
  Directed by Peter Mark Schifter
  Set and costumes by Zach Brown
  Lighting by Ronald M. Bundt

Bonjour, là, Bonjour
Michel Tremblay
  Translated by John van Burek
  and Bill Glassco
  Directed by Steven Robman
  Set by Marjorie Kellogg
  Costumes by Jennifer von Mayrhauser
  Lighting by Ronald M. Bundt

Hamlet
William Shakespeare
  Directed by Stephen Kanee
  Set by Jack Barkla
  Costumes by Carrie F. Robbins
  Lighting by Ronald M. Bundt
  Music by Hiram Titus

Marriage
Nikolai Gogol
  Adapted by Barbara Field
  Directed by Anatoly Efros
  Set and costumes by Valery Leventhal
  Lighting by Robert Bye

A Christmas Carol
Charles Dickens
  Adapted by Barbara Field
  Directed by Stephen Kanee
  Set by Jack Barkla
  Costumes by Jack Edwards
  Lighting by Duane Schuler
  Music by Hiram Titus

The Beggar's Opera
John Gay
  Directed by Alvin Epstein
  Set by Tony Straiges
  Costumes by Jennifer von Mayrhauser
  Lighting Duane Schuler
  Music by Darius Milhaud
  and William Bolcom
  Musical settings by John Gay

Guthrie 2

**Flashbacks: Christmas
Past, Christmas Present**
  Adapted by Scott Rubsam
  and Gail Smogard
  Directed by Scott Rubsam
  and Gail Smogard

My Cup Runneth Over
Robert Patrick
  Directed by Michael Feingold

Surprise, Surprise
Michael Tremblay
  Translated by John Van Burek
  Directed by Emily Mann

Vienna Notes
Richard Nelson
  Directed by Bruce Siddons

Litko
David Mamet
Action
Sam Shepard
  Directed by Michael Feingold

On Mount Chimborazo
Tankred Dorst
  Translated by Peter Sandor
  Directed by Emily Mann

**Angel Honey, Baby,
Darling Dear**
Robert Patrick
  Directed by Christopher Covert

A Kurt Weill Cabaret
Kurt Weill
  Directed by Alvin Epstein
  and Martha Schlamme

Martha Schlamme in Concert
  Performance by Martha Schlamme

Little Eyolf
Henrik Ibsen
  Directed by Bruce Siddons

Émigrés
Slawomir Mrozek
  Directed by Cara Duff-McCormick

On Tour

Marriage
Nikolai Gogol
  Adapted by Barbara Field

Outreach Tour

Under the Greenwood Tree
William Shakespeare
  Directed by Jack McGlaughlin

Americana
  Adapted by Scott Rubsam
  Directed by Scott Rubsam

Marriage.
Cara Duff-MacCormmick,
Peter Michael Goetz.

The Rivals
Richard Brinsley Sheridan
 Directed by Alvin Epstein
 Set by Dahl Delu
 Costumes by Jack Edwards
 Lighting by Duane Schuler
 Music by Dick Whitbeck

Right of Way
Richard Lees
 Directed by Steven Robman
 Set by Marjorie Kellogg
 Costumes by Jennifer von Mayrhauser
 Lighting by Duane Schuler

The Glass Menagerie
Tennessee Williams
 Directed by Emily Mann
 Set by Ming Cho Lee
 Costumes by Jennifer von Mayrhauser
 Lighting by Duane Schuler
 Music by Mel Marvin

Monsieur de Molière
Mikhail Bulgakov
 Adapted by Barbara Field
 Directed by Anatoly Efros
 Set by Valery Leventhal
 Costumes by Valery Leventhal
 Lighting by Ronald M. Bundt
 Music by Dick Whitbeck

Endgame
Samuel Beckett
 Directed by Rae Allen
 Set by James Guenther
 Costumes by Jared Aswegan
 Lighting by Ronald M. Bundt

Romeo and Juliet
William Shakespeare
 Directed by Ron Daniels
 Set by Tony Straiges
 Lighting by Craig Miller
 Music by Dick Whitbeck

A Christmas Carol
Charles Dickens
 Adapted by Barbara Field
 Directed by Richard Russell Ramos
 Set by Jack Barkla
 Costumes by Jack Edwards
 Lighting by Neil McLeod
 Music by Hiram Titus

You Can't Take It with You
Moss Hart and George S. Kaufman
 Directed by Edward Gilbert
 Set by Jack Barkla
 Costumes by Jack Edwards
 Lighting by Gilbert V. Hemsley, Jr.

<u>On Tour</u>

The Glass Menagerie
Tennessee Williams

Americana (revival)
 Adapted by Scott Rubsam
 Directed by Elizabeth Bussey

I Remember
Stephen Willems
 Directed by Stephen Willems

Even as the Sun
Warren Green
 Directed by Jon Cranney

Endgame.
Jeff Chandler, Richard Russell Ramos.

Clockwise from upper left:

The Screens, photo and poster, 1989.

Anniversary poster, 1988.

Costume staff dressed up for Variety Show.

G.A.T.E. students, South High, 1989.

Program, 1980.

Ticket tracking sheet, 1984.

Symposium on stage, 1984.

Robert Burns, Robert Curtis-Brown, *The Importance of Being Earnest*, 1984.

Gerry Bamman, *Peer Gynt*, 1982.

In the costume shop.

Patti LuPone, Val Kilmer, *As You Like It*, 1982.

Richard III program, 1987.

Camille

BROWN/1980

Eighteenth Season

TARTUFFE	6	A
TARTUFFE	39	AU
TARTUFFE	28	AU
TARTUFFE	29	AU
TARTUFFE	19	AUG
TARTUFFE	14	AUG
TARTUFFE	30	SEP
TARTUFFE	15	SEP

1980s

TARTUFFE		AUG07E
TARTUFFE	5	AUG14E
TARTUFFE	6	AUG21E
TARTUFFE	7	AUG15M
TARTUFFE	8	AUG08E
TARTUFFE	9	AUG15E
TARTUFFE	10	AUG22E
TARTUFFE	11	AUG02E
TARTUFFE	12	AUG09E

XTARTUFFE	20	AUG22E
TARTUFFE	3	AUG23E
TARTUFFE		SEP27E
		AG16E

Liviu Ciulei
Artistic Director 1981 – 86

In 1981, Liviu Ciulei presented his first season as Guthrie Artistic Director, and brought unprecedented visits and praise from local, national, and international theater critics. Ticket revenue was the highest in Guthrie history. The season was the longest the Guthrie had ever produced, with mainstage performances running from June 1981 to April 1982. *Newsweek:* "In a move that may be as culturally significant as the coming of Guthrie, [the directors] have chosen Rumanian director Liviu Ciulei, one of the boldest and most challenging figures on the international scene, as the Guthrie's new artistic director." Changes were made to the Guthrie stage; Ciulei, who was trained as an architect and scenic designer, squared off the asymmetrical thrust and opened up the backstage to accommodate additional scenery.

What I wanted was to confront the audience ... I think we opened some interesting doors for the Minneapolis audience, to understand the aesthetics of our time, which are the choice of artists – our capricious way of seeing things, which are a result of what's happening in the world.

When you look at history and when you look at an art book, the paintings of the seventeenth or eighteenth century, you can read what happened in that time just by looking at pictures. Art has a power of concentrating the events, and the mentality, the taste, the habits, the customs of a time, and that's our role, to include that in our artistic product and to speak to generations and generations about what we are. [Liviu Ciulei]

Choosing a season – artistically rewarding, pleasingly-balanced, and logistically possible – may be the most critical skill of the theater's artistic leadership. Choosing the title for a touring show adds another filter to the decision. Christine Tschida was the Outreach Director.

I cringe now when I consider the ultimatum with which I greeted our new artistic director before the ink had dried on his contract. "Mr. Ciulei, even though it's barely 1980, we need to know what production we'll tour in 1982. The title has to be well-known, familiar, but not over exposed, nor the kind of show done by community theaters or the local high school. It has to be sophisticated and interesting enough to attract audiences in several different big cities, but inoffensive to the more conservative communities we might visit

Opposite: Liviu Ciulei directing *As You Like It.*

in the Bible Belt. The show also must appeal to teachers and students, so that we can play student matinees.

If the title is too new we won't be able to get the touring rights, and people will really expect the Guthrie to tour a classic, anyway. But be careful if you choose a classic, because they are generally large-cast shows. The touring production can't have more than ten characters (too many salaries and per diems – six or eight would be better), and the characters should be no older than 50 because it is so hard to get mature actors to tour.

The setting, of course, has to be a unit one-location set, and that set has to fit within a 40-foot trailer because it would be impossible to freight more than that amount around the country. This production will represent to thousands of people just what the Guthrie Theater is. And of course, Mr. Ciulei, we expect you to fit this production into your very first, most difficult season to choose, designed to introduce Guthrie audiences to the kind of director you are and the kind of work you want to produce."

The tour show in early 1982 was *The Rainmaker*.

In 1982, an anonymous note was delivered to the stage door for Ebenezer Scrooge, setting in motion a chain of circumstances that would eventually lead to literally tons of food donated to the Twin Cities emergency food shelves. The theater's publicity director Dennis Behl helped it happen.

It all began when I got a call from the house manager following a matinee of *A Christmas Carol,* in December of 1982. "Seth Allen wants you to come down to his dressing room." I knew that a full-fledged Minnesota cold was taking its toll on the actor, and figured he might need a follow-up doctor's appointment or a ride back to his apartment to rest between shows.

Instead, he smiled and motioned to his make-up table and an envelope addressed to Ebenezer Scrooge.

"Dear Mr. Scrooge, thank you for reminding me in a most dramatic way that change is possible. Please see that this gets to the Cratchits and Tiny Tims who need it most in our town," said the handwritten, unsigned note. Four fifty dollar bills were tucked in the fold inside.

The following December, someone in the audience again sent a note backstage, with thanks to Scrooge, played that year by Richard Ooms. Again there was a gift of cash – $260, as I recall – "for the Cratchits of the Twin Cities." We all recognized that something quietly powerful was happening. Dickens' message of transformation was touching the audience so profoundly that they wanted to help, to share, and to respond immediately. The Christmas Carol food drive to supply the Twin Cities emergency food shelves was born.

In the theater, no one ever works alone, and we made it happen as collaborators. Linus [Vlatkovich] and the scene shop guys created a huge green drop-off bin for the lobby; the box office stuffed flyers into every ticket envelope. Manager Pam Truesdell made sure that every phone customer was asked to bring a nonperishable food item or make a cash donation. Ever since 1982, Guthrie audiences have responded with literally tons of food for the neediest in the Cities, playing out, each in his own way, Tiny Tim's refrain, "God bless us, everyone!"

David Warrilow played Jaques in Ciulei's 1981 production of *As You Like It*. He spoke later about the pleasure of playing the thrust and the connection with the Guthrie audience.

> You see, I loved the fact that I could go down to the edge of that thrust stage with 1,400 people in the house and start quite quietly to say "all the world's a stage" and have this ripple go through the audience, this sort of thrill, people recognizing the tune, do you know what I mean? And then suddenly they're realizing that they didn't know how it went on, and so they needed to be quiet to listen. And then they would really listen and it was magical.

Actor Josie de Guzman describes coming from Broadway to Minneapolis to work.

The Guthrie Theater
Peer Gynt
by Henrik Ibsen

> The opportunity came to work with Liviu Ciulei in *Peer Gynt*, and I went to the Guthrie. I was thrilled about playing Solveig. I wasn't thrilled about being in Minnesota during the winter – I spent five months there.
>
> It was hard to understand Liviu at first, because he's so European in his directing. He knows exactly what he wants, even physically, even line readings, and he wasn't open to any suggestions. When I read that I had to be blind and seventy years old at the end of the play, I asked Marilyn [Fried, her Method teacher], "What am I going to do?" She said, "Go look at apes. Apes are good for age." I worked on them, and I also did sensory exercises for blindness. I got to the Guthrie and Liviu said, in his wonderful accent, "No no no no, I don't want you to eemitate seventy years. She ees ageless." I had done all this work and he just wanted me to be myself! So I was myself, only a little slower. I did practice being blind, and it was helpful.
>
> Solveig spins and I learned how to spin thread. In one rehearsal, I was working on the spinning because I wanted to get it real, and Liviu said, "Thees you eendicate. You do not have to speen thread out of the wool. Een the theatre you eendicate." But I still got that yarn to come out, very nicely if I may add.

Jack Edwards was the Guthrie costume director for many years. In film footage from the late eighties, Edwards ushers the camera through a workroom constructing *Richard III,* knitting chain mail for armor, building a body suit for the hunchback king, bending over the tables in concentration, surrounded by a thousand tools.

The costume shop under his leadership was a tight-knit close community that produced brilliant work, and played nearly as hard as they stitched. Opening night parties up in the costume shop were legendary, and the seasons were marked by regular festivities, Strawberry Festivals, etcetera. And they loved the British royals. Dwight Larsen:

> We were all Charles and Diana fans. We were off Guthrie work when the big wedding happened, but some of us were stitching on *Sesame Street Live* costumes, and we all got up in the middle of the night, and gathered in someone's living room at five o'clock in the morning. We had breakfast and watched the wedding, and that was the beginning of it. And when the baby was born, we decided we should make a quilt and send it to him. We made a very intricate hand-pieced border and all got together one evening and hand-quilted the whole thing. We wrote a nice letter, packed it up and sent it off. A month or so later, we got a letter back from Buckingham Palace thanking us. It was signed by a lady-in-waiting. One of the guys in the shop did some research and made up a board that had photos of the quilt, scraps of the fabric, the letter. And a photo of The Heir! It hung in the shop for years and years. [1984]

When Ciulei became the Artistic Director, the arrival of European-born directors and designers on Vineland Place accelerated. Throughout the eighties, the Romanian scenic designer Radu Boruzescu and his costume designer wife Miruna were regular guest artists. Radu spoke some English. Miruna did not. Up in the costume shop, Jack Edwards got ready.

> She spoke five different languages, but not English. I wasn't going to speak Romanian and I didn't want to speak German – anyway, I decided to take French lessons so we could talk back and forth to each other. It was almost unnecessary, because Miruna and I were like the same soul. And there is the language of dressmaking, and that we both understood. Intuitively, we knew what the other was thinking all the time.
>
> I was studying French and she was studying English.
>
> In the very beginning, we were having a fitting and we were trying to rush it because we had to get the actor back to rehearsal. The cutter was fitting the bodice and Miruna was on one side of the skirt and I was on the other pinning the hem. We were on our hands and knees working our way around and at one point, we came sort of head-to-head. And Miruna said, "See the black dog? This is not a black dog. This is a pink pig." And she smiled and laughed. "See, Jack, how much help this is for the costumes?"
>
> That was her English lesson for the day, you see.
>
> One day she said, "Jack, what is 'avalabala?'" I said "Miruna, I haven't the slightest idea." She said "Everywhere, everywhere, 'avalabala'." And she took

me to the fitting schedule where it said "Harry Smith, three o'clock. Joan King, three-thirty. Peter Piper, as available." Avalabala!

⌒

Mark Bly was a dramaturg for Liviu Ciulei, Garland Wright, and many guest directors, researching plays and periods and working very closely with the process of making plays at the Guthrie.

There was an incredible diversity of people there during those years. You weren't always seeing only Romanian artists; it was a very wide spectrum coming. Directorial talents, design talents! So many Romanian designers, French designers, Italian designers, American designers. And so many actors from so many different worlds. You had a David Warrilow, Priscilla Smith, Joan McIntosh from the avant-garde world. You had Werner Klemperer, from his own world. The Juilliard actors, like Harriet Harris. The Yale actors, like David Hyde Pierce. Plus the Minneapolis actors – the great old guard like James Lawless and the new guard like Sally Wingert. Richard Ooms, Claudia Wilkens. It was a constant intersection of people you'd never expect to be working with in a million years.

Liviu brought in people like Andrei Serban and Lucien Pintilie because he knew how good they were and how those productions would affect American theater. It wasn't just the critics from *Time* and *Newsweek* flying in to see opening nights in Minneapolis. There were directors and actors flying in to see the work.

To me, that was the real excitement. Looking around and saying, Oh my God, anything really is possible here. With Liviu, you knew you were going on a journey. And it was going to be full of surprises.

When I was there, it worked quite unlike any other theater I had ever worked at. There was life going on there on Saturdays, on Sundays. There were always people around – backstage people, ushers, everyone. There were people downstairs in the shops who had been there forever. There were always people that I didn't know but I understood mattered in ways that were inconceivable to me.

I'll never forget the night we were doing *Marriage of Figaro* and the actor Robert Dorfman was swinging out on his trapeze, doing his ten minute speech. Suddenly one of the wires connecting to the trapeze sort of flinched and for a second he had a look of panic on his face as he was swinging out over the audience. Garland and Serban and I were looking and looking. I went backstage and found out that the wire had snapped on the trapeze and the lead stagehand had grabbed the wire and held on to it while Robert Dorfman swung in space. The kind of commitment that took! And not disrupting the performance.

That is the closest thing I can come to understand the Guthrie at its best. At its best, it's beyond family. It's theater workers, people who just say 'I will be there and I will give what I have.' That guy, and Sheila Livingston, are my definition.

"That guy" was Bill Kephart.

In May of 1982, the Guthrie was honored with the American Theatre Wing's Tony Award for its outstanding contribution to the American regional theater. "The Guthrie Theater has played an important role in the development of America's regional theater. For twenty years, the Guthrie, with its true rotating repertory and many fine actors has shared its benefits contributing to the development of theater as a whole – on Broadway and throughout the nation."

Tony Award.

Theater folk have long memories for their own "worst moments," and – in this case, anyway – a gentlemanly reluctance to place blame. In 1983, Matt Barber was conducting the orchestra for the annual production of *A Christmas Carol* from an offstage room, connected with the stage only with monitors; this incident he describes as "surely the worst moment of my career, but after twenty years it seems rather hilarious." It just proves that anything can happen, even in a show as often-repeated as the holiday production.

> Perhaps you've heard of the entrance of the Fezziwig party in the 1983 production of *A Christmas Carol?*
>
> [Music director] David Bishop had recorded the singers singing "Deck the Halls" to beef up the singing voices of the cast, and the live orchestra was intended to play along with the finished tape. I was conducting the orchestra from the orchestra room down below and was hooked up to the tape monitor via headphones, since the tape was being operated from the booth. I would then bring the orchestra in when I heard the count-off through the headphones.
>
> Well, one fine night, when the cue came, nothing! No count-off, no voices, nothing. I waited perhaps five seconds. My assumption was that the tape had broken and I decided to just bring the orchestra in. Little did I know that the recorded music was blaring away just fine in the house. I just couldn't hear it.
>
> It wasn't long before I realized what was happening and upon tearing off my headphones, I heard a sound that Charles Ives would have loved. The bizarre and fascinating clash of two versions of "Deck the Halls" completely out of synch, coupled with the riotous entrance of the (somewhat confused) Fezziwig partygoers. The cacophony of sound was described as "kinda cool" by one followspot operator, but "dare we show our faces again?" by an actor.

Barber reports an error by "a certain sound technician who shall remain unnamed" as the reason for Charles Dickens' unexpected encounter with Charles Ives.

The rarely-seen, circa 1980's, Wardrobe Crew ("no one ever comes down to visit us") stepped up to present a number featuring a steamer and a washboard at a backstage Picnic Cabaret. Photo by Kerry Dikken, who was then the stage doorman.

Theater press materials called the 1983 *The Seagull,* directed by Romanian Lucien Pintilie in his American debut, a "controversial reinterpretation." Staff remembers that the production started with the fourth act instead of the first. And that the run was full of incident.

In those days, designers used a lot of acid-treated mirrored Plexiglass in the scenery; the entire backstage area of the set was a forest of birch trees surrounded by a Plexiglass wall. In one of the first scenes of the play, Treplev, played by David Hyde Pierce, is berated by his family and friends, gets very frustrated, and runs offstage. My job was to look through a crack in the set where I could see him approach, and open a flush-mounted door in the mirror wall just as he got there so it looked like he disappeared in the forest.

Well, one night as David raced upstage toward me, I saw him disappear to my left instead of to the right. I heard a loud noise and the wall shook violently. I opened the door, and David stepped through holding his head and bent over. He had missed the opening. He didn't stand up. He stayed bent over and simply said, in a somewhat muffled voice, "Don't say a word, not a word." I had to bite my tongue not to laugh out loud – we had a great laugh over it. Later.

It was an eventful run for some reason. The play started with a storm, with numerous thunder clap sound effects and flashing strobe lights, etc. One night we had a substitute sound operator and instead of hearing the thunder clap cue, the Guthrie Theater audience experienced perhaps the largest and noisiest cricket known to man.

Seagull closes with an offstage suicide, which interrupts a quiet card game being played on stage. We had a 16 gauge, double-barrelled shotgun with both barrels loaded as a backup. As luck would have it, both barrels failed in a single performance. The card players waited. And waited. Treplev had to die in order for the play to end. Then the 'doctor' wrote his own line of Chekhov to get offstage, and returned. He faced the other actors, seated at the table, and announced that Treplev must have taken some poison out of his medical bag, and was dead.

The lesson? Gun maintenance is crucial. [Russell Johnson]

The comic and actor Jerry Stiller as Nathan Detroit, with the company of *Guys and Dolls*.

The Threepenny Opera.
Barbara Andres (seated), Claudia Wilkins (on her left) and company.

The Threepenny Opera, directed by Liviu Ciulei, and *Guys and Dolls,* directed by Garland Wright, were both enormous musical productions. They were rehearsed at the same time, they opened just a few days apart, and then played in repertory over the summer of 1984.

Jerry Stiller came to Minneapolis, he said, "to play the best role ever written in an American musical. During rehearsals, I pictured the ghost of Sam Levene, the original Nathan Detroit, hovering over me. Lots of young actors came backstage during the run, many of whom had played Nathan Detroit in a school play or a community theater production. The young Nathans would invariably advise me on how to get more laughs."

Liviu Ciulei was a brilliant communicator, and his English – perhaps his fourth language – was excellent. It was also inventive, idiosyncratic, and occasionally incomprehensible. There is a story of an actor, eager to please Ciulei, who was directed in one scene to "be more eccentric." Willingly, and then somewhat desperately, the actor tried unusual physicalities and odd vocal choices, without seeming to satisfy the director. Finally Ciulei stopped and said, "No, no. Be more eccentric. Go toward the center of the stage!"

The annual production of *A Christmas Carol* can be a time of theatrical family togetherness. In 1984, Barbara Kingsley played Mrs. Cratchit. Her husband Stephen D'Ambrose played Bob Cratchit. And not-yet-four-year-old Cooper D'Ambrose played Tiny Tim, who is, after all, supposed to be ill during most of the play.

Cooper was a ball of fire; he just had a tremendous amount of energy. The question was not whether he could do it; it was whether the theater would still be standing. There was the one night, though, when he forgot the audience was there.

In rehearsal, Cooper learned to use his little crutch, to ride on his (real and stage) father's shoulders, and to pretend to have a sore leg.

"No, honey, you can't run after that apple while we're on stage. You have a sore leg, remember?"

And he learned to deliver his big line. Restored to health, Tiny Tim perched on kindly Scrooge's shoulder, vigorously cried, "God Bless Us, Every One!" and skipped straight upstage and off, there to stand in the wings and wait for his curtain call.

Sometimes Cooper got tired of waiting, though. In rehearsal, he would scamper offstage and around, and run down an aisle into the auditorium, watch a few moments, and then run back in time to take Scrooge's hand for their call.

He got into the habit and that's what he did on the first preview night. During the final scene, a small shaft of light from the door came into the house from the top of Aisle 1. From the control booth, staff watched helplessly as Cooper, dressed as Tiny Tim, entered the auditorium and ran down the aisle to sit on the bottom step and watch, just as he had done in rehearsal, and entirely heedless of the fact that every seat in the house was full. Audience members near the first section were noticeably distracted by the appearance of Tiny Tim in their midst.

Cooper, in the spill from the stage light, sat and watched for a minute, until a laugh line came from the stage and the audience chuckled. He looked to his right and realized he was within inches of the audience and some of them were looking back at him.

Cooper whirled and fled up the steps, out of the auditorium and to the backstage to appear moments later, completely unruffled, for his curtain call. A brief lecture was delivered later that night.

~

In the theater, all decisions are formative, even though the audience may not be aware of them. From resident Director Christopher Markle's production notebook for *Hedda Gabler*, some notes on the new translation commissioned by the Guthrie. The notebook records a lively exchange between the translators on the merits of calling the character "Auntie Juju."

The Cratchit family together backstage: Stephen D'Ambrose, Barbara Kingsley, Cooper D'Ambrose.

Hedda Gabler, Act I:

Frøken Tesman. God morgen, god morgen, Jørgen!
Tesman (i døråpningen). Tante Julle! Kjære tante Julle! (går hen og ryster hennes hånd.) Helt her ute — så tidlig på dagen! Hva?

Frøken Tesman. Ja, du kan da tenke at jeg måtte se litt innom til jer.

Tesman. Og det enda du ikke har fått deg noen ordentlig nattero!

Frøken Tesman. Å, det gjør meg ingen verdens ting.
Tesman. Nå, du kom vel ellers godt hjem fra bryggen? Hva?

Hedda Gabler translation, Act I, second draft:

MISS TESMAN
Good morning, good morning, George!

see Note ①

TESSMAN (IN THE DOORWAY)
Auntie JuJu! Dear Auntie JuJu! (goes to her and shakes her hand vigorously). All the way out here--and so early in the day! Huh! Hmm!

This is too literal— not meaning of Norw. line

MISS TESMAN
Yes, I'm sure you knew I had to peek in for a minute (on you two)

16

TESMAN
And without even a good night's sleep!

17

?

MISS TESMAN
Oh, that doesn't matter to me one bit.

why? (so modern, cliché'ish)

you know,

→ I like to reinforce her. Typical of her.

TESMAN
Well--you got home then from the pier all right? Huh?

Several times in most weeks, school buses pull up to the Guthrie and release a torrent of young people into the theaters; this has been going on, and increasing, since 1963. The theater hears regularly from students who say their lives were changed.

> I want to tell a story about a standing ovation that put me where I am today. I came down with my class to see a Wednesday matinee of *The Rainmaker*, largely a school audience. I was sitting off Aisle 7, under the overhang, and I could hear every word. When the rain came at the end, you could feel the rain in the auditorium. It wasn't just the lighting and the sound, but the way the actors were reacting and well. I get goosebumps even now and I almost well up thinking about the end of that play. It remains the most crystallizing performance; I remember images. I remember the look and feel of the set. I remember that moment when it was supposed to be raining and you really thought it was. And there was no water.
>
> At the end, we were immediately all up on our feet. It didn't take someone starting it; it was a collective thing, a true standing ovation. It was fascinating and life-changing. And now I'm a part of that thing that happened to me back then. [Director and teacher Jef Hal-Flavin]

Cyrano de Bergerac brought a first-and-last to the Guthrie stage, with the addition of "Dolly" the horse to the cast, to pull a carriage (with ingénue) onto the set. Dolly was chosen in part for her equanimity, since she had to walk through the narrow – even for actors – hallways of the backstage and duck through several doorways to make her entrance. Dressing her handler as the Cyrano-era character who would lead her across the stage presented a special challenge to the costume designer and shop; the handler had a regular sideline as a John Wayne impersonator. Guthrie insiders took a great deal of pleasure in watching "John Wayne," elaborately bedecked in a long, curling, and disguising wig making his brief and secret debut on the Guthrie stage.

Managing tickets for opening nights and sold out runs is a special art for the box office. In early 1987, the theater presented *The Gospel at Colonus*, an adaptation from Sophocles by way of an African-American church setting. It was a smash. One busy night, 124 duplicate tickets mysteriously appeared for a sold-out performance. Twenty minutes to curtain; the clock was ticking.

> This was a very difficult show because it was so popular and we had lots of people coming who weren't necessarily used to coming to the Guthrie. I remember one woman who took a bottle of white-out and marked out her seat locations. She re-wrote them for the locations she wanted. And somebody in the show told people just to go ahead and bring their own chairs, so people would be in the lobby with their lawn chairs.
>
> We had sold tickets through Dayton's Ticketmaster. I was sitting at my desk on a Saturday night, about twenty minutes before the show was going to

Werner Klemperer and Marianne Tatum backstage during *Hang On To Me*, 1984 season. Directed by 24-year old Peter Sellars, the show was billed as "an inspired marriage of Gorky's *Summerfolk* and songs of George and Ira Gershwin." Backstage, it was referred to as "the Gorky-Gershwin."

Opposite: Final preparations are made on the ship's exterior for *Anything Goes*. The entire set, with all actors aboard, weighed eight tons; it tracked downstage, revolved to show new locations, and flew. On the night of the first preview, the ship made its first revolve to reveal an unpainted plywood side; the shop ran out of preparation time. Three weeks of performances were added at the end of the run, to respond to ticket demand. Author and then-stage manager Peg Guilfoyle at lower left. Note the orchestra pit created down front.

start. The house manager came in and brought me two tickets and said, "I've got dupes." And I thought, "oh, boy" and I dealt with it. Pretty soon she comes back with six tickets – six more dupes. Then she came back with ten. All of a sudden there's a crowd of people outside my door. There were 124 tickets that we had given to Dayton's to sell and when the audit came back, we mistakenly put them back on sale. We had double-sold them.

So I'm standing there and all these people are yelling at me, "my tickets are good!" I was trying to yell because they're all standing around the box office door. There are people writing passes like mad for what seats we had, and for chairs, and I turned around to come to the box office and I tripped and flew into the office. One of my staff said, "Oh my God, she's been hit. Somebody's hit her. Slam the door, they're attacking the office."

I refunded all of them. They could either stay and sit on the stair steps that night or they could come to another performance. Backstage, they graciously held the show for about twenty minutes while we got people in. The actors standing on stage for that show saw no aisles anywhere. It was packed, stair steps and all. [Pam Truesdell]

Garland Wright came to the Guthrie leadership as an American director already familiar with the theater, which by 1987 was enormous, sometimes unwieldy, and an institution. Having directed plays in Minneapolis as part of his freelance career, and been an artistic associate to Liviu Ciulei, Wright knew the way the Guthrie worked, and saw its enormous potential. In his time, he placed the actor at the center of the business of the theater, and the artistic directorship firmly at the helm; it was the first time that the artistic director was placed at the very top of the organizational chart.

The theater asks the questions that curious and life-filled people ask: Who are we? Why are we here? Why is life so difficult and sometimes so painful? Why is it sometimes absurdly silly? Why is it, or is it, wrong to be afraid? Can love conquer all? Can it at least conquer a little? We ask these questions out of our experience because our experience is not enough. Our experience tells us only that these things are so, but we want to know why they are so, and if not why, we want solace in knowing that others, too, want to know why. And we long to hear many different people's attempts at an answer, even if the answer is impossible. As Joseph Campbell says, "We seek perhaps not a meaning for our lives, but a shared experience of having been alive."

Given that such a curiosity exists and has been encouraged, the theater then does become a need in our lives. And here I specifically mean the theater as opposed to other arts. The theater shows us real people right before us – acting, doing something. I find that a very powerful metaphor to teach us that action requires the real person. So, do we share, even in a culture as diverse as ours, common questions? Yes, I think we do. And the theater should be a powerful unifying force. [Garland Wright]

The Gospel at Colonus. Janice Steele, Jevetta Steele, Morgan Freeman.

Opposite: Garland Wright (center) directing *Uncle Vanya.* From left: Cristine Rose, John Carroll Lynch, Stephen Yoakam

Garland Wright
Artistic Director 1987 – 95

Auditions, those nerve-wracking try-outs when actors have perhaps five minutes to display their skills, make a connection, and get a job, are a fact of life in the theater. Nathaniel Fuller remembers his first (successful) audition for the theater.

I'd been auditioning at the Guthrie for 10 years off and on without success. It was a miserable process. What did they want? What kind of actor were they looking for? What piece could show off my skills and make me stand out any more than the hundreds of actors parading through the annual general auditions?

I'd done the speeches of Hamlet, Mark Antony, Richard III, Macbeth, Oberon, Bottom, etc. Each audition had received a version of the "Very good, thank you" response, which translates into, "Don't call us and we won't call you."

Finally I decided that if I had to keep going through this process I was going to do it as much for me as for them. I wanted to have a little fun and maybe create a bit of a surprise.

Garland Wright was casting *Richard III* and I had an opportunity to audition for him. This is how I introduced my monologue. "My next piece is classical." I said. "It's Shakespeare. What you are about to see is an experiment to test Stanislavski's theory that there are no small parts. What follows are some dozen or so scenes of roles I'd most likely be cast in my first year in a major repertory company."

I then turned my back on Mr. Wright, walked away a few steps, wheeled and shouted, "Arm! Arm! The enemy doth make assault!" I turned away again, turned back and went through a series of thirteen Shakespearian messenger and servant speeches in a variety of over-the top characterizations and scenery-chewing accents.

I threw myself sprawling across the floor and doubled up in pain after being struck and kicked by Richard III as I tried to tell him of Buckingham's capture. I entered a palace and silently passed from hope to horror to despair before uttering an abject, "I will, my liege," and departing. The moving Birnam Wood was described to the Scottish king in the thickest throat-tangling brogue I could muster. One of the two mimed heads of Andronicus' sons kept falling over until I desperately smooshed the neck into the floor. I tersely informed Brutus of his wife Fulvia's death. Frantically and manically I screamed to Lady Capulet of the chaos in her kitchen. I hissed a warning to Caesar of dangerous portents in the entrails of a beast.

Finally, I ran into a mob-filled street shouting for "Jack Cade! Jack Cade!" With a sudden grunt I arched sharply back from a sword blade in my back, doubled forward with a groan from a thrust to the guts, and wheezing, collapsed to sitting on my rear. With a look of pain and bewilderment I began to gurgle. Slowly, slowly, I toppled sideways into a contorted, sprawling, open-eyed demise concluded by the inevitable drawn out death rattle.

Garland hired me.

What goes in to a new, ground-breaking and controversial production at the Guthrie?

In the fall of 1987, director JoAnne Akalaitis staged Henry Schmidt's translation of the George Buchner play, *Leonce and Lena* for the Guthrie. The production was titled *Leon and Lena (and lenz)* and included a short film version of Buchner's novella, Lenz, which was integrated into the staging.

The dramaturg providing research for the production was Mark Bly. In 1990, Yale's Theater magazine published excerpts of his log, documenting the exploratory intellectual process that Akalaitis and her collaborators undertook.

When the Guthrie lights go down, the audience is invited to participate in the result of months, and sometimes years, of the artists' consideration and collaboration. Everything is deliberate; Bly's log provides a window into the complexity of those decisions, and into the way that artists' work is sometimes remarkably influenced by events from the world outside the rehearsal room.

> JoAnne has a series of meetings in early 1987 with her collaborators: George Tsypin [set designer]; Adelle (Bonnie) Lutz [costume designer]; Terry Allen [composer]; and Jennifer Tipton [lighting designer]. Early discussions with George and Bonnie go through a phase of looking at Russian Constructivist art books, but this does not last. JoAnne's initial reading of the play made her feel it should be set in the American Southwest and accompanied by Terry Allen's music and she goes back to this idea.
>
> JoAnne shows George the book *Zany Afternoons* by Bruce McCall, which George describes as a "stream-lined, zany, made vision." They also spend time looking at many books on the Southwest. JoAnne talks to George about the sense of "big sky" in the Southwest and about the pop culture "Cadillac Ranch" sculptures outside Amarillo, Texas. One evening in February, JoAnne cooks supper for George and Jennifer. Drawing upon the feeling that the "Cadillac Ranch" sculptures gave him, George discusses a set with a highway suspended in air and a blazing yellow sun setting, amidst a whole highway system of road signs and hotels.

In March and again in April, JoAnne and her collaborators come to Minneapolis to work, discuss, talk with theater staff, and look at the Guthrie's enormous thrust stage.

> JoAnne describes the interior settings. The rooms are filled with rich people's eclectic playthings: architectural models; aquarium with a shark; Jacuzzi, rare plants; video monitors. The exterior settings reflect our fantasies about wide open spaces and endless horizons. A highway that leads nowhere will be suspended over the stage and there will be a motel and road signs. The effect of the exterior will be "endless sky and road on an empty plain, moving clouds, all is vast and brilliant."

In August, rehearsals begin. In October, technical-dress rehearsals.

At last, after eight weeks of rehearsal we get to work on stage with the set. What George Tsypin has created is amazing. Suspended over the Guthrie thrust stage is a sixty-foot highway, creating another whole level in the space, a road upon which people can travel. The highway is askew, reflecting the Guthrie auditorium itself, which is non-symetrical, filled with odd angles. The road has an astonishing power as it floats obtrusively, jutting out ominously at the audience.

In October, during the previews and opening period, Bly notes the following.

It is often said that art never exists in a vacuum, and the world events of this week seem determined to prove the old adage true. Perhaps it is "poetic justice" that "real world" distractions have suddenly intruded upon us. After all, we moved this 1836 play into 1987 America in part to make a point about the state of our contemporary world. On October 19, "Black Monday," four days before the opening, the Dow Jones Industrial Average plummets 508 points, the largest single one-day decline in history. During rehearsal on Tuesday, JoAnne pulls out a copy of the *Wall Street Journal* and selects several headlines which the Executive Secretaries and Chairman of the Board now repeat to one another as they make their entrance in I-3. It is not necessary for JoAnne to make a speech pointing out the audience's heightened awareness of corporate and monetary issues after "Black Monday" – the media already has anxiety at fever pitch.

It makes a good story now, but no one was laughing at the time. Even when the onstage work is utterly serious – as in the first preview of *Hamlet* in the Guthrie's 25th Anniversary season – life backstage has its own rhythms, and its own incidents.

It was the summer of 1988. We were doing our first preview of Garland's *Hamlet* featuring Zeljko Ivanek as Hamlet and Julianne Moore as Ophelia. Richard Hicks and I were playing, respectively, Guildenstern and Rosencrantz. We'd finished our big 'hello long time no see' scene with Hamlet. We came off stage and went downstairs to our dressing room deep in conversation about how we thought our big scene had just gone – serious young actors that we were. We continued the discussion as we got out of our costumes – and continued somewhat casually dissecting our work, based on the many weeks of rehearsal we'd just finished. This was our first audience. This was *Hamlet* at the Guthrie. Garland's *Hamlet,* 25 years after the theater's inaugural production of Tyrone Guthrie's own *Hamlet*. The same Tyrone Guthrie who had directed Laurence Olivier in his *Hamlet*.

Our big scene just finished was a comic scene and we were busily gauging, among other things, how many of our 'laugh lines' had in fact, well, gotten laughs. Serious young actors that we were. We hung up our costumes as we talked and were sitting there, somewhere one level underneath the stage in the cement bunker dressing room we shared, in our briefs, t-shirts and black socks. Next costumes for us both were tuxes.

In this sort of situation – backstage in a dressing room during a show – one goes about various activities, but always with part of one's ears semi-consciously monitoring the dressing room speaker system for the familiar landmark words of the famous scenes being played out upstairs onstage – words that were distance markers between now and your next entrance. We talked and began to relax and come down a bit from the high of a first audience. Suddenly, Richard and I – sitting there face to face in our underwear, somewhere mid conversation were interrupted by very familiar words indeed. Over our dressing room speaker system, we heard the worst thing any actor can ever dream. Worse even than "thanks for coming" at an audition. We heard the first line of the scene we were in. Or were supposed to be in.

The King has the first line in Act III Scene 1 as he and Gertrude storm angrily downstage: "And can you by no drift of circumstance get from him why he puts on this confusion?" at which point they both whip around to face us. We, Richard and I heard the line – in disbelief. In horror. In our dressing room. In the basement. In our underwear. Rick spoke first. He said "Oh my god – WE'RE ON!" I shook my head. "No–No!" Richard: "Yes – yes! We ARE!" We heard more lines over the speakers – but lines that weren't in Shakespeare's *Hamlet*. Claudius: "Rosencrantz?!" Gertrude: "Guildenstern?!?" Rick and I moved both in double-time, and somehow, slow-motion at once. We flailed at the costume racks for parts of our tuxes and took off in a crazed dash out of the dressing room. Over the monitors in the hallway we heard another "Rosencrantz!" "Guildenstern!!" "Come here this instant!" We wailed up the stairs, flailing at whatever clothing we'd managed to grab. We entered upstage center in white tee-shirts and black socks, hopping and tugging our tux pants up.

The King and Queen's eyes spun in their heads. From the audience – more of a laugh than we'd been able to get during our "comic scene" with Hamlet. It must have looked to them like Claudius and Gertrude had interrupted Rosencrantz and Guildenstern doing off in their room just what parents are afraid happens in all-boy boarding school dorm rooms – the love that dared not speak its name. I only remember the Queen, eyes spinning wildly, finally staring at us and saying: "Well! Well!"

We, Richard and I and our underwear entrance, were the talk of the company backstage and after the show. And especially the next morning at notes session back in the rehearsal room. With Garland. When he finally, after an excruciating wait, came to that point in the notes he just said something like: "Act three." (Long pause) "Rosencrantz and Guildenstern" (Another longer pause) "I take it ... that that won't happen again." We, Richard and I, shook our heads contritely. The rest of the cast released in an eruption of laughter. They laughed long and hard at us. You can count on Shakespeare to always provide some comic relief, no matter how high the tragedy. [actor Tom Fervoy]

Actor Zeljko Ivanek and vocal coach Liz Smith preparing him for *Hamlet*.

Hard on the heels of 1987's double opening of *The Misanthrope* and *The Piggybank*, both directed by Wright, came the realization of a goal that every artistic director had named and none had yet fully achieved. The Second Stage 'acting laboratory' opened in temporary quarters at the Minneapolis College of Art and Design, under the supervision of young director Charles Newell. According to the *Star Tribune*, "the space will be used by the acting company to develop projects and give actors an opportunity to try roles they normally wouldn't attempt on the mainstage." The MCAD space was the first of a wide variety of temporary spaces which housed occasional open rehearsals for small works and company-oriented workshops, and the predecessor to the Guthrie Lab, which housed productions until the Guthrie consolidated to the river location in 2006.

The Lab, housed in a former warehouse in the Minneapolis warehouse district, opened in June 1988, although not necessarily for an audience. "The Lab's emphasis is on the material and the actor rather than the production value," said the *Skyway News*. Guthrie Press Director Dennis Behl said "It's a place for the development of new theatrical experience. In some cases, the work here will not correlate to the Guthrie stage very directly. But in some cases, the correlation will be very direct. There are also times when the public will be invited in to see what we are doing." The first of those was the performance of Shakespeare's *Cymbeline*, the first of a series of Resident Director's projects.

A few years later, actor Brenda Wehle would say:

> The Lab is delicious. It's so liberating to pursue an idea or an approach to a part without pressure to produce a finished product. It's like exercise; ultimately the time spent building strength and flexibility benefits your overall work.

Cymbeline rehearses in the new Guthrie Lab.

In the eighties the Guthrie, like many theaters, became engaged in AIDS education and fundraising. The theater donated Lab space and personnel for an Equity Fights AIDS benefit, initiated and participated in various task forces, and provided readers, including Garland Wright, at the ceremony marking the first visit of the AIDS quilt to Minneapolis. A December 1988 newspaper article said:

> While AIDS still seems remote to most of us, it has long been a reality too immediate to ignore in the national performing arts community. In theater, many have lost more than one friend or colleague to the disease. And what the Guthrie, and other theaters around here do to raise both money and awareness is exemplary – not only of what a community can do collectively to combat AIDS, but how theater can inform and educate within that community.

For some curious reason that can only be explained by genetic miscalculation, there have always been, and I firmly believe will always be, a staunch group of dedicated dreamers who will find it within themselves to make theater, and to make it regardless of what the prevailing climate of demand for such a product may be. These artists, as we call them because we can't find any less exotic category for them, flourish on their own dreams. The laws of supply and demand elude them completely. Sometimes they are very lucky, as in the case of a Michaelangelo or a Shakespeare, where their own mode of expression is readily seen not only by the intelligentsia and the connoisseurs, but by the masses. Their genius is the genius of their times. They were embraced. At other times, their genius is out of synch. It is reviled, only to be discovered and treasured after they've gone, as in Van Gogh, Rimbaud, Buchner, Nijinsky. But artists, regardless of any acceptance they may receive, have found, and I believe always will find, the strength to speak from their hearts and minds their view of the world and try to communicate it to others. They do it from an innate need to speak out and from a strong sense that what any individual might say about the human condition does indeed have value.

So I don't really worry about the theater or its capacity to survive. Artists will insist that there is art in the world whether anyone thinks it's necessary or not. [Garland Wright]

South High School students take a rest from marching in front of the Guthrie on Vineland Place. Two were providing legs, and one was providing guidance, using a costume from *Rhinoceros* to promote an open house and auction to benefit the Minnesota AIDS project.

Garland Wright and actor Richard Ooms in the old Rehearsal Room 1 on Vineland Place, preparing for *The Imaginary Invalid* in the 1988 season.

Wild Oats
John O'Keeffe
   Directed by Kenneth Frankel
   Set by Jack Barkla
   Costumes by Lewis Brown
   Lighting by John McLain
   Music by Thomas Fay

Camille
Alexandre Dumas fils
   Adapted by Barbara Field
   Directed by Garland Wright
   Set by Jack Barkla
   Costumes by Lewis Brown
   Lighting by John McLain
   Music by Hiram Titus

The Tavern
George M. Cohan
   Directed by Stephen Kanee
   Set by Jack Barkla
   Costumes by Jack Edwards
   Lighting by John McLain
   Music by Dick Whitbeck

Desire Under the Elms
Eugene O'Neill
   Directed by George Keathley
   Set by James Guenther
   Costumes by Virgil Johnson
   Lighting by John McLain
   Music by Dick Whitbeck

Mary Stuart
Friedrich von Schiller
   Translated by Joseph Mellish
   Directed by Garland Wright
   Set by Jack Barkla
   Costumes by Jane Greenwood
   Lighting by Craig Miller
   Music by Steven M. Rydberg

A Christmas Carol
Charles Dickens
   Adapted by Barbara Field
   Directed by Tony Mockus
   Set by Jack Barkla
   Costumes by Jack Edwards
   Lighting by Paul Scharfenberger
   Music by Hiram Titus

Arms and the Man
George Bernard Shaw
   Directed by Michael Langham
   Set and costumes by Desmond Heeley
   Lighting by Duane Schuler
   Music by Dick Whitbeck

Macbeth
William Shakespeare
   Directed by Edward Hastings
   Set by Sam Kirkpatrick
   Costumes by Robert Fletcher
   Lighting by John McLain
   Music by Dick Whitbeck

On Tour

The Tavern
George M. Cohan
   Directed by Stephen Kanee
   Set by Jack Barkla
   Costumes by Jack Edwards
   Lighting by John McLain and
   Paul Scharfenberger
   Music by Dick Whitbeck

A Midsummer Night's Dream
   Adapted and directed
   by Stephen Willems

Soldiering
   Written and directed
   by Stephen Willems

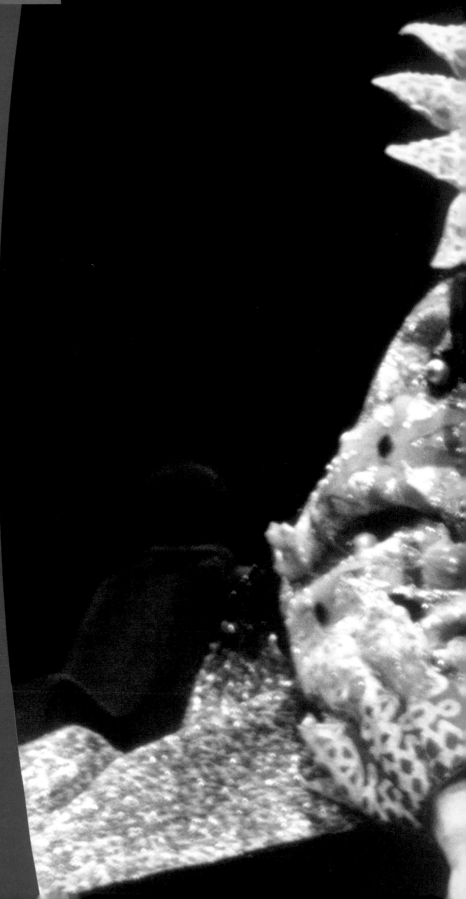

Mary Stuart.
Barbara Bryne, Michael Goodwin.

123

The Tempest
William Shakespeare
   Directed by Liviu Ciulei
   Set by Liviu Ciulei
   Costumes by Jack Edwards
   Lighting by Duane Schuler
   Music by Theodor Grigoriu

Don Juan
Molière
   Translated by Donald M. Frame
   Directed by Richard Foreman
   Set by Richard Foreman
   Costumes by Patricia Zipprodt
   Lighting by Duane Schuler
   Music by Dick Whitbeck

Our Town
Thornton Wilder
   Directed by Alan Schneider
   Set by Karl Eigsti
   Costumes by Marjorie Slaiman
   Lighting by Richard Riddell
   Music by Dick Whitbeck

Foxfire (U.S. premiere)
Hume Cronyn and Susan Cooper
   Directed Marshall W. Mason
   Set by John Lee Beatty
   Costumes by Jennifer von Mayrhauser
   Lighting by Dennis Parichy
   Music by Jonathan Holtzman

Eve of Retirement
Thomas Bernhard
   Translated by Gitta Honegger
   Directed by Liviu Ciulei
   Set by Jack Barkla
   Costumes by Jared Aswegan
   Lighting by Paul Scharfenberger

Eli
Nelly Sachs
   Translated by Christopher Holme
   Directed by Garland Wright
   Set by Jim Guenther
   Costumes by Jared Aswegan
   Lighting by Paul Scharfenberger
   Music by Dick Whitbeck

A Christmas Carol
Charles Dickens
   Adapted by Barbara Field
   Directed by Jon Cranney
   Set by Jack Barkla
   Costumes by Jack Edwards
   Lighting by Karlis Ozols
   Music by Hiram Titus

Candide
Voltaire's novel
   Adapted by Len Jenkin
   Directed by Garland Wright
   Set by John Arnone
   Costumes by Kurt Wilhelm
   Lighting by Craig Miller

As You Like It
William Shakespeare
   Directed by Liviu Ciulei
   Set by Santo Loquasto
   Costumes by Santo Loquasto
   Lighting by Jennifer Tipton
   Music by Theodor Grigoriu

On Tour

The Rainmaker
N. Richard Nash
   Directed by David Chambers
   Set and costumes by James Guenther
   Lighting by Paul Scharfenberger

Trouble Begins at Eight: A Mark Twain Offering
   Written and directed by
   Christopher Markle

The Tempest.
Francois de la Giroday, Frances Conroy,
Boyd Gaines, Ken Ruta, company.

1982-83 SEASON

Summer Vacation Madness
Carlo Goldoni
  Directed by Garland Wright
  Set by Adrianne Lobel
  Costumes by Ann Hould-Ward
  Lighting by Craig Miller
  Music by Hiram Titus

Requiem for a Nun
William Faulkner
  Directed by Liviu Ciulei
  Set by Jack Barkla
  Costumes by Jared Aswegan
  Lighting by Duane Schuler
  Sound Composition by Terry Tilley

The Marriage of Figaro
Beaumarchais
  Translated by Richard Nelson
  Directed by Andrei Serban
  Set by Beni Montresor
  Costumes by Beni Montresor
  Lighting by Duane Schuler
  Music by Richard Peaslee

Room Service
John Murray and Allen Boretz
  Directed by Harold Stone
  Set by Jack Barkla
  Costumes by Jack Edwards
  Lighting by Paul Scharfenberger

Heartbreak House
George Bernard Shaw
  Directed by Christopher Markle
  Set by Michael Yeargan
  Costumes by Lawrence Casey
  Lighting by William Armstrong

A Christmas Carol
Charles Dickens
  Adapted by Barbara Field
  Direct by Christopher Markle
  Set by Jack Barkla
  Costumes by Jack Edwards
  Lighting by Paul Scharfenberger
  Music by Hiram Titus

Entertaining Mr. Sloane
Joe Orton
  Directed by Gary Gisselman
  Set and costumes by Santo Loquasto
  Lighting by Paul Scharfenberger

Peer Gynt
Henrik Ibsen
  Translated by Rolf Fjelde
  Direct by Liviu Ciulei
  Set and costumes by Santo Loquasto
  Lighting by Jennifer Tipton
  Music by Fiorenzo Carpi

On Tour

Talley's Folly
Lanford Wilson
  Directed by David Feldshuh
  Set by Jack Barkla
  Costumes by Jack Edwards

Master Harold ... and the Boys
Broadway tour production
Athol Fugard
  Directed by Athol Fugard
  Set by Jane Clark
  Costumes by Sheila McLamb
  Lighting by David Noling

The Threepenny Opera
Bertolt Brecht and Kurt Weill
  Translated by Marc Blitzstein
  Directed by Liviu Ciulei
  Set by Liviu Cuilei
  Costumes by Carrie Robbins
  Lighting by Richard Riddell
  Music direction by Dick Whitbeck

Guys and Dolls
Damon Runyon
  Adapted by Jo Swerling,
  Abe Burrows and Frank Loesser
  Directed by Garland Wright
  Set by Paul Zalon
  Costumes by Kurt Wilhelm
  Lighting by Frances Aronson
  Music direction by David Bishop
  Choreography by Randolyn Zinn

The Entertainer
John Osborne
  Directed by Edward Payton Call
  Set by Ming Cho Lee
  Costumes by Ann Wallace
  Lighting by Dawn Chiang
  Music by John Addison

The Seagull
Anton Chekhov
  Directed by Lucien Pintilie
  Translated by Jean-Claude van Itallie
  Set by Radu Boruzescu
  Costumes by Miruna Boruzescu
  Lighting by Paul Scharfenberger
  Music by Vasile Sirli

A Christmas Carol
Charles Dickens
  Adapted by Barbara Field
  Directed by Christopher Markle
  Set by Jack Barkla
  Costumes by Jack Edwards
  Lighting by Paul Scharfenberger
  Music by Hiram Titus

The Importance of Being Earnest
Oscar Wilde
  Directed by Garland Wright
  Set by Michael Miller and
  Garland Wright
  Costumes by Jack Edwards
  Lighting by Craig Miller

Hedda Gabler
Henrik Ibsen
  Translated by Siri Senje and
  Tom Creamer
  Directed by Christopher Markle
  Set by Douglas Stein
  Costumes by Gene Lakin
  Lighting by William Armstrong

On Tour

The Importance of Being Earnest
Oscar Wilde

Guys and Dolls.
Mike Mazurki, Jerry Stiller,
company.

129

1984-85 SEASON

Negro Ensemble Company
A Soldier's Play
Charles Fuller
   Directed by Douglas Turner Ward
   Set by Felix H. Cochren
   Costumes by Judy Dearing
   Lighting by Allen Lee Hughes

Hang On to Me
Book by Maxim Gorky
Music by George and Ira Gershwin
   Translated by Maria M.
   Markof-Belaeff and Peter Sellars
   Directed by Peter Sellars
   Set by Adrienne Lobel
   Costumes by Dunya Ramicova
   Music direction by Craig Smith

Three Sisters
Anton Chekhov
   Translated by Richard Nelson
   Directed by Liviu Ciulei
   Set by Liviu Ciulei
   Costumes by Jack Edwards
   Lighting by Dawn Chiang
   Music by Paul Goldstaub

Tartuffe
Molière
   Translated by Richard Wilbur
   Directed by Lucian Pintilie
   Set by Radu Boruzescu
   Costumes by Miruna Boruzescu
   Lighting by Beverly Emmons

'night Mother
Marsha Norman
   Directed by Christopher Markle
   Set and costumes by Jack Edwards
   Lighting by Bill Armstrong

Twelfth Night
William Shakespeare
   Directed by Liviu Ciulei
   Set by Radu Boruzescu
   Costumes by Miruna Boruzescu
   Lighting by Dawn Chiang

A Christmas Carol
Charles Dickens
   Adapted by Barbara Field
   Directed by Christopher Markle
   Set by Jack Barkla
   Costumes by Jack Edwards
   Lighting by Paul Scharfenberger
   Music by Hiram Titus

Anything Goes
Cole Porter
   Directed by Garland Wright
   Set by Thomas Lynch
   Costumes by Patricia McGourty
   Lighting by Craig Miller
   Music direction by David Bishop
   Choreography by Dirk Lumbard

On Tour

Foxfire
Hume Cronyn and Susan Cooper
   Directed by Terry Schreiber

Tartuffe.
Gerry Bamman,
Harris Yulin.

1985-86 SEASON

Great Expectations
Charles Dickens
  Directed by Stephen Kanee
  Adapted by Barbara Field
  Set by Jack Barkla
  Costumes by Jack Edwards
  Lighting by Dawn Chiang
  Music by Hiram Titus

Cyrano de Bergerac
Edmond Rostand
  Translated by Brian Hooker
  Directed by Edward Gilbert
  Set by Jack Barkla
  Costumes by Jack Edwards
  Lighting by Judy Rasmuson
  Music by Thomas Fay

A Midsummer Night's Dream
William Shakespeare
  Directed by Liviu Ciulei
  Set and costumes by Beni Montresor
  Lighting by Beni Montresor

Candida
George Bernard Shaw
  Directed by William Gaskill
  Set and costumes by Deirdre Clancy
  Lighting by Dawn Chiang

Execution of Justice
Emily Mann
  Directed by Emily Mann
  Set by Ming Cho Lee
  Costumes by Jennifer von Mayrhauser
  Lighting by Pat Collins

A Christmas Carol
Charles Dickens
  Adapted by Barbara Field
  Directed by Howard Dallin
  Set by Jack Barkla
  Costumes by Jack Edwards
  Lighting by Marcus Dilliard
  Music by Hiram Titus

On the Razzle
Tom Stoppard
  Directed by Stephen Kanee
  Set and costumes by John Conklin
  Lighting by Craig Miller

The Rainmaker
N. Richard Nash
  Directed by Timothy Near
  Set by Kate Edmunds
  Costumes by Jeff Struckman
  Lighting by John Gisondi

On Tour

Great Expectations
Charles Dickens
  Adapted by Barbara Field
  Directed by Stephen Kanee

A Midsummer Night's Dream.
Jay Patterson, Harriet Harris, company.

133

1986-87 SEASON

Saint Joan
George Bernard Shaw
  Directed by Patrick Mason
  Set by Eugene Lee
  Costumes by Donna M. Kress
  Lighting by Duane Schuler
  Music by Robert Dennis

The Merry Wives of Windsor
William Shakespeare
  Directed by Derek Goldby
  Set by Eugene Lee
  Costumes by John Pennoyer
  Lighting by John Custer

The Birthday Party
Harold Pinter
  Directed by Stephen Kanee
  Set and costumes by Andrei Both
  Lighting by Marcus Dilliard

On the Verge, or the Geography of Yearning
Eric Overmeyer
  Directed by Stan Wojewodski, Jr.
  Set by Hugh Landwehr
  Costumes by Jack Edwards
  Lighting by Pat Collins
  Music by Roberta Carlson

Rhinoceros
Eugène Ionesco
  Translated by Derek Prouse
  Directed by Kazimierz Braun
  Set by John Conklin
  Costumes by Jack Edwards
  Lighting by Marcus Dilliard
  Music by Roberta Carlson

A Christmas Carol
Charles Dickens
  Adapted by Barbara Field
  Directed by Richard Ooms
  Set by Jack Barkla
  Costumes by Jack Edwards
  Lighting by Marcus Dilliard
  Music by Hiram Titus

Infidelities
Pierre Marivaux
  Translated by William Gaskill
  Directed by William Gaskill
  Set and costumes by John Conklin
  Lighting by James F. Ingalls
  Music by David Bishop

The Gospel at Colonus
Adapted by Lee Breuer from
the Robert Fitzgerald translation
of *Oedipus at Colonus*
  Directed by Lee Breuer
  Set by Alison Yerxa
  Costumes by Ghretta Hynd
  Lighting by Julie Archer
  Music by Bob Telson
  Music direction by Bob Telson

The Gospel at Colonus.
Morgan Freeman, company.

135

The Misanthrope
Molière
Translated by Richard Wilbur
Directed by Garland Wright
Set by Joel Fontaine
Costumes by Jack Edwards
Lighting by Peter Maradudin

The Piggybank
Eugéne Labiche and Alfred Delacour
Translated by Albert Bermel
Directed by Garland Wright
Set by John Arnone
Costumes by Martin Pakledinaz
Lighting by Frances Aronson
Music by John McKinney

The Bacchae
Euripides
Translated by Kenneth Cavander
Directed by Liviu Ciulei
Set by Liviu Ciulei
Costumes by Patricia Zipprodt
Lighting by Marcus Dilliard
Music by Janika Vandervelde

The House of Bernarda Alba
Federico García Lorca
Translated by Timberlake Wertenbaker
Directed by Les Waters
Set by Annie Smart
Costumes by Martin Pakledinaz
Lighting by James F. Ingalls

Leon & Lena (and lenz)
Georg Büchner
Translated by Henry J. Schmidt
Directed by JoAnne Akalaitis
Set by George Tsypin
Costumes by Adelle Lutz
Lighting by Jennifer Tipton
Music by Terry Allen

A Christmas Carol
Charles Dickens
Adapted by Barbara Field
Directed by Richard Ooms
Set by Jack Barkla
Costumes by Jack Edwards
Lighting by Marcus Dilliard
Music by Hiram Titus

Richard III
William Shakespeare
Directed by Garland Wright
Set by Douglas Stein
Costumes by Ann Hould-Ward
Lighting by James F. Ingalls

On Tour

Frankenstein –
Playing With Fire
Barbara Field
From the novel by Mary Shelley
Directed by Michael Maggio
Set by John Arnone
Costumes by Jack Edwards
Lighting by Marcus Dilliard

Richard III.
Byron Jennings, company.

137

The Glass Menagerie
Tennessee Williams
   Directed by Vivian Matalon
   Set by Desmond Heeley
   Costumes by Ann Hould-Ward
   Lighting by Duane Schuler

The Imaginary Invalid
Molière
   Translated by John Wood
   Directed by Garland Wright
   Set by Garland Wright
   Costumes by Jack Edwards
   Lighting by Marcus Dilliard
   Music by John McKinney

Frankenstein – Playing With Fire
Barbara Field
   From the novel by Mary Shelley
   Directed by Michael Maggio
   Set by John Arnone
   Costumes by Jack Edwards
   Lighting by Marcus Dilliard

Hamlet
William Shakespeare
   Directed by Garland Wright
   Set by Douglas Stein
   Costumes by Ann Hould-Ward
   Lighting by James F. Ingalls

The Wild Duck
Henrik Ibsen
   Translated by Lucian Pintilie
   and David Westerfer
   Directed by Lucian Pintilie
   Set by Radu Boruzescu
   Costumes by Miruna Boruzescu
   Lighting by Beverly Emmons

A Christmas Carol
Charles Dickens
   Adapted by Barbara Field
   Directed by Richard Ooms
   Set by Jack Barkla
   Costumes by Jack Edwards
   Lighting by Marcus Dilliard
   Music by Hiram Titus

Pravda
David Hare and Howard Brenton
   Directed by Robert Falls
   Set by John Arnone
   Costumes by Jane Greenwood
   Lighting by James F. Ingalls
   Music by Rob Milburn

Guthrie Lab: Resident Director's Project

Cymbeline
William Shakespeare
   Directed by Charles Newell

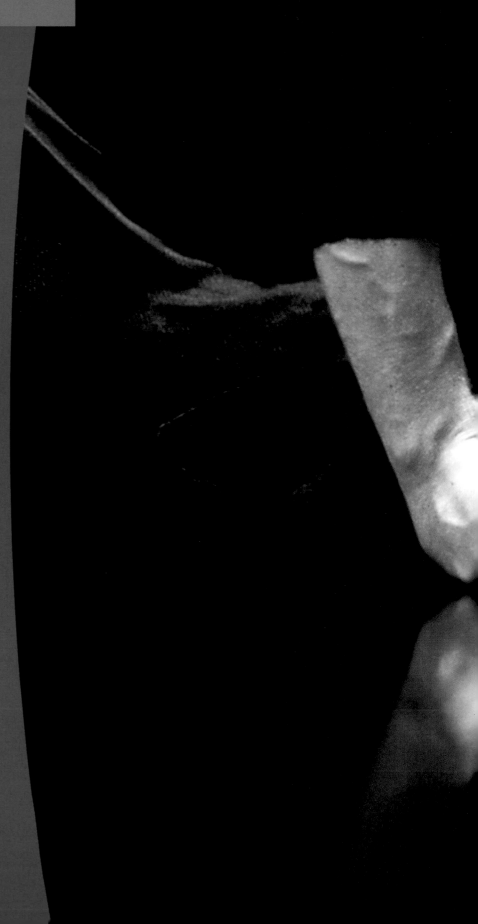

Hamlet.
Zeljko Ivanek, Julianne Moore.

1989-90 SEASON

Harvey
Mary Chase
  Directed by Douglas Hughes
  Set by Hugh Landwehr
  Costumes by Linda Fisher
  Lighting by Marcus Dilliard

Uncle Vanya
Anton Chekhov
  Translated by Jean-Claude van Itallie
  Directed by Garland Wright
  Set by Douglas Stein
  Costumes by Martin Pakledinaz
  Lighting by Marcus Dilliard

The Duchess of Malfi
John Webster
  Directed by Michael Kahn
  Set by Derek McLane
  Costumes by Martin Pakledinaz
  Lighting by Frances Aronson

Volpone
Ben Jonson
  Directed by Stan Wojewodski, Jr.
  Set by Christopher H. Barreca
  Costumes by Catherine Zuber
  Lighting by Stephen Strawbridge
  Music by Kim Daryl Sherman

The Screens
Jean Genet
  Translated by Paul Schmidt
  Directed by JoAnne Akalaitis
  Set by George Tsypin
  Costumes by Eiko Ishioka
  Lighting by Jennifer Tipton
  Music by Philip Glass and
  Foday Musa Suso

A Christmas Carol
Charles Dickens
  Adapted by Barbara Field
  Directed by Richard Ooms
  Set by Jack Barkla
  Costumes by Jack Edwards
  Lighting by Marcus Dilliard
  Music by Hiram Titus

Candide
Hugh Wheeler
  Adapted from Voltaire
  Music by Leonard Bernstein
  Directed by Garland Wright
  Set by John Arnone
  Costumes by David Woolard
  Lighting by Marcus Dilliard
  Music direction by David Bishop

Guthrie Lab:
Resident Director's Project

Measure for Measure
William Shakespeare
  Directed by Paul Draper

The Screens.
Jesse Borego (at left),
Isabell Monk, and company.

141

Guthrie Theater

Karen Bachman, President, and the Guthrie Board of Directors invi[...]

Guthrie Theater Annual Meeting
and Dedication of the Guthrie Hall of A[...]

Joining Artistic Director Joe Dowling as special guests will be members [...]
acting company, past and present, who are recognized on this new lobb[...]
honoring Guthrie actors. Your attendance is important to all of us at t[...]

Monday, July 20, 1998

Meeting 6:00 p.m. in the auditorium
Reception follows in the lobby
725 Vineland Place

Please call (612) 377-2224 to place your reservati[...]

celebrating our 35th se[...]

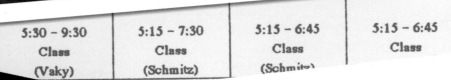

5:30 – 9:30	5:15 – 7:30	5:15 – 6:45	5:15 – 6:45
Class (Vaky)	Class (Schmitz)	Class (Schmitz)	Class

THE GUTH[...]

Guthrie Theater
program

YOU CAN'T TAKE
IT WITH YOU
BY GEORGE S. KAUFMAN AND MOSS HART

MEDEA

ICEBREAKER

July 15, 1998

The Importance of Being Ea[...]

This opening of *The Importance of Being Earne[...]*
beginning of the Guthrie Theater's 35th season. [...]
heater's illustrious and colorful history, tonight [...]
nowledge of this community treasure. (For yo[...]
heila is sitting at the table with all the people h[...]

1. Name the four shows of the inaugural season [...]
2. What Guthrie production was written by (and [...]
   Rose Lee's sister?
3. What play was being performed at the Guthri[...]
   War started?
4. In what Guthrie musical did Christopher Plum[...]
   leading role?
5. Who played B[...]

JULY 11 – AUGUST 17, 1997

7:00 1/2 hour   7:00 1/2 hour

Clockwise
from upper left:

Daily rehearsal schedule.

Production staff,
partial, 1995.

Dedication invitation,
1998.

Medea, 1990.

Prop notes,
Babes In Arms, 1995.

Cutter Annette
Garceau at work in
the costume shop.

Production
schedule, 1995.

Program, 1997.

Tour promotion, 1995.

Guthrie History
quiz, 1998.

Christopher Evan Welch,
Peter Schmitz, *The
Venetian Twins,* 1998.

Program covers,
1997, 1990.

PROPS:
Notes from I.1:
- CUT: Red pepper - for TESS
- The "Basta Pasta" bag should not have handles. We tried the paper
  bags. They don't stand up to the activity of the scene.
- The One-man-band is now a guy with a sandwich board which says "The
  world is coming to an end." He beats a single drum.

Notes from I.5:
- The piano lid needs to open 180 deg
  she stands up in it.

Notes form I.7:
- The newspapers for the TOTS shoul
  of paper.

Notes from I.9:
- Garland likes the little brown
  table.
  double tailor's measuri
  double notebooks and p

  bit-out-of-a-hat" bi'
  trick involved --

  II.4:
  cloth for the bir'

  II.5:
  stapler (204.07
  EXTRA with a
  yer of his sar
  ter that the k
  same EXTRA h
  Arms" poster

  I.9 ("Lady
  strips
  BOBBIE.
  coffee c

we see VIOLET when

THURSDAY   FRIDAY   SATURDAY

                                    Tour

                            T/D
                            Old Times

                        Archive Video
                        FIREBUGS
                        Audio Desc.

                        12 Tour

                    Short Plays
                    ROYAL FAMILY

                Teachers Conference

                    FIREBUGS

                19 Tour/Sensory Tour

1990s

SE   Preview Of
DESIGN MTG   FIREBU
21 • EDO   22
Light Plot due:
Fog   Publicity-Phot
                    Call: Fog
Post Play Disc.   RAY ON VACA

The Missouri Symphony Society and
the Missouri Theatre Building Trust present

K
Impressions
of THE TRIAL

Old Times

February 3 & 4
Missouri Theatre

Tour sponsored by AT&T

THE
GUTHRIE
THEATER

Joe Dowling Artistic Director   Edward A. Martenson Executive Director

FROM THE ARTISTIC DIRECTOR

Dialogues

Here we are again!

I am very pleased to welcome you to this first production of the 1997-98 season at the Guthrie. With my inaugural season firmly behind us, I look forward with excitement and some trepidation to my second year as artistic director.

To those of you coming to the Guthrie for the first time, I offer you a warm welcome. I hope you will come back to see us again and again. To our old friends, welcome back. Your loyalty and dedication has made this theater survive and prosper. Your response to last season was a source of great joy to all

Putting together the second season,

(*A Christmas Carol* included) in this year's program have never been seen at the Guthrie before. *Thunder Knocking on the Door* is by a young playwright named Keith Glover, who is fast establishing a reputation as one of the most important new voices in American theater. Another work new to our region is *Racing Demon* by David Hare who is widely regarded as a top contemporary British writer. This play was a huge success in the British National Theatre and on Broadway. It is a fascinating work, which deals with a crisis within the Anglican Church and, by extension, within society. The issues are as immediate for this country as for Britain.

Guthrie Artistic Director Joe Dowling

We will finish, as we did last season, with a Shakespearean comedy, *Much Ado About Nothing*. There is no writer in the English language whose work excites me as much as Shakespeare. The wisdom, the profound understanding of human behavior, the essential theatricality of his stories, the poetry and the majesty of his language all conspire to make his work as vivid now as when it was written.

There is nothing like the first rehearsal for a new production. Nothing like it for possibility, for audacity, and for sheer nerves.

In 1990, Garland Wright staged three of the Shakespeare History Plays to be played in repertory, a massive undertaking. The plays were *King Richard II*, *King Henry IV*, and *King Henry V*. On occasion during the run, all three would be performed in a single day. Here's what the first rehearsal looked like.

There's a skylight in Rehearsal Room One. On bright sunny days, the room is decorated with a large square shaft of light that travels across the playing area as the afternoon goes on. Actors move through it as they go about rehearsal; sometimes a climactic moment in the play happens to take place in a blaze of brilliant light.

The stage management staff has been at work all morning. At each place at the circle of tables, high up on the mock stage, is a pencil and a little pad of paper. There are 28 stacks of three bound scripts, mute testimony to the sheer size of the coming project. Off to the side is a table for the stage manager's set-ups, prompt scripts and yellow pads, telephone and a bowl of hard candy. At stage manager Jill Rendall's chair is a vase of daffodils. In the brown and muddy white and gray of the room, they are violently yellow. At one edge, someone has set an effigy prop from last season's production of *The Screens*, a styrofoam soldier with bared teeth that towers over the tables. On the director's table, where Wright will settle, the prop crown from 1983's satiric *Merry Wives of Windsor* is sitting. The crown is ridiculously velvet and topped with a stuffed corgi; it will disappear before rehearsal begins.

On one scarred wall of RR1, dramaturg Michael Lupu is putting up research materials, a large spreadsheet of historical information about each principal character in the plays and a long hand-made banner reading "All things are ready if our minds be so." The quote is from *Henry V*. "Jill," he calls out in his Romanian-accented English. "The daffodils, they should have been fleur de lis. But no! That is my job, that whatever we do, I explain how right it is. My job is to explain how daffodils are fleur de lis!" Laughter.

Good humor abounds on first rehearsal days. The stage managers joke that they will deliver the *Henry V* St. Crispian's Day speech on the first day of dress rehearsals, presumably the part about "He that outlives this day, and comes safe home." There is an air of anticipatory excitement in the room.

A little after eleven, the crowd starts to come in. Many of the theater staff come to meet and welcome the company back from their break. Veteran company member John Lewin gasps a little when he sees the shape of the rehearsal stage and exclaims, in broad British, "It's Tanya's stage!" Lewin has

Opposite: *King Henry IV.*
Stephen Yoakam, Barton Tinapp.

spent eleven seasons here, of the theater's twenty-six. He performed on Tanya's stage in its first three seasons, 1963-1965. When he climbs up the steps, he glances around in a satisfied manner – he knows this shape. "I've bruised my shin on it so many times!"

The company chatters. You've lost weight, you've gained weight, you've had a baby! I'm getting a nosebleed up here, from the height of the mock stage. Stephen Pelinski has been cast as fiery Hotspur. Someone says, "Oh, you're playing the wild man" and Pelinski replies, grinning, "No, he's just misunderstood, man, just misunderstood."

There is an announcement that new script pages can be found on top of each tall stack of scripts. Groans ensue. "Additions rather than subtractions?" Actor bags, the industry equivalent of gym bags, appear by all the chairs, stuffed with clothes and shoes and reference texts. Sandwiches, bottles of water, cups of coffee and gooey donuts from the big box in the corner appear on the tables. Actor Steve Yoakam takes one look at the set-up and marches down from the stage. He is going for a more comfortable chair. With three plays to read, it will be a long haul.

There is some business to be done. Forms to fill out, introductions to be made, a few words about cuts and vocal work and the evolving design. Finally, Garland Wright smiles a little and says "Let's read *Richard II*." There is much clearing of throats, much rustling and bustling. Then the room falls absolutely quiet. The stage manager looks inquiringly at Wright and then nods, smiling, to Charles Janasz who, as King Richard, has the opening lines in the first of the three plays. Charlie smiles, and takes a breath. The shaft of sunlight, very bright, is about center in the room. And the work begins. [Peg Guilfoyle]

Some moments in the theater stand out, even over the decades. Standing ovations, for example, generally occur at the end of the play. The History Plays provided a startling exception. Charles Newell co-directed with Garland Wright.

The essential impulse behind doing the History Plays was, through doing them, to create a company of actors for the Guthrie Theater. Because I had been part of the start of the Resident Artist project and the start of the Laboratory, I guess Garland thought it would be a good partnership for he and I to do. It was an outrageously long rehearsal period, and a tech month. And it generated probably the single most extraordinary moment in my life.

Garland prided himself in being able to anticipate and know everything, but this was a time when I saw him most surprised, and genuinely surprised, by something that happened in the theater. The first time we did the three plays together, in previews, it was a noon curtain for *Richard II*, 4:00 for *Henry IV,* and 9:00 for *Henry V. At* the opening for Henry V – "O, for a muse of fire." – the entire company of actors would all come out, fill the stage and just take different parts of the speech and share it around the stage. Well, they all came out and the lights came up and just before they were ready to begin, the audience began to applaud. And then the audience began to stand up and there was a standing ovation at the beginning of the play. It was a completely spontaneous moment, a complete celebration of the theatrical event between audience and actors. It was completely extraordinary. It was true theater.

And theater for everyone. One staff person had had no theater background before he joined the Guthrie, and said, "I always felt that while I was doing my job in the finance and facilities area, I didn't feel I was contributing anything to the program. It was not until the History plays were performed for the full cycle on opening night that that feeling changed. I knew, at that time, that the entire theater staff, myself included, were all a part of what was happening on that stage. The hair on the nape of my neck stood up." [Chuck Majeske]

His was not the only hair standing up. Backstage, crew member Mary Herzog was getting ready to put a robe on one of the actors. "It just sent electricity through me. It was just so magical."

From the booth, stage manager Jill Rendall found it "phenomenal. There was just this unbelievable surge of energy that pushed us through to the end of the play."

And from the house, a teacher was watching. "At the first glimpse of the company, we broke into applause that filled the space and pulled us into a spontaneous ovation, an ovation to recognize the power of what we had seen and the contract for what was to come. These were our actors and we were their people." [Kathy Detloff]

At one point during the run of the History Plays a Guthrie staffer was flying back to Minneapolis on the red-eye from Las Vegas. Across the aisle was a man reading *Henry IV*. He was a blackjack dealer and a theater fan, flying in to see the Histories. "I wouldn't miss it," he said.

It is no wonder that John Lewin exclaimed over the return of "Tanya's stage" for the History Plays. By 1990, the off-center thrust with its surrounding steps, the original shape of the stage she'd designed for 1963, had been much altered. Designer Doug Stein talked about the choice to bring it back.

> The starting point for designing the history plays was the world of the old Guthrie stage that Garland Wright and Charlie Newell wanted to set the cycle in. I think an analogy would be that it's like picking up somebody else's musical instrument and figuring out how to play it. I found there are many revelations about this theater, its history – about working on this old stage in this fixed configuration. I hear the revelations coming from all directions – from actors, from the directors, from the staff – of how the actual space is behaving, how the room is behaving. It's a great stage for a dialogue with the audience. I think Tanya Moiseiwitsch and Tyrone Guthrie knew that. And that's why I think it's so beloved by so many of the Guthrie audience.
>
> I asked the actors for responses, and I've gotten many interesting observations. Stephen Yoakam said to me, "It's the only stage I've ever worked on where when somebody walks away from you, you feel like they're going somewhere." A couple of other observations about the stage: Richard Iglewski used the analogy of real estate. He said it was like a piece of New York real

estate – it was more expensive per square inch than – I think he said – somewhere in Iowa. He said that the focus, when you're the actor, is much greater than most stages he's worked on. Richard Ooms said it's like a piece of sculpture and it feels like being on a pedestal. June Gibbons said that it makes you intensely aware as an actor of the choices you're making. Wherever you are – if you're down on the second step there – you're in high relief.

In June of 1992, the theater celebrated the successful conclusion of the largest endowment campaign ever undertaken until that time by any American theater – by a factor of four. Over $26,000,000 was raised in five years; more than half the total was pledged by individual donors. Many were making their first capital gift of any kind. John Murphy was an officer with the Hennepin County Sheriff's office.

> I didn't have what I'd call a close relationship to the arts in my early years. I was more interested in sports, particularly football. But ten or fifteen years ago, I went to see *A Christmas Carol*. I loved the spectacle. Since then, I've begun sampling plays. For the last several years, I've had season tickets. More and more, I am interested in the questions raised on stage. Take *Faustus*, for example. What does it mean to sell your soul to the devil? Plays deal with the big questions.
>
> I'm 47; I've heard about these plays all my life, and now I'm seeing them. I wish I'd been able to see them when I was in school. It is true what they say about the classics broadening one's horizons. I've come to think that without art, we're all wearing blinders. Our scope tends to be limited and tuned inward, but great art can expand your vision, which is tremendously exciting. This gift was the first capital gift I've made; I feel like the Guthrie earned it.

Actors can be opinionated, even at a young age. Stage manager Jeff Alspaugh received this note from some outraged choir boys in *A Christmas Carol*, who were released to go home after their appearance in the opening moment of the show, and not required to wait for the curtain call. But they wanted to bow!

Most actors distinctly remember their first entrance on the Guthrie stage. Do they imagine it as dignified, portentous, full of weight and gravity? Stage manager Jenny Batten watched this one, a true Big Moment, from the control booth during *A Christmas Carol* in 1993.

> In that year, Young Ebenezer Scrooge was played by J.C. Cutler in his Guthrie debut; it was the first preview and his first entrance onto the stage. There was a kind of tunnel up center on the stage with curtains that the stagehands would open and close for any actors entering or exiting. J.C.'s first scene on the Guthrie stage was right after a scene that had a lot of dry ice in it. Dry ice creates a fog effect that can also get the floor a little bit slippery. Young Ebenezer was to run onstage to meet his girlfriend for the first time. He had a little teacup in his hand. Well, he got a running start at it from backstage behind the curtain, but he slipped and when the crew person opened the curtain, he flew through the opening, well, it was like Superman. He was never vertical. The curtain opened and he was horizontal in mid-air. He fell, he broke

the teacup, he cut his hand and did the whole scene bleeding. Actually it kind of worked because young Ebenezer was supposed to be kind of a klutz. What an entrance.

Cutler recalls that another actor, staying determinedly in character, mysteriously carried a towel into the Fezziwig party scene to stanch the bleeding; Young Ebenezer danced with his hand up in the air until his exit came.

At some point in the nineties, the standard theatrical term 'extra' – a non-union actor permitted to appear in some scenes – turned into the term 'essential' – more descriptive to the function of actors who fill out crowd scenes, shift furniture and scenery, and provide atmosphere and texture to the stage. Use of 'essentials' is carefully planned, as illustrated by this story from an extra in *As You Like It,* directed by Garland Wright.

> Cast and crew had met in the theater before we started and we were told we would be working a couple of small scenes and then the two large group wintertime scenes in which we 'essentials' were so bundled up our faces were not visible. I was part of the second, largest group scene, in which Charles Janasz delivered his 'all the world's a stage' monologue, but I wasn't in the first scene.
>
> Since the scenes were running a little behind the announced schedule and I was dressed in costume early, and not paying attention, I joined my fellow essentials in the darkness at the back of the vom. It wasn't until I got into the light on stage that I realized I was in the wrong scene.
>
> I decided that since my face couldn't be seen I'd try to blend in somewhere and not be noticed. I kept my head down and I sat just outside a small clump of other essentials. Finally Garland stopped the scene but instead of hearing him give directions as usual there was nothing. I heard footsteps on the stage but with my head down I couldn't see anything. He stopped next to me, touched my shoulder, and said "Who is this person?" "It's me," I said as I looked up. "I think I'm in the wrong scene."
>
> What he said next shouldn't be repeated in polite company. [Vince Grundman]

From a backstage point of view, shows are sometimes judged by how complicated (read "interesting to run") or how simple (read "quiet and, eventually, boring to run") they are for the crew. While deadly serious about making the show right for the audience, the crew folk have a strongly whimsical side. In 1994, stage manager Chris Code was having his first Guthrie experience, with *The Play's the Thing.*

> It was a very simple comedy with one big joke in it, and during technical rehearsals we tried to have a good time as usual. And through the services of Gary Baird, one of our stalwart crew members, we had a really big laugh.

There was a moment in the show where Sally Wingert, as the leading woman Elona Zabo, was to do a sort of ballet that was backlit against a screen, so you could only see her shadow outline. She was doing these very beautiful, highly stylized, choreographed movements for about a half minute and then the light would fade out. Backstage, we were really bored during tech. Gary had been watching this six or seven times in a row while they worked it, and he had the moves down perfectly. Gary is a fairly rotund man – he has no shape like Sally Wingert, for sure – and when the lights came up, they revealed the shape of Gary Baird going through the movements, very elegantly, while we were just falling over backstage with laughter. It was a great little moment.

Making art, on budget and on time, with fifty or so high-profile personalities, is high-pressure business. Still, sometimes community forms; sometimes, community is needed, when an actor is far from home.

All these stories are about community and how close we became over the five months we were there. There was a rush to buy hats and scarves and humidifiers. Most of the cast was brought in from New York; it's amazing how close you can get, and how well you get to know people in a cold environment. I remember the big Secret Santa party, and going to the Dram [the in-house actor bar] every night. The Guthrie was like this living theatrical organism; it was really a safe place to create.

When we were already running and the show was up and going, I got a phone call one night that my grandparent's house had burned down. It was a

Kevin Cahoon (center) and the company in an early dance rehearsal for *Babes in Arms,* Kristin Chenoweth at his left.

really devastating fire that destroyed everything, and the insurance company wouldn't cover the house. I was debating whether I should go home and help them and be with them. The next morning I went to do a matinee for the weekend and I planned to leave that evening. I'd miss the Saturday night show and both shows on Sunday and hopefully come back the next week.

After the matinee, I was called to the stage, and the entire performing cast, the front of house crew, the running crew, the orchestra, the staff and the offices, everyone had all taken up a collection. It was a beautiful moment. I was standing on the stage of the Guthrie and everyone was standing there wishing me well on this journey that I had to take. It was so greatly appreciated; it exemplified what a family is, and what a family we were at the Guthrie. [Actor Kevin Cahoon, *Babes in Arms*.]

Babes in Arms had a young and ambitious cast, a brand-new re-write, and truly gigantic scenery. Big shows fill every corner of the theater, from the very first long day of rehearsal.

By 7:00 on that first night, Music Director David Bishop is briskly teaching the company the vocal parts to the *Babes in Arms* signature number. "Go to the downbeat," he calls to them. And to the chorus women: "Can I have chorine, please? Gum-chewing chorine!" Bishop points to his nose, reaches back down to the keyboard, gives a downbeat, and the singing women simultaneously go nasal.

Later on in the evening, he will start to teach the vocal parts to "Dancing Lady." As far as Bishop knows, the song has never been heard on a stage. It was cut from a movie called *Hollywood Party* and recorded once in the sixties as part of a Rodgers and Hart retrospective. In all probability, before this night, it has not been sung in 30 years.

In the back of the rehearsal room, Wright is listening, sitting on a gold ice-cream chair. Set designer John Arnone is half-reclining, with his feet up on a prop fainting couch. Choreographer Liza Gennaro is sketching movements in the back of the room with assistant Andrea Goodman, whirling once and then again. Heaped around them, on tables and in boxes, are stacks of rehearsal props. A stuffed gendarme dummy from *Candide* becomes Gennaro's partner as she continues to work a dance section from "Johnny One-Note."

At one point, around 9:00, Wright and Arnone walk back into the scene shop, past the office where Technical Director Ray Forton is working on budgets. They stand and look at the layout for the *Dancing Lady* platform, which takes up a substantial portion of the shop floor space. "Is this big enough?" John says, and they smile. It's a line from the show. The sound of the chorus echoes through the closed doors into the shop. They are standing and singing, and going for the downbeat.

Putting on a musical is the hardest thing I have ever encountered in the theater. Joy is what we get *from* it, not necessarily how we feel along the way. [Garland Wright]

In 1996, the Irish director and producer Joe Dowling took the helm of the Guthrie. Dowling, who had been the artistic director of the Abbey Theater, had directed widely in North America, including Broadway, the Stratford Festival, and the New York Shakespeare Festival. While the artistic director of the Gaiety Theatre in Dublin, Dowling founded the Gaiety School of Acting. Under his leadership at the Guthrie, subscriptions rose and the theater greatly expanded its offerings, including full seasons at the Guthrie Lab and the WorldStage series. Dowling led the theater to the realization of many of the Guthrie's long-held dreams, including a strong affiliation with training programs for young actors and artists, the regular creation and presentation of new plays, and the move to a new three-theater complex on the Mississippi River.

Joe Dowling greeted the audience on his arrival with the words excerpted here, beginning with a Shakespearean quote that adorned the theater's lobby for the next ten years.

"Give me your hands if we be friends." The words spoken by Puck at the end of A Midsummer Night's Dream *come to mind as I begin my first year in the Twin Cities at the helm of the Guthrie. In this spirit and with open arms, I am eager to make friends with the Guthrie audiences of all ages, old and new alike.*

Theater matters because it affects people on so many different levels. It affects us intellectually but, more importantly, it touches deep emotional strands in all of us. It makes us aware of aspects of the world around us and inside us that perhaps, under the routine circumstances of our daily existence, we might not focus on. In the theater we learn about our own emotions, we learn about our own feelings. When we participate in a theatrical event we recognize it as an opportunity for revisiting, reexamining and reinforcing the values held in common by our society. The Irish poet and dramatist W.B. Yeats once said talking about art: "If we understand our own minds and the things that are striving to utter themselves through our minds, we move others. Not because we've understood or thought about those others, but because all life has that same root. [Joe Dowling]

Opposite: Joe Dowling and Sally Wingert in rehearsal for *Julius Caesar*.

For staff, and for actors, the arrival of a new artistic director is a precarious moment. In many ways, the new leader is an unknown quantity. What will he like? Where will he lead the theater? And an essential theater question, will he like my work? In 1996, there was a bit of misunderstanding one day about the new Joe.

We already had a Joe in the building when Joe Dowling came, namely Joe Dillon the dog. Joe Dillon was a long-time resident in the lower offices, who came and went with Kirk Dillon who was on staff for twenty years. Joe Dillon has a thing about balloons. If he sees then, he leaps up in the air and pops them, grabs them, he just loves playing with balloons. And everybody knew that.

Joe Dowling
Artistic Director 1996 –

One day someone had delivered a bouquet of balloons to the stage door for the kids in *A Christmas Carol,* and it was sitting out there. And somebody came by and said, "Oh, those are really nice balloons." And Kerry Selseth, who was working stage door, said, "Well, as long as Joe doesn't see them." The other person said, "Why?" and Kerry said, "Well, he'll go crazy."

"But they're for the children!"

"Well, Joe won't care!"

And this went on and on until they realized they were talking about different Joes. We loved the image of Joe Dowling going crazy over the kids' balloons and tearing them out of the bouquet. [Lou Ambrose]

In November of 1996, the over-crowded prop and scenery departments of the theater, spread all over town for shops and storage, were eased by an auction of some of its larger pieces. It was a bizarre scene on a bitterly cold night; a remote commercial warehouse crowded with oversized oddities – giant eagles, a cartoonish car built on a golf cart *(Babes in Arms)*, a five-foot model steam ship *(Peer Gynt)*, a chastity belt *(Duchess of Malfi)*. Under the fluorescents, some pieces looked a bit worn, but their cachet was intact, and the auctioneer was professionally enthusiastic if a little at a loss for description. An iron lung, from Frankenstein? "This is unusual! No doubt about it! Uh, where are you going to find another one?!"

For preview performances, great numbers of the technical staff are in the audience – all those people with yellow legal pads, taking notes. In one preview for *A Doll's House,* a technical snafu had all those people looking fixedly down at their laps, so as not see what was happening on stage. No help could be given; carrying the moment was all up to the actor. Production Stage Manager Russell Johnson tells the tale:

> The director is there, the assistant director, the designers, the tech staff are all watching the show. And there was a chandelier that flew in and out as part of a shift, changing location for a scene. In this scene, Torvald, played by Stephen Pelinski, is decorating for Christmas. He's supposed to get all of these garlands, three big ones, that come to one hook and then they hook on to the chandelier.
>
> And it's all during this three-page monologue that he has – just an incredible amount of words.
>
> Every prop that Pelinski uses is something that he has taken ownership of, and all during rehearsal there had been discussion about his ladder. It was too heavy, then too light, or too flimsy, and was it safe? We were all focused on this ladder. So, it's in the middle of the monologue and he's getting wound up. He gets the ladder out there. All the garlands were already tied together so all he had to do was really pick up the hook and connect it. Well, he climbed the ladder and he was getting to the peak of the monologue, and he just reached

A customer test-drives a car at the Guthrie prop auction.

© 2005 STAR TRIBUNE/Minneapolis–St. Paul.

up and he moved his hand and there was nothing there to hang it on. There was no chandelier; it was nowhere to be found.

In every section, you could see at least one head, a staff head, go straight down. The audience knew nothing; sometimes they seem programmed to accept whatever happens in the theater. Maybe they were a little confused, but then he just came back down the ladder and put the garlands against the wall and folded up the ladder. He just kept talking and went on to the next thing.

When this story was told around a table full of laughing stage managers, Jenny Batten, stage manager for *A Doll's House,* smilingly asked for the opportunity to make a formal apology to Stephen Pelinski in this book. "Stephen, I'm sorry," she said. "Thank you."

It can be a shock when the costume shop discovers what actors will be doing in their carefully crafted creations. In addition to being period-correct, pleasing for the designer and director, wearable for the actor, and finished on time and on budget, costumes must also be built to last. For thirty performances or more, the garment must hold up to stress, sweat, cleaning and, sometimes, unusual physical activity.

The brilliant costume cutter Annette Garceau came to Minneapolis to work with Tyrone Guthrie in 1963 and was still creating in the costume shop forty years later.

For the wedding dress in *Much Ado About Nothing,* [costume designer] Desmond Heeley wanted layers and layers of skirt, very light, soft, and so on. We used delicate nets which I was terrified wouldn't hold out through the entire show. Just one little finger pushing through would break it. And then the actor told me, "Well, I'm pushed to the floor and I roll around" and all in this big huge wedding dress. You do what you can to make things director-proof, and you hope the maintenance people will mend it and watch it and so on.

I had no sketch for that dress. I could show you a little tiny squiggle with a ball point pen that Desmond did. It was about four inches, and that was it. But he said "Oh, you know, Nettie, another eighteenth century Desmond dress. You know what to do." And of course I did.

Not everyone does this, but I like to try and give the actor an effect, even at a first fitting, a sort of beginning look at what the whole effect will be. You do the shape in muslin even if it's just the silhouette, so they don't have to wait and wonder what the costume is going to be like. When you do that, they see. "Oh, look at this wonderful sleeve and I can use this, and oh yes, we were just rehearsing a scene where I wave my arms around and this sleeve will just drape beautifully." The minute they know what their costume is going to be like, they can think of that when they're rehearsing, and think of how to use their bodies to advantage with that costume. It's tremendously important to them.

Thousands of people enjoy Guthrie open houses, touring the backstage, visiting with actors, quizzing craftspeople about their work and, in this case, making a special theatrical hat to take home.

Storyteller, actor, and playwright Kevin Kling began to work closely with the Guthrie in the mid-nineties.

> Joe Dowling asked me if I would be interested in working on *The Venetian Twins* with Michael Bogdanov. He wondered if I could put the play into a Minnesota vernacular and I said, "Cripes, I suppose." And so then I went out and read the play.
>
> Any successful collaboration is like two molecules that have to come together, and the problem is you don't want to bump anyone's nucleus. When collaborations fall apart, I feel it's because people have interloped on other people's nucleus. I firmly believe the theater is not a democracy. It's a hierarchy in which everyone has their job. Of course actors will influence the direction, the designers will influence the direction, the play will influence the direction, but when push comes to shove, it's the one who stages the piece who's got the final say. That's the job a director has. Basically, in these situations, the playwright is the first one out of the picture – just kind of waving from the dock. You have to let something that might have lived only in your head go.

In 1999, as part of its 35th Anniversary Celebration, the Theater established an education fund in the name of long-time staffer and stalwart Sheila Livingston, and gave her the opportunity to select the fund's projects. Livingston created the annual Shakespeare Classic – $5 seats to one special Shakespeare performance each season, and aimed specifically at young audiences. In a letter to that first audience, her three daughters talked about why.

> Our mother, raised in a small Canadian town, did not see a professional theater performance until she was twenty. Her future husband, Ken Livingston, took her to Ontario's Stratford Festival Theatre for an evening of Shakespeare. That evening with *Richard III* was a transforming event and became the prologue for her own life in the theater. After moving to Minneapolis, she discovered that Tyrone Guthrie, the man who had directed that *Richard III,* was in the Twin Cities to build a new theater. She enthusiastically signed on to Guthrie's vision, eager to expose her own children to the pleasures of live theater.
>
> What exposure we got! We were still scraping our knees on the elementary school playground when our parents introduced us to the magic of the stage. We saw many plays before we read them in school so, to us, plays were first and foremost a vibrant living art form. During school classes, we saw more than the Bard's 17th century words on the page – we recalled vivid images of Malvolio's yellow stockings in *Twelfth Night* and the way Caliban slithered across the stage in *The Tempest*.
>
> But our education was shaped by more than mental images. Theater gave us insights into relationships and human suffering. It offered us windows to worlds we had never experienced and exposed us to diverse people and ideas. Theater taught us the power of words and the incomparable communal

experience of a live performance. It helped us to hone our ability to make critical judgments about what we liked – and didn't like – and to express our views about what we encountered on the stage and in life. We learned not to be intimidated by art but to embrace it whether wearing blue jeans or a fancy dress. [Franci, Sandy, and Robin Livingston]

Philip Goodwin played Scrooge in the 1999 production of *A Christmas Carol*.

I remember hoisting Max Friedman, as Tiny Tim, onto my shoulder to deliver his final line. He leaned down to whisper in my ear, "I think I'm going to throw up." He sat up to say, "God bless us, everyone!" to all the assembled. Then in my ear again, "Just kidding." Such a good kid. My most salient memories of my *A Christmas Carol* in Minneapolis have to do with kids. Bright, talented, caring and funny kids.

Every moment on stage is the result of an incredibly complex interaction of the physical – scenic elements, lights and sound, costumes – and the living work of the actor. Most shows, however complex, run smoothly night after night, allowing those moments to find full flower for the audience. The crews take pride and joy, in that. Here is one source of that joy.

We spend a good deal of time worrying in a constructive manner about how we can be prepared for the bad stuff that can happen. Walls have fallen down on stage. People don't make their entrances. Props get lost, hats get misplaced. That's where I draw the real gratification of the job – fixing the problems. Being a spontaneous troubleshooter. When things are going wrong and you're in the hot seat, you're the one that people look to for the answers as in 'what are we going to do now?' It's a live show. People are expecting to see that person walk on stage, or go through that door that suddenly won't open, or use that piece of scenery that isn't there. To successfully figure those things out and make the show work night after night is immensely personally gratifying to me. [Stage Manager Chris Code]

And sometimes, there's just nothing to be done.

It was our production of *The Plough and the Stars*. An actor named Leo Leyden, a very sweet man, was dressed in one scene in a ceremonial outfit; he was going to a lodge meeting and was wearing a big ceremonial sword. In the scene, he's in a bar and [actor] Sally Wingert carries in this prop baby, all wrapped up. She gets into an argument with another woman, so she hands Leo the baby. Well, Leo doesn't want this baby, so he's wandering around trying

Max Friedman and Philip Goodwin.

Brian Crow, head of the stage crew, takes a rare break backstage with Craig Rognholt.

© 2005 STAR TRIBUNE/Minneapolis–St. Paul.

to hand it to other people but nobody will take it, so he sets the baby on the bar and he's going to sneak out leaving it behind.

Well, the baby clothes got hung up on his sword. So he sits the baby on the bar, turns and starts to walk away, and the baby falls off the bar and is swinging on the end of Leo's sword. It was a baby doll that had a crying mechanism. So the baby is wailing and swinging and Leo doesn't realize at first that he's dragging this baby behind him. He didn't know where to go, and everybody on stage just started, you know, looking away, until the baby fell off the end of the sword. [Brian Crow, Stage Crew Supervisor]

Randy Reyes (below) revs up the crowd at a student matinee performance of *A Midsummer Night's Dream* in Austin, Minnesota. Austin is well-remembered by the touring staff, which had to cut the giant flower scenery in half in order to get it into the high school auditorium, and put it back together for the performances. A visiting critic from *The New York Times* was nearly seated in an undesirable location and was overheard being asked how he'd liked the show (a definite *faux pas*). His review in the *Times* was so positive, however, that theater staff copied and distributed it to the top of every desk at the Minnesota State Legislature, which was then considering funding for the proposed new Guthrie Theater facility. "We think it made the difference," said one member of the staff.

The theater keeps statistics on its tours, of course, and they are impressive. Taking a Guthrie show on the road is an enormous undertaking. *A Midsummer Night's Dream*, in 2000, played 62 performances in 16 cities over 12 weeks, carrying 37 people in the company and crew. 50,043 people saw the show, including 20, 277 students.

Actors Randy Reyes and Cheyenne Casebier polled their fellow actors and crew members for a slightly more personalized set of tour statistics.

- 5,338 miles on the road
- 723 hours on the bus
- 25 hotel check-ins
- 1,600 do not disturb signs on door handles
- 1,595 ignored do not disturb signs
- 4,222 hotel mini-soaps unwrapped
- 4 different seasons experienced every three days
- 500 SPAM paraphernalia items acquired (450 donated)
- 902 gallons of coffee consumed
- 1,815 gallons of water consumed
- 1,816 gallons of beer consumed
- $58,058 spent at Quicky Marts
- 59 standing ovations

The Guthrie on Tour truck. It took three trucks to carry *A Midsummer Night's Dream;* one was completely filled with a truss that allowed selected fairies to fly onto the stage.

The *Dream* tour returned the Guthrie to regional touring on a grand scale, but touring shows, like all plays, are experienced by people one at a time. Tour Director Beth Burns tells a story that demonstrates why the Guthrie went back on the road.

> We were in Des Moines, Iowa with *Dream* in 2000. We attended the performance with the director of the National Endowment for the Arts and right in front of us was a couple that absolutely embodied a typical, even stereotypical, Iowa farm couple. They were very engaged throughout the entire performance, laughing a lot. At the end of the performance (and this was typical of every performance on that tour), the audience leapt to its feet for a full standing ovation. However, the woman did not get up or even clap or move as the applause began. Because I was with the NEA director (who funded the tour!), I was extremely nervous. Had she hated the show after all? Her husband, who was standing already, leaned down to ask her what was wrong. We leaned forward to eavesdrop on her reply. She looked at her husband and we saw that she was crying — not little tears of fun, but all out weeping. She turned to her husband and said, "I want to call my high school English teacher and tell him to (expletive) off." Yikes, we thought. Now what?
>
> Then she said, "I failed the Shakespeare unit of my high school English class and I have always thought I was too stupid to understand Shakespeare. But no one ever showed me Shakespeare could be like this!" Then we were all crying, because *that* is why we tour.

A Midsummer Night's Dream plays the mainstage, 1997.

1990-91 SEASON

King Richard II
King Henry IV
King Henry V
William Shakespeare
    Directed by Garland Wright and
    Charles Newell
    Set by Douglas Stein
    Costumes by Ann Hould-Ward
    Lighting by Marcus Dilliard
    Music by Michael Sommers

The Skin of Our Teeth
Thornton Wilder
    Directed by Robert Woodruff
    Set by Douglas Stein
    Costumes by Susan Hilferty
    Lighting by Rob Murphy
    Music by Douglas Wieselman

The Front Page
Ben Hecht and Charles MacArthur
    Directed by Douglas Hughes
    Set by Hugh Landwehr
    Costumes by Michael Olich
    Lighting by Marcus Dilliard

A Christmas Carol
Charles Dickens
    Adapted by Barbara Field
    Directed by Richard Ooms
    Set by Jack Barkla
    Costumes by Jack Edwards
    Lighting by Marcus Dilliard
    Music by Hiram Titus

Medea
Euripides
    Directed by Garland Wright
    Set by Douglas Stein
    Costumes by Susan Hilferty
    Lighting by Jennifer Tipton
    Music by Marcus Wise

Guthrie Lab:
Resident Director's Project

Troilus and Cressida
William Shakespeare
    Directed by Erin Mee

King Richard II.
Jacqueline Kim, Sally Wingert.

161

1991-92 SEASON

Death of a Salesman
Arthur Miller
  Directed by Sheldon Epps
  Set by James Leonard Joy
  Costumes by Judy Dearing
  Lighting by Allen Lee Hughes

The Man Who
Came to Dinner
George S. Kaufman and Moss Hart
  Directed by Laird Williamson
  Set and costumes by Andrew Yelusich
  Lighting by Marcus Dilliard

The Illusion
Pierre Corneille
  Translated by Ranjit Bolt
  Directed by Garland Wright
  Set and costumes by Anita Stewart
  Lighting by Marcus Dilliard

Fantasio
Alfred de Musset
  Translated by Richard Howard
  Directed by Garland Wright
  Set by Douglas Stein
  Costumes by Susan Hilferty
  Lighting by Allen Lee Hughes

The Tempest
William Shakespeare
  Directed by Jennifer Tipton
  Set and costumes by John Conklin
  Lighting by Scott Zielinski

A Christmas Carol
Charles Dickens
  Adapted by Barbara Field
  Directed by Sari Ketter
  Set by Jack Barkla
  Costumes by Jack Edwards
  Lighting by Marcus Dilliard
  Music by Hiram Titus

Marat/Sade
Peter Weiss
  Directed by Garland Wright
  Set by John Arnone
  Costumes by David Woolard
  Lighting by Marcus Dilliard
  Music by Richard Peaslee

Guthrie Lab:
Resident Director's Project

Pericles
William Shakespeare
  Directed by Bartlett Sher

Marat/Sade.
Barton Tinapp, Cindy Katz, company.

163

1992-93 SEASON

Iphigeneia at Aulis
Euripides
Translated by W.S. Merwin

Agamemnon
Aeschylus
Translated by Robert Lowell

Electra
Sophocles
Translated by Kenneth McLeish

Directed by Garland Wright
Set by Douglas Stein
Costumes by Susan Hilferty
Lighting by Marcus Dilliard
Music by Michael Sommers

Private Lives
Noel Coward
Directed by Michael Engler
Set by Stephen Earle and
Derek McLane
Costumes by Robert Wojewodski
Lighting by Peter Maradudin

The Winter's Tale
William Shakespeare
Directed by Douglas Hughes
Set by Hugh Landwehr
Costumes by Catherine Zuber
Lighting by Marcus Dilliard
Music by Louis Rosen

The Seagull
Anton Chekhov
Translated by Jean-Claude van Itallie
Directed by Garland Wright
Set by Douglas Stein
Costumes by Susan Hilferty
Lighting by James F. Ingalls

A Christmas Carol
Charles Dickens
Adapted by Barbara Field
Directed by Sari Ketter
Set by Jack Barkla
Costumes by Jack Edwards
Lighting by Marcus Dilliard
Music by Hiram Titus

The Good Hope
Herman Heijermans
Directed by Bartlett Sher
Set by Douglas Stein
Costumes by Susan Hilferty
Lighting by Marcus Dilliard
Music by Peter Still

Guthrie Lab:
Resident Director's Project

The Merchant of Venice
William Shakespeare
Directed by Risa Brainin

Too Clever by Half
Alexander N. Ostrovsky
Translated by Rodney Ackland
Directed by Garland Wright
Associate direction by Sari Ketter
Set by Douglas Stein
Costumes by Susan Hilferty
Lighting by Peter Maradudin

Naga Mandala
Girish Karnad
Directed by Garland Wright
Associate direction by Bartlett Sher
Set by Douglas Stein
Costumes by Susan Hilferty
Lighting by Peter Maradudin
Music by David Philipson

The Triumph of Love
Pierre Carlet de Marivaux
Translated by Paul Schmidt
Directed by Dominique Serrand
Set by David and Wendy Coggins
Costumes by Sonya Berlovitz
Lighting by Marcus Dilliard

Othello
(the Moor of Venice)
William Shakespeare
Directed by Laird Williamson
Set by Richard Seger
Costumes by Anita Stewart
Lighting by Marcus Dilliard

A Christmas Carol
Charles Dickens
Adapted by Barbara Field
Directed by Sari Ketter
Costumes by Jack Edwards
Set by Jack Barkla
Lighting by Marcus Dilliard
Music by Hiram Titus

A Woman of No Importance
Oscar Wilde
Directed by Garland Wright
Set by Garland Wright
Costumes by Susan Hilferty
Lighting by Marcus Dilliard

Dream On Monkey Mountain
Derek Walcott
Directed by Bill T. Jones
Set and costumes by Marina Draghici
Lighting by Robert Wierzel
Music by Jay Johnson

Guthrie Lab:
Resident Director's Project

Peer Gynt
Henrik Ibsen
Directed by Anne Juntine D'Zmura

Naga Mandala.
Stan Egi, Nirupama Nityanandan.

167

1994-95 SEASON

The Rover
Aphra Behn
  Directed by JoAnne Akalaitis
  Set by George Tsypin
  Costumes by Gabriel Berry
  Lighting by Jennifer Tipton
  Music by Bruce Odland

The Play's the Thing
Ferenc Molnar
  Adapted by P. G. Wodehouse
  Directed by Michael Engler
  Set by Robert Brill
  Costumes by Candice Donnelly
  Lighting by Peter Maradudin

Home
David Storey
  Directed by Garland Wright
  Set by Douglas Stein
  Costumes by Susan Hilferty
  Lighting by James F. Ingalls

The Broken Jug
Heinrich von Kleist
  Translated by Jon Swan
  Directed by Liviu Ciulei
  Set by Liviu Ciulei
  Costumes by Marina Draghici
  Lighting by Beverly Emmons

As You Like It
William Shakespeare
  Directed by Garland Wright
  Set by Douglas Stein
  Costumes by Susan Hilferty
  Lighting by Jennifer Tipton

A Christmas Carol
Charles Dickens
  Adapted by Barbara Field
  Directed by Sari Ketter
  Set by Jack Barkla
  Costumes by Jack Edwards
  Lighting by Marcus Dilliard
  Music by Hiram Titus

Macbeth
William Shakespeare
  Directed by Kristoffer Tabori
  Set by Yael Pardess
  Costumes by Mark Wendland
  Lighting by Peter Maradudin

K - Impressions of The Trial by Franz Kafka
  Adapted by Garland Wright
  Directed by Garland Wright
  Set by John Arnone and
  Garland Wright
  Costumes by Susan Hilferty
  Lighting by Marcus Dilliard
  and Garland Wright

Guthrie Lab: Resident Director's Project

Mother Courage and Her Children
Bertolt Brecht
  Translated by Ralph Manheim
  Directed by Dipankar Mukherjee

As You Like It.
Company.

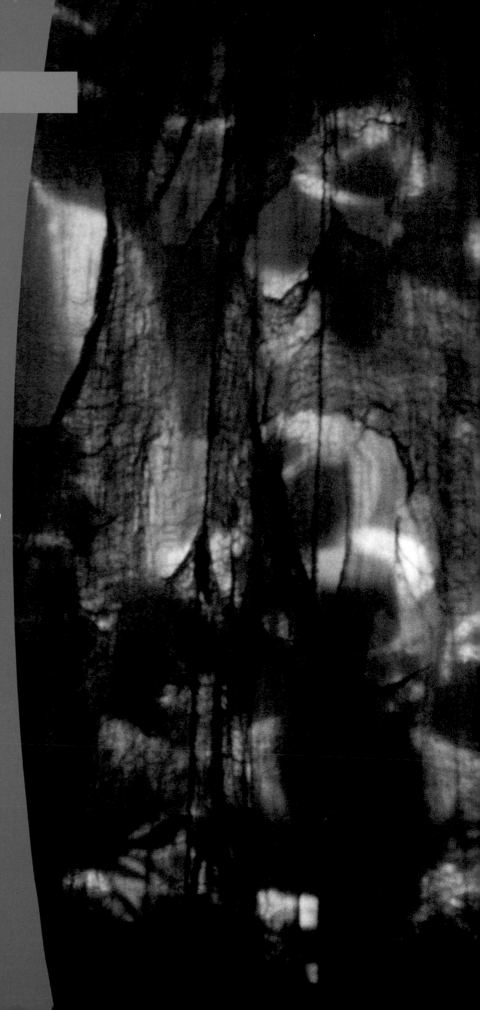

1995-96 SEASON

King Lear
William Shakespeare
  Directed by Garland Wright
  Set by Douglas Stein
  Costumes by Susan Hilferty
  Lighting by Marcus Dilliard

The Royal Family
George S. Kaufman and Edna Ferber
  Directed by Sari Ketter
  Set by Douglas Stein
  Costumes by Kim Krumm Sorenson
  Lighting by Marcus Dilliard
  Music by Victor Zupanc

The Firebugs
Max Frisch
  Translated by Michael Feingold
  Directed by David Gordon
  Set by Marina Draghici
  Costumes by Adelle Lutz
  Lighting by Jennifer Tipton

The Big White Fog
Theodore Ward
  Directed by Lou Bellamy
  Set by Douglas Stein
  Costumes by Paul Tazewell
  Lighting by Allen Lee Hughes

A Christmas Carol
Charles Dickens
  Adapted by Barbara Field
  Directed by Risa Brainin
  Set by Jack Barkla
  Costumes by Jack Edwards
  Lighting by Michael Klaers
  (based on a design by Marcus Dilliard)
  Music by Hiram Titus

Babes in Arms
Richard Rodgers and Lorenz Hart
  New book by Ken LaZebnik
  Directed by Garland Wright
  Associate direction by Sari Ketter
  Set by John Arnone
  Costumes by Susan Hilferty
  Lighting by Howell Binkley
  Choreography by Liza Gennaro
  Music direction by David Bishop

Guthrie Lab

Short Plays
  Directed by Risa Brainin
  Set by Nanya Ramey
  Costumes by Kathleen Egan

Tone Clusters
Joyce Carol Oates

Naomi in the Living Room
Christopher Durang

The Zoo Story
Edward Albee

Old Times
Harold Pinter
  Directed by Garland Wright
  Set by Garland Wright
  Costumes by Devon Painter

K – Impressions of The Trial by Franz Kafka (revival)
  Adapted by Garland Wright
  Directed by Garland Wright
  Set by John Arnone and
  Garland Wright
  Costumes by Susan Hilferty

*K – Impressions of
The Trial by Franz Kafka.*
Charles Janasz and company.

171

The Cherry Orchard
Anton Chekhov
  Translated by Jean-Claude van Itallie
  Directed by Joe Dowling
  Set and costumes by Desmond Heeley
  Lighting by Marcus Dilliard
  Music by Keith Thomas

She Stoops to Conquer
Oliver Goldsmith
  Directed by Douglas Hughes
  Set by John Lee Beatty
  Costumes by Linda Fisher
  Lighting by Christopher Akerlind

Philadelphia, Here I Come
Brian Friel
  Directed by Joe Dowling
  Set by John Lee Beatty
  Costumes by Catherine Zuber
  Lighting by Christopher Akerlind

A Doll's House
Henrik Ibsen
  Translated by Vanessa Burnham
  Directed by Michael Langham
  in association with Helen Burns
  Set by Neil Peter Jampolis
  Costumes by Susan Benson
  Lighting by Neil Peter Jampolis

A Christmas Carol
Charles Dickens
  Adapted by Barbara Field
  Directed by Sari Ketter
  Set by Neil Patel
  Costumes by Jess Goldstein
  Lighting by Marcus Dilliard
  Music by Victor Zupanc

The Price
Arthur Miller
  Directed by David Thacker
  Set by Fran Thompson
  Costumes by Laurie Bramhall
  Lighting by Marcus Dilliard

A Midsummer Night's Dream
William Shakespeare
  Directed by Joe Dowling
  Set by Frank Hallinan Flood
  Costumes by Paul Tazewell
  Lighting by Howell Binkley
  Music by Keith Thomas

Guthrie Lab

Simpatico
Sam Shepard
  Directed by Gary Gisselman
  Set by Nayna Ramey
  Costumes by Devon Painter
  Lighting by Matthew Reinert

Mystery of the Rose Bouquet
Manuel Puig
  Translated by Allan Baker
  Directed by Risa Brainin
  Set by Nayna Ramey
  Costumes by Devon Painter
  Lighting by Michael Klaers
  Music by Marcela Kingman Lorca

Many Colors Make The Thunder King
Femi Osofisan
  Directed by Bartlett Sher
  Set by Nayna Ramey
  Costumes by Devon Painter
  Lighting by Michael Klaers
  Music by Peter Still

Penumbra at the Guthrie

Fences
August Wilson
  Directed by Claude Purdy
  Set by W.J.E. Hammer and Greg Ray
  Costumes by Deidrea Whitlock
  Lighting by Mike Wangen

The Cherry Orchard
Helen Carey,
Christopher Evan Welch.

173

You Can't Take It with You
George S. Kaufman and Moss Hart
Directed by Douglas C. Wager
Set by Thomas Lynch
Costumes by Patricia Zipprodt
Lighting by Allen Lee Hughes

Blithe Spirit
Noel Coward
Directed by Joe Dowling
Set by John Lee Beatty
Costumes by Paul Tazewell
Lighting by Kenneth Posner
Music by Victor Zupanc

Racing Demon
David Hare
Directed by Mark Brokaw
Set by Allen Moyer
Costumes by Devon Painter
Lighting by Kenneth Posner

A Christmas Carol
Charles Dickens
Adapted by Barbara Field
Directed by Sari Ketter
Set by Neil Patel
Costumes by Jess Goldstein
Lighting by Marcus Dilliard
Music by Victor Zupanc

The Playboy of the Western World
John Millington Synge
Directed by Joe Dowling
Set by Frank Hallinan Flood
Costumes by Susan E. Mickey
Lighting by Blake Burba

Thunder Knocking on the Door
Keith Glover
Directed by Marion McClinton
Set by Neil Patel
Costumes by Michael Alan Stein
Lighting by Christopher Akerlind
Music and lyrics by Keb' Mo'
Additional music and lyrics by
Keith Glover and Anderson Edwards
Choreography by Ken Roberson

Much Ado About Nothing
William Shakespeare
Directed by Joe Dowling
Set and costumes by Desmond Heeley
Lighting by Chris Parry
Music by Keith Thomas

Guthrie Lab

Black No More
Syl Jones
Directed by Tazewell Thompson
Set by Donald Eastman
Costumes by Gabriel Berry
Lighting by Robert Wierzel
Music by Joshua Bloay
Choreography by Julie Arenal

Thunder Knocking on the Door.
Eric Riley, Lovette George.

175

1998-99 SEASON

The Importance of Being Earnest
Oscar Wilde
  Directed by Joe Dowling
  Set by Frank Hallinan Flood
  Costumes by Mathew J. LeFebvre
  Lighting by Christopher Akerlind
  Music by Victor Zupanc

A Month in the Country
Brian Friel, after Ivan Turgenev
  Directed by Mark Brokaw
  Set by Frank Hallinan Flood
  Costumes by Ellen McCartney
  Lighting by Christopher Akerlind

The Venetian Twins
Carlo Goldoni
  Adapted by Michael Bogdanov
  with additional material by Kevin Kling
  Directed by Michael Bogdanov
  Set and costumes by Kendra Ullyart
  Lighting by Marcus Dilliard
  Music by Terry Mortimer

A Christmas Carol
Charles Dickens
  Adapted by Barbara Field
  Directed by Sari Ketter
  Set by Neil Patel
  Costumes by Jess Goldstein
  Lighting by Marcus Dilliard
  Music by Victor Zupanc

The Magic Fire
Lillian Garrett-Groag
  Directed by Libby Appel
  Set by Richard L. Hay
  Costumes by Deborah M. Dryden
  Lighting by Ann G. Wrightson

Julius Caesar
William Shakespeare
  Directed by Joe Dowling
  Set by Michael Yeargan
  Costumes by Paul Tazewell
  Lighting by Chris Parry
  Music by Keith Thomas

Summer and Smoke
Tennessee Williams
  Directed by David Esbjornson
  Set by John Arnone
  Costumes by Elizabeth Hope Clancy
  Lighting by Christopher Akerlind

Guthrie Lab

Molly Sweeney
Brian Friel
  Directed by Joe Dowling
  Set by Frank Hallinan Flood
  Costumes by Laurie Bramhall
  Lighting by Marcus Dilliard

Gross Indecency: The Three Trials of Oscar Wilde
Moises Kaufman
  Directed by Ethan McSweeny
  Set by John Arnone
  Costumes by Mathew J. LeFebvre
  Lighting by Matthew Reinert

Lysistrata
Aristophanes
  Directed by Wendy Knox
  Set by Michael Sommers
  Costumes by Kathy Kohl
  Lighting Rich Paulsen
  Music by Joshua Bloay

Julius Caesar.
Lance Reddick, Alex Podulke, company.

177

1999-2000 SEASON

The School for Scandal
Richard Brinsley Sheridan
  Directed by Joe Dowling
  Set by Frank Hallinan Flood
  Costumes by Mathew J. LeFebvre
  Lighting by Kenneth Posner

Ah, Wilderness!
Eugene O'Neill
  Directed by Douglas C. Wager
  Set by Ming Cho Lee
  Costumes by Zack Brown
  Lighting by Allen Lee Hughes

Martin Guerre
Alain Boublil and
Claude-Michel Schönberg
  Music by Claude-Michel Schönberg
  Lyrics by Alain Boublil
  and Stephen Clark
  Directed by Conall Morrison
  Set by John Napier
  Costumes by Andreane Neofitou
  Lighting by Howard Harrison
  Choreography by David Bolger
  Music direction by Kevin Stites

A Christmas Carol
Charles Dickens
  Adapted by Barbara Field
  Directed by Sari Ketter
  Set by Neil Patel
  Costumes by Jess Goldstein
  Lighting by Marcus Dilliard
  Music by Victor Zupanc

Misalliance
George Bernard Shaw
  Directed by Neil Munro
  Set and Costumes by Peter Hartwell
  Lighting by Matthew Reinert

The Darker Face
of the Earth
Rita Dove
  Directed by Lou Bellamy
  Set by Douglas Stein
  Costumes by Paul Tazewell
  Lighting by Mike Wangen

The Plough and the Stars
Sean O'Casey
  Directed by Joe Dowling
  Set by Frank Hallinan Flood
  Costumes by Matthew J. LeFebvre
  Lighting by Chris Parry

Guthrie Lab

Sweeney Todd
Stephen Sondheim and
Hugh Wheeler
  Music and lyrics by Stephen Sondheim
  Book by Hugh Wheeler
  From an adaption by Christopher Bond
  Directed by John Miller-Stephany
  Set by Frank Hallinan Flood
  Costumes by Mathew J. LeFebvre
  Lighting by Matthew Reinert
  Choreography by
  Marcela Kingman Lorca
  Music direction by Andrew Cooke

Mr. Peters' Connections
Arthur Miller
  Directed by James Houghton
  Set by Christine Jones
  Costumes by Matthew J. LeFebvre
  Lighting by Marcus Dilliard

Lake Hollywood
John Guare
  Directed by Itamar Kubovy
  Set by Neil Patel
  Costumes by Rich Hamson
  Lighting by Jeff Bartlett

Side Man
Warren Leight
  Directed by Ethan McSweeny
  Set by John Arnone
  Costumes by Amelia Busse Breuer
  Lighting by Matthew Reinert

On Tour

A Midsummer Night's Dream
William Shakespeare
  Directed by Joe Dowling
  Set by Frank Hallinan Flood
  Costumes by Paul Tazewell
  Lighting by Matthew Reinert and
  Michael Burgoyne
  Music by Keith Thomas

Ah, Wilderness!
Maria Thayer, T.R. Knight

179

Clockwise
from upper left:

WorldStage *Carmen Funebre* flyer, 2003.

Cotume page
from study guide,
Mrs. Warren's Profession,
2002, designed
by Ann Hould-Ward.

Season brochure, 2005.

Ticket for last
performance on
Vineland Place, 2006.

Season schedule
draft, 2005.

Playwright Arthur Miller
and Joe Dowling, 2001.

Hamlet, Santino Fontana
and Leah Curney.

In the costume
shop, 2002.

Amadeus, 2001.

New building
brochure, 2003.

From the
Guthrie newsletter.

Guthrie WORLDStage Series
and the Walker Art Center co-present

from Poland, Teatr Biuro Podrozy's

CARMEN Funebre
(Funeral Song)

A TALE OF

WAR
IN
THE
MOD
ERN
WO
RLD

A powerful visual spectacle seen in 27 countries no[...]
Minneapolis for 5 night-time performances onl[...]

Performed in English and Polish

Stage Directions
Following the Guthrie family

-WARD (most recently *Mrs.*
rofession 2003) designed the
Dance of the Vampires, a new
ed on Roman Polanski's film
Vampire Killers, in New York.
ELET (*Martin Guerre* 1999)
t director …

kespeare Theatre in Washington
winter, EDWIN C. OWENS (most
isalliance 2000) was in the cast
do About Nothing by William
MARK LAMOS (most recently
d Cleopatra 2002) directed,
OMADA (*The Carpetbagger's*
001) composed the music and
ZUBER (*Philadelphia, Here I*
96, *The Winter's Tale* 1992)
ostumes …

Edwin C. Owens
in *Misalliance*
(Michal Daniel).

BRENDA WEHLE (numerous
productions) and DANIEL
DAVIS (*Pravda* 1988, *Misan-*
thrope 1987 among others)
are in the cast of Alan Bennett's
Talking Heads Off-Broadway …

JOSE LLANA (*Martin Guerre* 1999) was in
the cast of the recent Broadway revival of
Flower Drum Song by Richard Rodgers
and Oscar Hammerstein II, with a new
book by David Henry Hwang …

NEIL PATEL (most recently *A Christmas*
Carol 2002) designed the set for *Ain't*
Misbehavin' at Center Stage, Baltimore,
earlier this winter. PAUL TAZEWELL (*Three*
Sisters 2003, *Amadeus* 2001 among others)
designed the costumes …

PETER KACZOROWSKI (*Mrs. Warren's*
Profession 2003) designed the lighting for the
national tour of Mel Brooks' *The Producers*
which visited the Twin Cities last year …

Earlier this spring PAUL DE CORDOVA
(most recently *Once in a Lifetime* 2001),
TRACEY MALONEY (*Antony and Cleopatra*
2002, *Simpatico* 1996), EMIL HERRERA
(most recently *Resurrection Blues* 2002)
and former Guthrie company member and
dramaturg FAYE M. PRICE were in the cast
of *[sic]* by Melissa James Gibson at
Pillsbury House Theatre …

Brenda Wehle with Charles Janasz in
Too Clever by Half (Michal Daniel).

T.R. KNIGHT (most recently *Amadeus*
2001) was in the Off-Broadway cast of Anto
Howard's *Scattergood* directed by DOUG
HUGHES (most recently *Da* 2001) …

Emil Herrera with Sally Wingert in *A Christmas Carol* (Michal Daniel).

DON'T MISS A MOMENT!

2005-2006 Season (ver. 24)

	Rehearse	1st Tech	1st Preview	Open	Close
FRIDAY May 31	June 28	July 2			July 31
					Sept 11
					Oct 23
					Oct 9
					Oct 30
					Nov 6
					Dec 24
					Nov 6
					Nov 20
					Feb 5
					Feb 12
Jan 17			Jan 22		Mar 19

Guthrie Theater

Hamlet
Sponsored by Target
Final Performance on Vineland Place
Sunday, May 7, 2006 - 7pm
725 Vineland Place, Minneapolis
612-377-2224 or 1-877-447-8243
SHEILA LIVINGSTON

MAIN FLOOR

AISLE 7
ROW   N
SEAT   68

8415//
50.00
000000H

BOATS

VESTIBULE

MEASUR

CAROL
Gisselmar

RECORDING
STUDIO

KLING

The New
Century

The Guthrie Theater

The Guthrie Theater stood at 725 Vineland Place in Minneapolis, next door to the Walker Art Center, from 1963 to 2006, with only the thrust stage. The theater originally built as a summer festival – one large theater with minimal backstage facilities – grew over time to an institution operating year-round, with enormous productions, and artistic ambition to present a wide variety of kinds of plays and performances, not all of which were suited to the thrust stage. Various expansions and adjustments and renovations of the Vineland Place location were made, but the theater's programs were clearly outstripping its spaces. Something had to give. Could the theater leave its home on Vineland Place? Where would it go? What would that take?

Joe Dowling:

One of my first meetings in 1995, when I came in as Artistic Director, was to talk to staff about how difficult the conditions were backstage. We were spread out at five different locations around the Cities, the administration was divided up. We were building sets in a room that was never designed for that so it was actually quite unsafe.

If we were going to continue to produce at a very high standard, we needed to do something quite dramatic about the facility. Otherwise the quality was going to drop and that was not going to happen on my watch if I had anything to do with it and of course, as the Artistic Director, I did.

My first production here was *The Cherry Orchard*. Now, I think Chekhov is one of the greatest geniuses the theater has ever produced, but you can't truly do Chekhov on a thrust stage. Moments of silence and moments of stillness are almost impossible on a thrust because, somewhere or other in the house, someone's not seeing what motivated that moment of stillness. I did an analysis, too, of the previous five seasons and realized that some of the plays were those that ought to have been done in a smaller venue, where the true merits of the play and the production would have been seen. There is a whole repertoire from Eugene O'Neill onward that works better on a proscenium stage than they do on a thrust.

So the artistic ambition of the organization had absolutely reached beyond its capacity in its facility. So having done that analysis I was able to say that what was needed was a viable second space. If the Guthrie were going to grow into what is truly its originators' intention, the intention of the founders, then we could not do it in the facility that they built. It was simply not possible.

Combine that with the fact that you had dangerous situations backstage, and we were spread all over the city. And now that our Vineland Place stage didn't work for all the kinds of work that we needed to do. It led us inexorably and logically to the idea of a new theater.

Opposite: Joe Dowling as the new building rises around him.

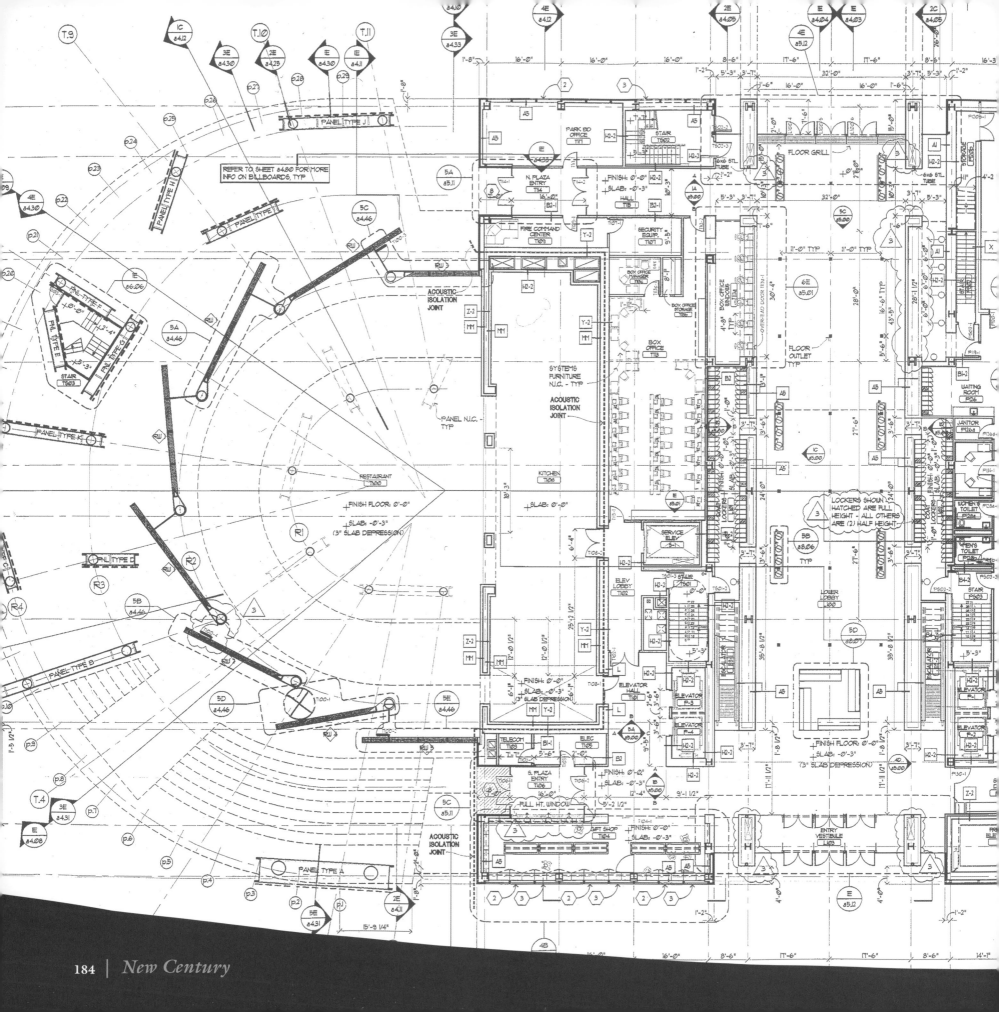

At that early point, we were still thinking about expanding on Vineland Place. We didn't know that the Walker was planning on growing, too. We were going to have to fight over the territory. Our facilities problems were too big for the Vineland Place footprint to solve.

I said, in a meeting that I distinctly remember, "Well, the only solution is to move." There was a stunned silence. Someone said do you really mean that you would move the Guthrie Theater from its present location? And I said, "If you take the logic of everything we're all saying, we're going to have to move somewhere else. The reason I'm saying that is that I know we will actually fail to do what we want to do, here. I've done the analysis. I know the history. This will fail."

So the philosophical idea of a national center for theater arts and theater education – which I genuinely believe was the intention of the founders – evolved as a result of painstaking analysis and a result of the facilities problems on Vineland Place. It evolved. Charlie Zelle said it best. This is not a facility looking for a program; this is a program already determined that needs a facility.

We started to talk about a venue, a building, that would encompass classical work, new work, student work, allow for a growth of the art form itself through studio work. At the same time, we wanted to create spaces that would allow audiences going to those different things to come together in a communal way, whether it's to share a meal or a drink or whatever.

Considering the future is the work of the theater's artistic leadership and its governing board. Charles Zelle led that board early in the new century; his father Louis was one of the original trustees of the Guthrie.

I grew up with the Guthrie. I was seven when I saw the *Hamlet* in 1963, and can still remember specifics of *The House of Atreus* from 1967. Guthrie people were part of my childhood, both the artists and the community leaders.

The stories that my father told around the dinner table were about a passionate mission. The board, and the people involved with the Guthrie now, are doing much more than checking a box marked "civic duty." There is a total belief that the Guthrie is very important, that it is a transforming and one of the great distinguishing features of our community. Everyone on the board comes from a different place, but there is a common thread, that the Guthrie is worth stretching for. It is worth risk.

The move to the river was in part about people wanting that excitement and that kind of pioneering spirit that happened in the early sixties. Like those early leaders, we felt we were on a mission and that we in Minnesota can do this like no other place can. Call it civic pride. We can all work together and be enthusiastic about making our place, making an international mark that can't be done in New York, can't be done in Washington. If not here, it just can't be done. Going to the river was about the same kind of wanting-the-very-best, in the same tradition that we had in 1963.

In the last ten years, we had started to really honor our history. The actor wall, the artistic directors' wall, the community leaders wall – there was renewed pride. Some of the actors and scenic designers who had been part of our history were coming back – Helen Carey, Desmond Heeley. The notion that we couldn't possibly leave Vineland, the resistance to changing the brick and mortar, it kind of melted away. The board and the organization had confidence that we were going to be able to continue to hold all that dear. It was not dependent on Vineland Place. It was about what goes on inside the building, not the building itself.

There was a long process of site selection. There was one day we got a bus and about eight or nine of us were driven around. We went downtown to look at a vacant lot near the theater district. We went to the back of St. Anthony Main and looked at a vacant lot there and thought about the other side of the river. And we drove to what eventually became our new site. It was ironic. We were driving along the river and drove around the block and parked right in front of this parking lot. It was full of cars. Everybody got out. There were silos and dust and the Liquor Depot and that was it. We wandered around. We couldn't even see the river, because it was just a parking lot. Why would we even consider it? But standing in the parking lot, we had a conversation. This is where the city is moving. It has close access with Interstate 35. There's an incredible park area that's being developed here. This could have tremendous views. And it would be our own space, our own neighborhood. We would be a destination, as we were on Vineland for all those years.

There was a tremendous belief on the board in the power of this project. There was a lot of conversation and what-if and certainly a full range of opinions and beliefs were expressed. We had turning points – when we had to approve the budget without having secured the state funding, and particularly when the governor vetoed the project in the spring of 2002. But underlying it all was the belief that this had such merit for the organization and for the state that we must go forward. It was perilous, but underneath the board was saying that this was too powerful to stop. I remember one of the board members saying, "For goodness sake, whatever you do, do not commit suicide for fear of dying!" If we don't make it, it wouldn't be because we didn't make the effort.

The committee for architect selection traveled far and wide, as related by board member Margaret Wurtele.

The architect selection committee went to New York and Europe to view works by the four or five architects who were the remaining finalists. We stopped in Paris and saw two of Jean Nouvel's buildings. The first was the Fondation Cartier on the Boulevard Raspail – very clean, very simple, very elegant. Then we saw the Institut du Monde Arabe. Again the structure was geometric and imposing. This time the surface was intricately modeled in Arab designs – very complex, eastern and exotic. The two buildings couldn't have been more different.

We flew to Lyon the next day to see the renovated opera house. Amazing! A new clean geometric building nestled inside the shell of the traditional old opera house. The whole thing was dramatic and gave a sense of occasion. The best, though, was yet to come. Downstairs in the back, we entered a rehearsal room for the chorus. It felt like a chapel – clad in elegant wood with a soaring ceiling. Joe Dowling looked around and said, "This is the first architect we've seen who spent as much time on the spaces for the artists as he did for the audience."

The night before our last stop, the Lucerne Performing Arts Center, sitting around the dinner table, we took a straw vote: if you were going to choose our architect right now, who would it be? The result was Jean Nouvel.

It wasn't until the next day that we saw the pièce de resistance: the Lucerne complex. It loomed over the lake like a boat about to take to the water. Everyone we spoke with told us how its clean, gorgeous spaces really worked for the art. No more votes were necessary.

In February 2002, the Guthrie unveiled the first presentation of schematic designs for the new building. Architect Jean Nouvel spoke and said, in part:

Everything comes from somewhere: cities, theaters, people. Our birth has a cause forever inscribed in our genetic makeup. Thus, if Minneapolis had not had its waterfalls, boats would not have stopped here, mills would never have been built, and it would have remained a village. And if Tyrone Guthrie had not had a certain conception of popular theater, a thrust hall as unique and revered as the Guthrie's would never have seen the light of day.

Today the Guthrie is coming to settle in the historic golden rectangle near the falls, next to the old mills, in the industrial quarter that invented Minneapolis.

This is why the architecture of the Guthrie, by its volumes and colors, can be read as a far-off echo of silos; and why the shared lobby advances like a bridge to contemplate the waterfalls; and why the lighted signs above the adjacent silos dialogue with those of the theater; and also why industrial bridges take the place of skyways, and why, finally, next to the direct re-interpretation of the thrust hall, two new theaters, one frontal, the other flexible, complete the industrial metaphor of the new Guthrie.

The construction of the new Guthrie on the river, with its theaters, its public spaces, and its extensive and specific workrooms, was difficult. Artistic Director Dowling stood in the leadership position, and at the very center. He was, he says, "determined to make a building that would work."

There were a number of occasions along the way when the complexity of the building was particularly clear to us. We needed three theaters and four classrooms and three rehearsal rooms. Well, I've worked in rehearsal rooms all over the world and I've never been in a decent one in my life. They're all ghastly and they are always forgotten. So I was insistent that ours would not be buried in the center of the building or the basement. It would be somewhere that had the potential of daylight. And a view!

There were years of back and forth negotiation and we had literally hundreds of people involved. The construction people, Nouvel's architects, the architects from Architectural Alliance, the structural engineers, the acousticians, the

Groundbreaking for the new Guthrie, in September 2003, on the Mississippi River. Joanne Von Blon, Rep. Ron Abrams, Jean Nouvel, Joe Dowling, Susan Engel, Charles Zelle.

© 2005 STAR TRIBUNE/Minneapolis–St. Paul.

theater consultants. Sometimes there would be thirty or forty people around the table and a whole row of people behind them. Luckily, I'm stubborn and I'm Irish and I don't give up easily. As I told Jean Nouvel once, the Irish don't give up. Ever. It's just part of who we are; we don't give in.

From the moment that Jean stood on our site, it was the magic of the Mississippi River that made this project attractive for him. "The Mississippi, that's America," he would say. He was interested in seeing up and down the river framing the views in the theater so that people would have the drama of the river before they had the drama that was on stage.

Jean was insistent about the views. But the difficulty of putting everything fifty feet in the air to take advantage of them was a real issue. Putting the theaters on upper levels made everything our staff was going to have to do exponentially more difficult, and it was going to add another couple of million to the project. So I was arguing strongly about keeping the theaters on the ground floor. And Jean was arguing equally strongly that if we wanted to take advantage of the site we were on, we would have to go up high. I think it was Peter Kitchak, who was on the board, who made the suggestion that we get a crane down to the site and that Jean and I go up together. And we did! Jean was in all black of course with his leather coat and his hat and his cigar. We were put into this bucket and taken up to the level of what is now the bridge and we were swung right out over to where the bridge would be. It was wonderful! It was wonderful. I had a complete road-to-Damascus conversion at that moment, because I knew he was right. We had to go up. We had to have those views. We couldn't build this building on that site and ignore those views. He was absolutely right.

Then, dammit, I had to tell him. He just said, in that wonderful Gallic accent, "Well, what did you expect? I am right! My friend, now you acknowledge that I know something!"

At the groundbreaking ceremony, representatives from every part of the theater put spades to dirt, young actors lifted their voices and sang, and Joe Dowling was presented with a symbolic cup of flour welcoming the theater to the historic mill district. Governor Tim Pawlenty got a laugh when he started his speech: "Ever since Ford's Theatre and Mr. Lincoln, Republicans have had an uneasy relationship with the arts."

Under Joe Dowling's leadership, the Guthrie bent itself toward the training of young actors through strong initiatives like the Bachelor of Fine Arts program in association with the University of Minnesota. Relationship beween the Guthrie and the University reaches back all the way to the sixties. The twenty-first century University of Minnesota/Guthrie Theater BFA Actor Training Program accepted its first class in 2000. By the time they graduated in 2004, they had appeared on the Guthrie stage as 'essentials' in crowd scenes, and in the occasional speaking role, presented new programs in collaboration with local theaters, and performed at the Guthrie Lab in two plays written expressly for them.

I've lived in Minnesota all my life and have grown up with the Guthrie. The first show I ever saw, like so many thousands of Minnesotans, was *A Christmas Carol* when I was five years old. Almost every year since, it has been a family tradition to see the show together around the holidays. I remember always jumping on my Dad's lap right before Marley's ghost appeared onstage, and gradually getting less and less scared of the ghosts every year. After I saw my first "real" show, *Othello*, at age 11, I remember telling Dad how I wished to one day walk on that stage.

My senior year in high school, when I auditioned to be in the Guthrie's inaugural class, was probably one of the most thrilling and exciting times in my life. Everything seemed to happen in a whirlwind and then, all of a sudden, two weeks after graduation, I was walking backstage at the Guthrie for the first time, getting fitted to be an extra in *Twelfth Night*. We walked out on to the stage and I felt like I got the wind knocked out of me. There's something about that stage that makes you feel this overwhelming, intense sensation whenever you stand on it. It's as if the presence of all the thousands of great actors, directors, staff members and shows that have graced the Guthrie lingers on in the floorboards. [Lindsey Obrzut, class of 2004]

Like many of us, I'm not from around here and I didn't know anything about the Guthrie Theater four years ago. Coal mining towns in Pennsylvania don't pay much attention to the workings of American theater. Most of my free time was spent in parking lot "carousing," as my mother liked to call it. But when I looked into this new program and asked teachers, friends and professionals about the Guthrie, something happened. Eyes opened a little wider, pace of speech increased, and everyone across the board said, "If you've got a shot at being part of the Guthrie, take it." And I did, because I needed to find out what kind of a theater could make people's hearts beat faster from 900 miles away.

It's funny, the things I didn't look for or expect have turned out to be the most valuable experiences. We know not all of us are going to be successful in this field. And we know that acting isn't physics. It's more difficult in a lot of ways, because there's never a right answer, never a clear solution to a problem. Struggling with that, trying to be okay with the fact that a lot of people aren't going to like my work no matter what I do, has been hard. But in the theater, as a teacher once told me, there's no such thing as good and bad. There's what you tried to do, and what you didn't. There's trying to be a success, and trying not to be a failure. That's good advice for any career field, and more than that, for being a stronger human being.

I don't know who I would be if, four years ago, I hadn't made that decision to figure out what this Guthrie place was, but thank God I did. I've grown more as an actor than I thought possible, but I've learned even more about what it takes to be alive. [Matt Amendt, Class of 2004]

Class of 2004, Guthrie/BFA program at the University of Minnesota.

In another injection of new young talent, the Guthrie began in 1996 to offer a program for actors from graduate training programs across the country, the Guthrie Experience for Actors in Training. Scheduled in the summer before their final year of studies at schools like The Juilliard School, New York University, Yale and Columbia, the project helps young artists build a bridge between their training and the professional world. "GExers" have gone on to television, to film, and to Broadway; many have returned often to the Guthrie stage.

Guthrie/BFA student Jeremy Catterton tries on the offerings at CostumeRentals. Note the racks of hats.

I have just finished a whirlwind week in New York meeting agents and casting directors following my third year showcase. The jump from the protected artistic environment of actor training into the acting profession can be very jarring. It was for me. Suddenly, I could no longer focus only on developing my ability as an actor; there were many "business" issues to deal with. As an actor whose experience, training and passion point me first to the stage, how do I survive in a business that caters primarily to film, TV and commercial work? In the Guthrie Experience, I felt I was under the wing of an organization large and respected enough to keep me from getting lost in the business. The Guthrie, Ken Washington and Joe Dowling are names on my resume that were discussed in every meeting I had this week. But beyond resumes and business, the Guthrie Experience connected me to eleven other young actors from training programs across the country and a host of theater professionals whose paths cross, as they seem to do, at the Guthrie. [Jeff Cribbs, Guthrie Experience 2001, writing in 2002]

The Guthrie Experience serves as a reminder to us – the future generation of theater artists – that we need it as much as it needs us. I now find myself in the position shared by many young artists. I would love to work in the theater throughout my entire career but have come face to face with the realities of the casting process. I've found that you have to have a recognizable name to be considered for a leading role on Broadway and that many important theaters across the country prefer to hire actors with television and film credits. The dilemma then becomes, "What do I have to do in order to participate in the theater community?" I believe this is why more and more young actors like myself go straight to television and films, to create a name for ourselves so we can pick and choose the theater we want to do. [Morena Baccarin, Guthrie Experience 1999, writing in 2002]

All the titles presented at the Guthrie are part of a grand seasonal scheme, preceded by a long and difficult planning process. Associate Artistic Director John Miller-Stephany describes the route that brought *To Fool the Eye* to the stage.

Every February or March, the Guthrie Theater holds a special event at which Artistic Director Joe Dowling announces the repertory of plays that will be produced in the Guthrie's next season. Joe wrestles for months with a staggering variety of titles, trying to balance the season – making sure there is a winning combination: comedies as well as serious dramas; escapist entertainments as well as challenging texts; classic plays as well as contemporary works. Joe certainly welcomes advice, but at the end of the day, he listens to his own heart and decides upon the plays he believes will best serve the Guthrie community in the next season.

Last fall, as he was going through this exhausting process, I approached him with an idea to commission a new translation of the Jean Anouilh play, *Léocadia*. Quite naturally, Joe asked me, "Who do you have in mind to do the adaptation?" Frankly, I hadn't thought it through that thoroughly but blessedly, a name popped into my head: Jeffrey Hatcher, a tremendously gifted locally-based playwright. I greatly admired his writing; he clearly knows how to make time-honored material fresh for modern audiences. Joe loved the idea of having Jeff write a new adaptation.

Jeffrey Hatcher loved the idea, too.

A playwright friend of mine says the three best things in life are "Sex, Food, and Re-Writing Someone Else's Play." An adaptor of someone else's play gets a modified version of that particular frisson: not as scholarly and precise as a translator, not as free and original as the author himself. Writing an adaptation is like a game of "telephone:" someone whispers a story to someone else, who in turn whispers it to someone else, etc. The fun is in finding out if the story you get at the end matches the story you started with at the beginning. *To Fool the Eye* is an adaptation. It's not a literal translation of Jean Anouilh's *Léocadia*. Stephanie Debner did that for us and did it marvelously. It's also not a free-form riff on the play, in which characters are cut or combined, scenes are added or dropped, and meaning is altered. The plot and order of scenes are the same, the characters are the same, and the ideas are essentially the same. The words, however, are very different. A sharp observer will first note they're not in French. But that observer might also note they're not in "British" – the default mode of English favored by countless translators of plays originally written in French, German, Spanish, Russian, Romanian, and any other language on the planet.

John Miller-Stephany and I wanted this adaptation to have a recognizably American sound while retaining the essential French tone of the original. This is tricky in most cross-cultural negotiations, but the American and French languages have a particularly uneasy relationship (see: "Le Big Mac.") My job has been to tailor the text, massage it, expand it here, condense it there, know when to hew close to the original and when to go off on my own for a bit. To retain the ineffable quality of French-ness without becoming, in the words of the Duchess, "precious;" and to please the American ear without coarsening Anouilh's lyricism. To create a world in which both a Veuve Cliquot in a Lalique flute and a shot glass full of something harder are perfectly acceptable and complementary.

Last: *To Fool the Eye* is an English equivalent of the French art term "trompe l'oeil." Painted images meant to imitate reality, like painted books on painted shelves or painted vines on painted bricks. The trick works from a distance, but the closer you get, the more artificial it appears. It's a fitting description of the play, in which so much is made to appear to be what it is not. But artifice can be beautiful, and sometimes – as in the case of *Léocadia* – a fake can give more pleasure than the real thing.

There can be many reasons why a particular play is chosen to be part of a Guthrie season, and many potential paths for a young director to find himself working in Minneapolis. Ethan McSweeny was an intern at the Folger Shakespeare Theatre in Washington, D.C., when he met Joe Dowling, before Dowling became the Guthrie Artistic Director.

Six Degrees of Separation.
Amy Van Nostrand, Stephen Pelinski.

I was on the phone with Joe about two weeks after he arrived in Minneapolis. I was on my way back from Utah and rerouted my flight to stop and see him. Joe picked me up at the airport and it was about 30 degrees below zero. Garland Wright was still here, directing his final show as Artistic Director, so Joe didn't have an office. He wasn't really the Artistic Director yet, his family was still in Ireland, and it was freezing. I think he was having buyer's remorse. We had dinner and many cocktails; this was my introduction to Minneapolis. I went to the gift shop and bought a postcard of the thrust stage and stuck it over my desk at the Shakespeare Theatre. It became my ambition to direct on that stage.

I was so young when I started working at the Guthrie and it was such an amazing experience. Eventually, I directed three shows at the Lab theater. Just before the last one, *Thief River,* opened, Joe invited me to breakfast at Sydney's at 8:00 in the morning. I'm completely bleary-eyed and of course Joe is all pert. He offered me *Six Degrees of Separation* on the thrust stage.

I saw the original production of *Six Degrees of Separation* at Lincoln Center in New York and it was one of the most important plays I ever saw. I was in college; it was the first time that I'd seen a play that was as artistically successful as it was commercially successful. I was thinking about directing at that time, and that production was flawless – it really influenced me. When Joe offered it to me, I was thrilled and terrified.

One thing I've always noticed about Joe is that he never has just one reason for doing a project – it's always three to five. It's about certain actors, audiences, and artistic staffs. With *Six Degrees,* he was interested in cultivating a relationship with John Guare. It's Guare's masterpiece, and it hadn't had a major revival, and that made it a great choice. Joe wanted a vehicle for the actor Danyon Davis, and it was a great role for him. And he wanted to get the Guthrie used to doing newer plays, and here was a new-ish one with bona fides established.

The Shakespeare Theatre was my education, and the Guthrie was my finishing school. I've been incredibly lucky to get to create there; if they tell you they're going to do something, they do it. And it works right the first time. As a young director, to be able to imagine something, feed the idea, and work at a place that could achieve it was an enormous gift. I'll always be profoundly grateful for it. On the individual craftsperson level, it's the most imaginative staff in the world. Some of those people have skills that no one else has, and I hope they are able to pass them on.

In 2002, two breaks in water mains let 55,000 gallons of water sweep through the theater's lower levels, including administrative offices, dressing rooms, production areas and archive storage. In the hallway to the rehearsal room, water poured from overhead light fixtures. "It was just like *The Poseidon Adventure*," said John Miller-Stephany, smiling. Below, the Guthrie staff swabs out the prop shop.

For actors, the thrust stage, much less common than playing on a proscenium 'picture frame,' is an exhilarating space to perform their work. Sally Wingert knows.

> It's like a narcotic once you get on that stage. Like slap the veins and push the needle in. It's the most exciting theater space I have ever been in in my life. You walk out; it's relatively small, but you are the focal point of this surround-sound of humanity. The way that space feels when all those people are there doing an energy exchange with you, that's the true high of it. This is going to sound cheesy. It's sort of spiritual. You're sending stuff out, you're talking

about ideas. You're being this other person and you're having a dialogue, but completely aware that there are 1,500 people who are eavesdropping on you.

The audience is another character that you're communicating with. So you get revved. You get charged. If the audience is willing to come in with sort of an open heart, it's just juicy! You just thrum!

I remember my first curtain call at the Guthrie, way back then. I remember this wave and this roar. The audience was pitch black; the lights were on us. There are other things. I adore getting a wave of laughter in that theater. And hearing that theater dead-silent, pin-drop silent makes all my hair stand up.

When I broke through the Guthrie, I felt like here I was in a fabulous theater with every ounce of support I could possibly need. Nothing happens in that theater that doesn't support the performance on stage. Every single technician, every single marketing person, every single human being is there to support the product that goes on stage.

Sally Wingert with Charles Janasz
in *Too Clever by Half*.

How does a designer move from a script to an idea to a design to the set on stage? From an idea to an entire world. No wonder there is such a sense of satisfaction when the crew finally puts the scenery in place, and the actors can start to inhabit it. The well-known scenic designer Ming Cho Lee wrote about *Ah, Wilderness!* and his process for the Guthrie study guide.

I have to begin by admitting something rather embarrassing: before I started to work on this production, I had never read *Ah, Wilderness!* Many of my students at Yale had designed sets for the play in class over the years and I always felt as if I knew it. I had pretended for so long that I half forgot I hadn't actually read the play. When I did get around to it, I thought, "My God! What a long play this is!" and then I thought, "My God! What a lot of props there are!" and then, "My God! What a lot of settings there are!" I mean, Richard is in his living room, then he's out in a bar, then he's at the beach, and then somehow, without any intermission, he's back in the living room again. I started to think that this is a very difficult play O'Neill has given us.

Fortunately for me, Doug Wager is a smart guy and came to the early design meetings with the idea that *Ah, Wilderness!* is a kind of dream play, O'Neill's dream of a childhood the way he would have liked his own to have been. This gave me some freedom in how I was to create the theatrical space, the environment where these characters could come to life. First, I thought, "Well, the play is about family, so I'll have all of these family portraits at the back" – that idea didn't really work out. And then I thought, "Well, it's about the Fourth of July, so why not have the whole stage look like an American flag" – but that didn't really work out either. Around that time, Zack Brown, the costume designer, gave me a book of snapshot photos of Connecticut in that time period. I also visited O'Neill's Monte Cristo cottage in New London. Then, I happened to see a photo of the musical *Ragtime* with this model of a house filling the background. I thought that this was really a great idea. (All designers borrow, by the way, but what has made me better than most is that I tend to borrow the good ideas.) The more I considered various options for this dream idea, the more I thought that for some reason, the house is very important. So, finally, I arrived at the design: I'm going to have a house on the beach.

Designing is something that you don't approach in a linear way like you approach climbing a ladder, one step at a time, and eventually you reach perfection. It's actually a constant exploring of ideas. It's about how you connect with a play, how you live the life of the play. Especially at my old age right now, I love exploring this, exploring that.

I think the important thing about working in the theater is to be connected with the text and the human events and the storytelling, and somehow, the designer is to create the world where these human events take place. That is perhaps my mission and why I enjoy being a designer.

Two seasons later, *Ah, Wilderness!* went on tour for eleven weeks, visiting eighteen cities throughout the Midwest from February to May. In Decorah, Iowa, the company played the performing arts center at Luther College where, twenty-five years earlier to the week, the grand opening celebration had featured the Guthrie tour of *Moon for the Misbegotten.* The *Ah, Wilderness!* actors attended a reception whose host had seen *Moon* as a student in 1978.

Some things about regional touring stay the same, even after twenty-five years. Offstage activities in Decorah included nine company-taught workshops in everything from Basic Acting to Arts Advocacy, plus a speech to the local Rotary Club and a potluck supper at the Lutheran Church.

And there are still a lot of hours spent in hotel rooms. On long tours, actors and crew people amuse themselves as they can. Actor Nathaniel Fuller is a touring veteran, and an avid golfer.

I'm thinking about writing a book called '101 Tips on Playing Golf in a Hotel Room.' My top tip? White toothpaste covers up marks in the ceiling after you've been practicing your swing.

The theater becomes a kind of family and sometimes, you can go home again. Bartender and usher Neal Baxter started work "in a lovely orange polyester uniform" in the seventies. Polly Brown Grose had lived nearly twenty years in London. In 2005, she returned to Minneapolis and the Guthrie.

According to custom, I stepped to the Guthrie lobby bar for a pre-performance glass of wine. "It's Polly Brown!" I heard. I looked up and met Neal Baxter's flashing eyes as his huge hand covered mine. "Put that away," he nodded to the ten dollar bill I had placed on the counter. "For you, it's on the house. Welcome back."

Before his entrance, actor Richard Ooms rattles his Jacob Marley chains in the "underworld" below the stage in the 2002 production of *A Christmas Carol.* By 2005, Ooms had played Scrooge ten times, directed the play four times, and appeared in seven other productions of the play.

© 2005 STAR TRIBUNE/Minneapolis–St. Paul.

From his command post behind an array of glasses and bottles, the unmistakable Neal towered over a lobby filled with theatergoers sipping drinks and greeting friends – his domain. Thanks to his gentle hospitality, the lobby was less a public space than a gracious 'great hall.' Laughing, his head tilted back, he filled my glass and I turned to the swirling voices. I was back, and I had never lost my forty-year bond to the Guthrie.

Several weeks earlier, as I entered my condominium from the airport, I picked up the ringing telephone. It was Andy Andrews, Guthrie Board member, who had been Board President during my years as Development Director. I thought, "This guy wants my pledge to the Guthrie on the River campaign." Wrong. Andy asked me to join the Board of Directors, to re-join the family. Such a timely welcome home – and to a Board now led by the son of my Guthrie comrade Louis Zelle, with whom I'd made countless calls over the years. The warm atmosphere of Neal Baxter's lobby was no accident. The Guthrie family still churned and moved as one.

We cannot ask Shakespeare or Shaw why they wrote the plays they did. But we can ask a living playwright about a new work. Directors, designers and actors start from the script. Where does the playwright begin?

Charles L. Mee's play *Wintertime* was presented at the Guthrie Lab, and published in 2003. Mee was asked a simple, open-ended question: *Wintertime,* why?

I wrote this play called *Summertime,* which was done at the Magic Theatre. There's this director named Ken Watt who did my *Orestes* in San Francisco six or seven years ago, which is a very nasty, twisted play, and he called me and said, "Would you write something for me to do at the Magic?" And I said, "Sure!" 'cause I thought that would be cool 'cause I don't have any friends in San Francisco so I can do any kind of nasty crazy thing I want without feeling embarrassed. So I started out to write this piece for him, and I thought this could be as foul, twisted and nasty as anything I'd ever done. And out came this kind of frothy romantic comedy about a dysfunctional family in a summer house and a young couple trying to get together. And so he took it into a workshop at the Magic Theatre and since he didn't believe I wrote frothy romantic comedies, he dug into all the subtext of all the pain and anguish that's naturally there in any little romantic love story. And I went out to see this workshop and it was just awful. And I said to him, "You know, I don't think you can load *King Lear* and *Macbeth* on top of this fragile nothing little structure of froth, because it just caves in." And he said, "Oh, I think you're right." So he just turned it upside down.

It was really quite amazing. I mean, I think he was fabulous to do it. And the actors, they just went "flip" and out came this frothy romantic comedy. But I looked at it and I thought, I could do that in the writing; I could go into all the pain and anguish and suffering with the same people in the same summer house, put it in the middle of winter instead of the middle of summer and call it *Wintertime*. And I will write this dark, anguished, tragic play. So I sat down to write that, and out came this frothy romantic comedy. And so I've quit trying to write the dark anguished play with these people. So that's it, and it came out of an impulse to write something, I guess what I found out was, if I just did whatever I felt like doing without even thinking about it, then it turns out that I'm just a frothy romantic person.

How do the theater artists make the audience gasp? Special effects, illusion, and primarily, the power of the performer. In the theater, they are accomplished live, safely, and repeatedly, for every performance. No virtual realities possible. It's all done with creativity, problem-solving and stagecraft.

The Night of the Iguana, in the 2003-2004 season, had audiences reaching unthinkingly for umbrellas during a crucial storm scene. It was complex to prepare, time-consuming to rehearse, and in perfect support of the theatrical illusion.

Although the storm lasts only 45 seconds, the preparation and clean-up arrangements are quite extensive. The problems involved with rain onstage are multi-faceted.

First, the water must be supplied in a way that looks realistic; secondly, there must be a way to catch the water; third, the water must be disposed of. To create the rain storm at the end of Act I, four rain tubes are hung by the first catwalk, each of which is run with a garden hose. There is a second auxiliary rain system mounted in the area under the edge of the roof. Electric valves close the water flow in order to make it stop raining. To catch the rain, there are 14 troughs under the deck of the stage that are sloped so that the water runs down into a drain into the trap room. Finally, a sump pump removes the rain after the show. Once the rain sequence is complete, the last challenge is to make certain that no drops of water hit the stage to obscure the dialogue and lessen the believability of the storm. Electric valves close to stop the flow of rain in the tubes, and there is a towel wrapped at the end of each tube to prevent any drops from falling on the stage. Water on stage is very problematic because any leakage could cause serious damage to the stage, and water on the performance surface could be a safety hazard for the actors. For this reason, two rubber membranes are under the deck for protection.

Through a collaboration between the lighting and sound departments, the storm effect is made realistic. The rain is enhanced by lighting it from the side; sound effects enhance the noise of rain hitting the ground. Further effects are created by the technical crew with fans in the moat to make the foliage move, rustle the palm trees, billow the mosquito netting, cause the shutter to slam and make the lanterns and chimes to sway.

All of this technical expertise to create 45 seconds of realism! [Adriane Levy, assistant technical director]

It's raining in *The Night of the Iguana.*
Armand Schultz, Joel Friedman, Kate Forbes.

At the Guthrie Lab

Beginning in the late nineties, plays presented at the across-town Warehouse District Guthrie Lab were fully-produced, expanding the number of annual productions, and the variety of titles. Directors, actors and audiences reveled in the possibilities of the flexible Lab.

Molly Sweeney.
Charles Janasz, Julie Briskman.

Sweeney Todd.
Jon Whittier,
Dan Sharkey,
company.

Thief River.
Bard Goodrich,
James Shanklin,
Alex Podulke.

Blood Wedding.
Morena Baccarin,
Rene Milan.

Wintertime.
Robert O. Berdahl,
Sam Freed,
Claudia Wilkens,
Jeff Cribbs, Isabell
Monk O'Connor.

When the Guthrie presents beloved and well-known stories, some audience members arrive with their own set of ideas. Many people love the book *Pride and Prejudice*, and it has been made into many movie and television versions. Jacque Frazzini, from the theater's education department, interviewed Costume Director Maribeth Hite.

Costume design for this show has a sort of "Minnesota connection" in that designer Mathew LeFebvre did some primary research through an Edina woman who has an extensive collection of fashion plates from the Regency period. She is a member of an online chat group "The Republic of Pemberley," which was extremely unhappy with the costumes for the A & E version of *Pride and Prejudice*. Matt hopes that after the local "Republic" members see the Guthrie production that he won't look out his window to see them rioting on his lawn!

There are 33 actors in the show including 14 extras, and all but four of these cast members have at least two costumes! Fifty percent of the costumes have been pulled from stock while the rest were rented or were created specially for this production. Sources for rentals were fabric shops in New York, Los Angeles, San Francisco, Canada and Hopkins fabrics in England. Hopkins specializes in historically accurate fabrics – voile or lawn – which is a lightweight cotton. Costume building was started two weeks before the first rehearsal, so that some of the actors actually had their costumes fitted before they began to rehearse!

A special challenge in costuming this show was that the action switches from day wear to formal and back again twice during the production. LeFebvre created a convention for this show to accommodate the quick changes that had to be made by the actors. The women wear daytime jumpers over the top of their formal dresses which enable them to change quickly, indicating the passage of time. Another accessory which helps to change the look of the costumes for the women is the wearing of fichus, light triangular scarves draped over the shoulders. Hats for the extras were pulled from stock, but two hats were specially made – for Charlotte Lucas and Lady Catherine De Bourgh.

The well-dressed family, *Pride and Prejudice*.

Actors come from everywhere and speak like everything, but when they enter the world of the play, they need to sound right. *Pride and Prejudice* takes place in England around the end of the eighteenth century. Gillian Lane-Plescia was vocal coach for that production.

My job has been to try to make the actors sound the way they should sound to be in this play. Of course we don't know exactly how they sounded then. There are no recordings from the period, accents change over the years. But we know they were members of what was known as the lesser gentry, so they should have posh accents, they should have upper-class accents. So we have to use what we think of as an upper-class accent. An upper-class accent in England is actually not the same even today as it was when I was growing up there. But it is what, especially in America, is recognized as being an upper-class accent, so that's what we've used as the basis. All of the characters in this production are members of some aspect of the gentry class; some are a little more high upper-class but they're all really the same class.

This is probably one of the best casts I've ever worked with in terms of their ability to do the accent. When I was listening to the first read-through – I knew some of the actors but not all of them – I thought, "Well they've done this little number on me, they've brought in all these real English people. I'm going to embarrass myself by giving them notes and they're going to tell me, but, I'm English." But it turns out they're not, they just do a very very good job.

I'm just there to make sure they don't slip back into whatever part of the world they come from, which is very hard not to do when you're emotionally connected with a moment. When you're really feeling it as an actor it's very hard to put on another kind of voice, especially this particular British voice because for many people to speak this way makes them feel as though they're being insufferably affected. It doesn't feel affected to me but that's because I've spoken this way pretty much all my life, but I know it does to Americans.

I also help the actors with the particular acoustics of the thrust stage, which are a challenge, to make sure that everybody is heard all the time. No matter where they're facing or where they are on stage, or how intimate the moment is, it still has to be shared with everybody.

Fight choreographers are specialists, able to make a staged brawl – whether with fists, clubs or swords – appropriately violent, credible, and safe. And "in period." How did people really fight in the time of *Romeo and Juliet?* Fight Director Rick Sordelet knows.

Today no one duels anymore. We don't solve our disagreements or conflicts with a meeting on the field of honor, wading through the morning mists to clang out our displeasure with the music of the sword or the final shot of a pistol. In Shakespeare's time and in the Verona of *Romeo and Juliet,* they do. These young men are well versed in the language of the sword. They understand the finer points of dueling in the same way that we know tennis or golf. They know when a thrust is a hit or a miss. More importantly, they know why they practice fencing. Mercutio and Tybalt fight for honor and for the attention and praise of the citizens; they fight to have the right to brag of having humiliated a rival competitor. Tybalt is more than ready to pour fuel on the flames of the ancient grudge between Capulet and Montague even without knowing why this feud once started. Shakespeare, in his wisdom, exposes universal issues on many levels: grudges, first loves, duels of honor, teenagers.

Creating the fights for this show means exploring and bringing to the forefront of physical actions the emotional state of the characters engaged in clashes. Their behavior which, in turn, informs the action. Once the actors know how the characters feel, with Shakespeare providing the words, we can create the action that carries forward their story. Fights are choreographed to accentuate the story, and they help explain the interaction between the characters. Once we understand the underpinnings of the fights, we may take sides, follow the character's deeds and, for a few hours, we are involved with their lives. We feel as they do, and we mourn them when they die.

The actors have been physically conditioning their bodies and breath in order to handle the rigors of our stage fights. They coupled the physical training with the rehearsal of the text and prepared daily in the same way a runner prepares for a marathon. The duels and clashes are not only very demanding physically, one must also maintain concentration and have a sharp focus of attention for all movements and their coordination in order to successfully execute a proper stage fight. The swords are not sharp, but they are real. The actors are allowed a tiny margin of error, but ultimately the fights need to be executed flawlessly. At the end of our fights the actor must portray the ultimate act of our existence: Death. It is no small feat for an actor to put his body through that. Most people have no idea of how hard this is on our bodies. Consider the full spectrum of emotions that the actors put themselves through as they flow through the action. They literally fill the range of a lifetime in the few hours of the performance.

Romeo and Tybalt duel, *Romeo and Juliet.*
Patch Darragh, Alex Podulke.

Adding light to a play does much more than simply allow the audience to see the actor's faces. Mood, focus, location, and even weather can be established in a heartbeat. The designer's tools are technical and complex – hundreds of specifically-chosen lighting instruments, miles of cabling and connections, an incredible range of color options – but the end result of the work is entirely aesthetic in nature. Lighting designer Matthew Reinert knows the challenges.

The key to designing the lights for the production of a Shakespeare play is to pay close attention to the text. Elizabethan theatrical technology was worlds apart from that utilized today. This is particularly true for lighting. The Globe, where *As You Like It* most likely premiered in 1599, was an outdoor theater with daytime performances. Performers as characters would tell the audience about the location, time of day, weather conditions and season of the action, to set the proper context.

Designing for the theater I always keep in mind that on stage there are different levels of abstraction. For example, the human body and voice are obviously the most immediate "real" elements of a production. Moving outwardly from the actors, their costumes, the air around them, towards the scenery, the levels of abstractions change, even if it is a most realistic setting. Theater doesn't do the "real" very well, and theater artists very seldom truly try that. For me, lighting is the "glue" holding the real and the abstract together. It's important for me to remember what that means for this production. There will be distinct differences between the lighting I'll use to illuminate the actors and the set elements, scenery backdrops, etc., since they represent different levels of abstraction.

Drafting the light plot is like taking a trip to the art supply store. There I may buy a few different brushes, some canvases, a bunch of tubes of paint; but it is only when I sit down in the theater during those technical rehearsals with the director, the other designers and the cast, that I get to do any actual "painting." I might discover that a "brush" that seemed such a great option in the store really doesn't work, or that a particular color I had chosen is completely wrong. You can't fall in love too much with your initial ideas because you may have to jettison them at a moment's notice once you start integrating your design with all other elements of the show. The process is very organic, and my design choices have to harmonize with what a character is wearing, or how the music underscores a scene, or how the director has chosen to stage a particular moment.

There is a corps of actors associated with Guthrie plays that the theater does not plan for the audience to ever see – the understudies. Every principal role is understudied and every production has a complex underlying plan of what to do when an actor is unable to perform. There are understudy rehearsals and understudy fittings. During the annual run of *A Christmas Carol*, however, colds and flu can travel rapidly through the company, making chaos of The Plan.

Christmas Carol is the time of year when everyone starts getting sick. For one matinee, both "Mrs. Cratchit" and her daughter "Martha" got sick. The actors went out, and their understudies went in. Then, at the beginning of the matinee, the two understudies started feeling sick. Really, really sick. We had an evening show that night; what to do?

Well, one actor in the show had been watching the Cratchit scene from offstage while waiting to make her regular entrance for the following scene. She said she'd watch it during the matinee and then perform it that night. Then someone else said that she had performed Martha in a different year's production, and she would look at the script, get up on line changes. They both said they could go out for the evening show. So we had our plan.

Sure enough, the evening comes along and the two real understudies are too sick to perform; they're out. So on go these other two actors in their new roles. They start playing the scene and we're all backstage listening and rooting for them, when we suddenly realized. The actress playing the daughter was three years older than the actress playing the mother. [Martha Kulig, Stage Manager]

Huge scenery for *Antony and Cleopatra* under construction on stage.
This scenery under stage light on page 211.

Actors visiting the Guthrie for the first time sometimes check their contract carefully for dates, and scour Los Angeles or New York for winter clothing before getting on the plane. Sore throats and flu can be disastrous for performers, particularly singers. Actor chandra thomas [sic] played the Guthrie in *Crowns* in the 2003-2004 season. It opened in January.

Crowns. chandra thomas, company.

> It seemed most impossible, but it happened – my eyelashes froze together. The forty below temperature (plus windchill!) had gotten the better of me, despite my winterized boots, two pairs of socks, thermal underwear, pants, three shirts, Thinsulate-layered long coat, ski gloves, scar, and hat. But, the moment I stepped into the Guthrie (and removed my excess clothing layers!) the chill of the outside was surpassed by the genuine warmth of the artists and staff inside the theater.
>
> The response to *Crowns* was overwhelming, and a further testament of collective truths that stretch beyond recognizable borders. The images, textures, sounds that continue to echo, resound, are of a passionate creation of a space to tell stories, good stories, great stories.

The Guthrie can be a place where different cultures meet. Sometimes they form something new; sometimes they just look at each other.

> In May of 2004, during the run of *Forbidden Christmas, or The Doctor and the Patient* at the Guthrie Lab, I offered to take the cast and crew to Nye's Polonaise Room after a performance to eat and hear some music. The star of that show was the world-famous Russian dancer Mikhail Baryshnikov. Baryshnikov asked "is the music really good?" I said, "It is something you have to see with your own eyes to believe. And bring your camera."
>
> Baryshnikov took a whole roll of pictures watching Ruth Adams and the World's Most Dangerous Polka Band, tipped them for their music and said "Dave, I am so glad you brought us here."
>
> I bought Baryshnikov one of the band's baseball caps as a gift; Ruth asked me, "That guy taking our pictures. Was he famous? Who was that guy?" When I told her, she said "Yeah. I knew I knew him from somewhere." She handed me some sheet music and asked for his autograph.
>
> So now, Ruth has a copy of "You Made Me Love You," signed by Mikhail Baryshnikov, and Baryshnikov is wearing a World's Most Dangerous Polka Band baseball cap. [David Russell, Director of Theater Services]

Many young people sit in the Guthrie house and dream of being an actor; very few return in leading roles. Peter Macon grew up in north Minneapolis, and attended *The Rainmaker* in 1985 with his class from North High. After working as an actor in the Twin Cities, New York and California, Macon returned to the Guthrie in the title role of *Oedipus* in 2004.

Butterflies. Chatter. Excitement. We are all in such a giddy mood because today we are not in school. Today we are on a field trip to the Tyrone Guthrie Theater and we are going to see some play called *The Rainmaker*. Never heard of it before but our theater teacher says it's good. Yeah, okay, whatever. Even if it ain't, at least there won't be math class today. It is 1985.

I remember thinking I had better be quiet, because they, the actors, could hear me. There was no television tube or movie screen separating them from us. Anything I said, anytime I moved, maybe even anything I thought would somehow catch the attention of one of the players and I'd surely be exposed. I wanted to be the mysterious magic man who'd come to town. He seemed to have a secret. One that made the town folk swoon and drown in a sea of possibility. He made it rain. How was this possible? A lot of water and electricity in the same space at the same time, but no one was electrocuted, amazing. This was not the world of bullies, bad lunch and math class from only a few hours before. This was a place where dreaming was thoroughly encouraged.

When the play ended, the real magic began for me. In all of their civilian glory (sneakers, jeans, bottles of water), the actors came back on stage and introduced themselves. I was at once polarized and enraptured. These were real people! This was their job! Upon realizing this it was very clear to me that I wanted to be an actor. I wanted to be one of those who bared their souls, their flaws and imperfections to the universe eight, and sometimes nine, times a week. They went to the scary places and happily lived in states of vulnerability on a daily basis. They were alive and doing what they loved, which made us love it.

It is now twenty-one years later in December on a still Minnesota Monday night, which is to say it is freezing. I am alone in the theater. I start rehearsal for *Oedipus* in the morning. Save for a naked lamp standing guard, the stage is bare. I am alone with the ghosts and the memories of this magnificent place. They say to me 'welcome, it is your turn.' There is a calm in the air here; it is so quiet that I can hear everything at once. Flashes of past experiences I've had in this theater rush into me, swirling inside my mind, bringing me back to the first time I was here. I sit there in the quiet storm. One thing rings true: I am standing in a space where people talk to and listen to God. A space I will forever call home, both as audience and actor.

Carmen Funebre.

The very first performance at the new Guthrie on the river took place on its building site, outdoors, in 2003. The Teatr Biuro Podozy company of Poland brought their astonishing *Carmen Funebre*, a wordless meditation on the human costs of war, as part of the WorldStage series. It had been a hot and dry late summer. At the performance on September 11, a night when many in the audience were thinking back two years to terrorist attacks in New York and Washington, a heavy rain blew through downtown Minneapolis. The drenched company finished the play in wind and water; the audience stood and watched and thought, as the drought was broken and the fire effects burned.

GUTHRIE THEATER PERFORMANCE REPORT

Production: Freezing Paradise

Date: Tuesday, February 15, 2005
Location: Austin, MN
Performance Number: 7

Part I:
Curtain Up: 7:02   Curtain Down: 7:54   Time: 52.09

Part II:
Curtain Up: 8:09   Curtain Down: 8:57   Time: 47.55

Running Time: 1h. 55m.

REMARKS:

Tonight's performance was ASL interpreted.
Kevin had a fantastic show this evening. The house was the polar opposite of this afternoon; these people were ready to have a good time. They were in hysterics about 10 seconds after Kev introduced himself. Our run time tonight was a little longer due to the insane laughter and applause throughout the show.

We had such a great time in Austin. Although we didn't get to the SPAM museum this year (2 show day- Who booked this thing?☺), we ran into a lot of familiar faces from past tours. This kid Andy went to Riverland when we were here for Stuff of Dreams and dropped out the following year. Because he wasn't at school last year, he missed Kevin's performance and was none too happy about it. He started back this year and was so excited to finally see this guy everyone was talking about. At intermission he came backstage and said he was having a great time and couldn't wait to get back for Part II. After the show was over he came back to the green room to see if he could meet Kevin. I introduced them and watched this kid stumble over himself telling Kev how inspirational he is, and how he now has a little more faith in his career path. Right before we left he grabbed me and told me he has a new hero.

Michaella K. McCoy
STAGE MANAGER

GUTHRIE THEATER PERFORMANCE REPORT

Production: Freezing Paradise

Date: Friday, March 11, 2005
Location: Hibbing, MN
Performance Number: 19

Part I:
Curtain Up: 7:35   Curtain Down: 8:26   Time: 50.57

Part II:
Curtain Up: 8:44   Curtain Down: 9:30   Time: 46.20

Running Time: 1h.55m.

REMARKS:
We held 4 minutes for the house, then played a 1 minute recorded curtain speech. The show tonight was awesome. We had a very nice crowd that were very honest. If they liked something, they let you know, otherwise they weren't too vocal. Kevin loved them because they were great listeners and low key. Kev is still feeling under the weather, but he's hanging in there.

At intermission I ran out to smoke and an older couple came out to join us. The guy told his wife that the Church story really hit home, especially the part about the claw coming into the back seat. He turned to me, and noticing my headset, said the only part of the story Kevin missed was dad screaming "Don't make me stop this car." We laughed and the guy said one time when his dad said that, he asked him if there was something wrong with the brakes – he got the claw. His wife said her favorite was the Valentine's day story at the end of the first act. She said she cried and that it was sweet. Her husband looked at her square in the face and said, "Yeah I don't know about that. He didn't say how long they were married." It was hilarious.

Michaella K. McCoy
STAGE MANAGER

Performance reports are written by stage managers for every show, and circulated to the artistic staff and a few others, keeping the playing company in touch with the no-longer-watching staff, and vice versa. Those from touring shows provide a vivid glimpse of the daily effort and reward of being on the road. Michaella K. McCoy has stage managed many tours for the Guthrie. Here are two samples from the six-week, small-town Minnesota tour of _Freezing Paradise,_ written and performed by Kevin Kling. "People", said McCoy, "laughed forever."

In every season, young people who love the theater come to the Guthrie as interns, to get a taste of what professional theater is all about. In 2005, Nong Vue interned in the community partnerships office with Sheila Livingston, who has mentored dozens of young people at the Guthrie. At the close of her internship, the staff took her out to lunch, and the shy Nong Vue made a speech.

> I would like to say thank you for coming to lunch and for this wonderful opportunity at the Guthrie Theater. You all gave me such an experience that no one could ever forget.
>
> I remember when I started my internship; I wasn't nervous, but scared. I was a merit girl, shy and quiet. I didn't want to ruin my first day impression, so I came 30 minutes early. When I arrived, I was greeted by big smiles and cheery eyes.
>
> At the Guthrie I was part of everyone. I've been with Dan Hershey in the office who is always showing me cool pictures on the internet and making me tea. He is always sharing yummy thing with me from an apple to chocolates. Here comes Ken Washington's name. It seems that every time I come in, he is so happy to see me and I happy to see him. There's Sheila Livingston, a wonderful lady. She is always busy talking on the phone and/or going to long meetings, but with such a schedule, she made room for me. I was like a favorite object she carries with her.
>
> When I came to the Guthrie Theater, I came to learn the business-wise of a successful company. But the Guthrie Theater changed my view of business. It made me realize, I wanted to do business like what you have been doing. I want to make a difference like you have done. You all gave me a view of my future. Thank you all for opening your door and adding me into the little corner of your office. This has been my Guthrie experience for I have been a part of the Guthrie Theater. Thank you.

Actor Bianca Amato played Eliza in the 2004-05 season production of *Pygmalion* and tells a story about actor process, actor breakthroughs – and a wardrobe malfunction.

Every time I begin a project I ask myself will I step out of the way and let the creative spark combust into life? Or will I push, pull, yank, angst and gnash my way through a process? No surprise as to which path is more fun. Mostly I find myself in self-propelling mode for the first half of the rehearsal process, but then somewhere along the line I jump off the precipice and start to free-fall. I can get obsessed with a pathway that blocks me from my character's leap, and it can take a dramatic shift of perspective to allow me to go over the edge. Sometimes the catalyst is revelatory, sometimes laughably simple, and sometimes, as in *Pygmalion,* downright hilarious.

Well into the run I struggled to feel at home with Eliza, and with Shaw. I wanted a lighter touch, but I had loaded my Eliza with such deep expectations that she was gasping for breath.

In the final scene, Eliza makes a triumphant discovery about herself in front of Higgins, who is apoplectic at her encroaching on his turf, and he charges toward her, hands going for her throat. But on this particular night, to my horror, I realized that dear Danny Gerroll (Higgins) was threatening to erupt into peals of laughter as opposed to violence, his face reddening and his eyes tearing and bulging at the effort of restraining himself. Furious, I continued into my big speech, and discovered as I tried to move toward him, that I couldn't. My skirt was around my ankles. There I was, in purple pantaloons, in front of a thousand people.

What to do? I kicked the skirt across the stage and continued with the scene, my mind racing as to how to get through this indignity with dignity. The audience was obscenely quiet. I strutted around the stage – this was, after all, Eliza's moment of triumph – and as soon as an opportunity presented itself, I picked up the skirt, folding it crisply: "Oh! When I think of myself crawling under your feet and being trampled on and being called names (fold, fold) when all the time I had only to lift up my finger to be as good as you, (fold! Fold!) I could just kick myself."

I felt acutely alive and in the moment. And in swooped Mrs. Higgins with the perfect, perfect feed line. "Are you ready, Eliza?" "Quite," I responded and, flinging my skirt over my shoulder, began my exit from Higgins' life, finally – literally – wearing the blooming pants.

The message to me from the Gods of the theater was clear: Lighten Up! Eliza and I let go after that. The balance of comedy and depth felt restored once more, and I got to revel in Shaw's acerbic humanity and light touch. With an extra clasp on my skirt.

Twelfth Night
William Shakespeare
  Directed by Joe Dowling
  Set by Richard Hoover
  Costumes by Karyl Newman
  Original lighting by John Gisondi
  Additional lighting by Matthew Reinert
  Music by Mel Marvin

Hedda Gabler
Henrik Ibsen
  English version by Doug Hughes
  Directed by David Esbjornson
  Set by John Arnone
  Costumes by Elizabeth Hope Clancy
  Lighting by Kenneth Posner

To Fool the Eye
Adapted by Jeffrey Hatcher
from Jean Anouilh's *Léocadia*
  Directed by John Miller-Stephany
  Set by John Lee Beatty
  Costumes by Mathew J. LeFebvre
  Lighting by Kenneth Posner
  Music by Andrew Cooke

A Christmas Carol
Charles Dickens
  Adapted by Barbara Field
  Directed by Sari Ketter
  Set by Neil Patel
  Costumes by Jess Goldstein
  Lighting by Marcus Dilliard
  Music by Victor Zupanc

Who's Afraid of Virginia Woolf?
Edward Albee
  Directed by David Esbjornson
  Set by Christine Jones
  Costumes by Jane Greenwood
  Lighting by Marcus Dilliard

Once in a Lifetime
George S. Kaufman and Moss Hart
  Directed by Douglas C. Wager
  Set and costumes by Zack Brown
  Lighting by Allen Lee Hughes

Guthrie Lab

The Invention of Love
Tom Stoppard
  Directed by Joe Dowling
  Set and costumes by Patrick Clark
  Lighting by Marcus Dilliard

Blood Wedding
Federico Garcia Lorca
  Translated by Lillian Garrett-Groag
  Directed by Marcela Kingman Lorca
  Set by Christine Jones
  Costumes by Paul Tazewell
  Lighting by Jeff Bartlett
  Music by Pedro Cortes
  and Victor Zupanc

In the Blood
Suzan-Lori Parks
  Directed by Timothy Douglas
  Set by Tony Cisek
  Costumes by Amelia Busse Cheever
  Lighting by Michael Gilliam

On Tour

Molly Sweeney
Brian Friel
  Directed by Joe Dowling
  Set by Frank Hallinan Flood
  Costumes by Laurie Bramhall
  Lighting by Marcus Dilliard

Who's Afraid of Virginia Woolf?
Patrick Stewart, Mercedes Ruehl

209

Amadeus
Peter Shaffer
  Directed by Joe Dowling
  Set by Patrick Clark
  Costumes by Paul Tazewell
  Lighting by Christopher Akerlind

Da
Hugh Leonard
  Directed by Doug Hughes
  Set and costumes by Monica Frawley
  Lighting by Michael Chybowski

A Christmas Carol
Charles Dickens
  Adapted by Barbara Field
  Directed by Gary Gisselman
  Set by Neil Patel
  Costumes by Jess Goldstein
  Lighting by Marcus Dilliard
  Music by Victor Zupanc

Antony and Cleopatra
William Shakespeare
  Directed by Mark Lamos
  Set by Ming Cho Lee
  Costumes by Jane Greenwood
  Lighting by Stephen Strawbridge
  Music by Hiram Titus

The Canterbury Tales
Geoffrey Chaucer
  Adapted by Michael Bogdanov,
  with additional material by Kevin Kling
  Directed by Michael Bogdanov
  Set and costumes by Ulrike Engelbrecht
  Lighting by Ann G. Wrightson
  Music by John Gould

All My Sons
Arthur Miller
  Directed by Joe Dowling
  Set by John Lee Beatty
  Costumes by Devon Painter
  Lighting by Matthew Reinert

Guthrie Lab

The Carpetbagger's Children
Horton Foote
  Directed by Michael Wilson
  Set by Jeff Cowie
  Costumes by David Woolard
  Lighting by Rui Rita

Merrily We Roll Along
Stephen Sondheim and
George Furth
  Music and lyrics by Stephen Sondheim
  Book by George Furth
  based on the play by George S.
  Kaufman and Moss Hart
  Directed by John Miller-Stephany
  Set and costumes by
  Mathew J. LeFebvre
  Lighting by Charles D. Craun
  Choreography by
  Marcela Kingman Lorca
  Music direction by Andrew Cooke

Thief River
Lee Blessing
  Directed by Ethan McSweeny
  Set by Michael Sims
  Costumes by Rich Hamson
  Lighting by Jane Cox

On Tour

Ah, Wilderness!
Eugene O'Neill
  Directed by Douglas C. Wager
  Set by Ming Cho Lee
  Costumes by Zack Brown
  Lighting by Allen Lee Hughes

Antony and Cleopatra.
Company.

Resurrection Blues
Arthur Miller
    Directed by David Esbjornson
    Set by Christine Jones
    Costumes by Elizabeth Hope Clancy
    Lighting by Marcus Dilliard

The Comedy of Errors
William Shakespeare
    Directed by Dominique Serrand
    Set by Dominique Serrand
    Costumes by Fabio Toblini
    Lighting by Marcus Dilliard
    Music by Eric Jensen

A Christmas Carol
Charles Dickens
    Adapted by Barbara Field
    Directed by Gary Gisselman
    Set by Neil Patel
    Costumes by Jess Goldstein
    Lighting by Marcus Dilliard
    Music by Victor Zupanc

Mrs. Warren's Profession
George Bernard Shaw
    Directed by Lisa Peterson
    Set by Michael Yeargan
    Costumes by Ann Hould-Ward
    Lighting by Peter Kaczorowski

Six Degrees of Separation
John Guare
    Directed by Ethan McSweeny
    Set by Christine Jones
    Costumes by Constance Hoffman
    Lighting by Jane Cox

Three Sisters
Anton Chekhov
    Directed by Joe Dowling
    Set by Patrick Clark
    Costumes by Paul Tazewell
    Lighting by Matthew Reinert

<u>Guthrie Lab</u>

Good Boys
Jane Martin
    Directed by Jon Jory
    Set by Neil Patel
    Costumes by Marcia Dixcy Jory
    Lighting by Matthew Reinert

The Chairs
Eugène Ionesco
    Translated by Jim Lewis
    Directed by Daniel Aukin
    Set by Kyle Chepulis
    Costumes by Katherine Kohl
    Lighting by Matt Frey

Wintertime
Charles L. Mee
    Directed by John Miller-Stephany
    Set and costumes by
    Mathew J. LeFebvre
    Lighting by Dennis Parichy

Top Girls
Caryl Churchill
    Directed by Casey Stangl
    Set by Troy Hourie
    Costumes by Devon Painter
    Lighting by Marcus Dilliard

<u>On Tour</u>

The Stuff of Dreams
Bill Corbett
    Directed by Jef Hall-Flavin
    Set by Patricia Olive
    Costumes by Maribeth Hite

Three Sisters.
Kathryn Meisle, Michelle O'Neill,
Julie Briskman, Meghan Wolf.

213

2003-04 SEASON

Pride and Prejudice
Jane Austin
Adapted by James Maxwell
Revised by Alan Stanford
Directed by Joe Dowling
Set by John Lee Beatty
Costumes by Mathew J. LeFebvre
Lighting by Kenneth Posner

The Night of the Iguana
Tennessee Williams
Directed by John Miller-Stephany
Set by James Youmans
Costumes by Mathew J. LeFebvre
Lighting by Marcus Dilliard

A Christmas Carol
Charles Dickens
Adapted by Barbara Field
Directed by Gary Gisselman
Set by Neil Patel
Costumes by Jess Goldstein
Lighting by Marcus Dilliard
Music by Victor Zupanc

Crowns
Regina Taylor
Based on the book by
Michael Cunningham
and Craig Marberry
Directed by Timothy Bond
Set by Christine Jones
Costumes by Reggie Ray
Lighting by Allen Lee Hughes
Choreography by Patdro Harris
Music direction by Sanford Moore

Romeo and Juliet
William Shakespeare
Directed by Ethan McSweeny
Set and costumes by Mark Wendland
Lighting by Jane Cox

The Pirates of Penzance
Gilbert and Sullivan
Additional material by Jeffrey Hatcher
New orchestrations by Andrew Cooke
Directed by Joe Dowling
Set by Michael Yeargan
Costumes by Paul Tazewell
Lighting by Stephen Strawbridge
Choreography by David Bolger
Music direction by Andrew Cooke

Guthrie Lab

Nickel and Dimed
Joan Holden
Based on the book by Barbara Ehrenreich
Directed by Bill Rauch
Set by Christopher Acebo
Costumes by Lynn Jeffries
Lighting by Marcus Dilliard

Othello
William Shakespeare
Directed by Joe Dowling
Set and costumes by Patrick Clark
Lighting by Matthew Reinert

Boston Marriage
David Mamet
Directed by Douglas Mercer
Set by James Noone
Costumes by Valerie Marcus Ramshur
Lighting by Matthew Reinert

Blue/Orange
Joe Penhall
Directed by Casey Stangl
Set by Troy Hourie
Costumes by Mathew J. LeFebvre
Lighting by Marcus Dilliard

On Tour

Othello
William Shakespeare
Directed by Joe Dowling

Guthrie WorldStage

Carmen Funebre
Teatr Biuro Podrozy, Poland

Twelfth Night
Shakespeare's Globe Theatre, England

Forbidden Christmas, or The Doctor and the Patient
Former Soviet Republic of Georgia,
New York

The Pirates of Penzance.
Dan Calloway,
Jennifer Baldwin Peden,
company.

215

Death of a Salesman
Arthur Miller
  Directed by Joe Dowling
  Set by Richard Hoover
  Costumes by Devon Painter
  Lighting by Matthew Reinert

Pygmalion
George Bernard Shaw
  Directed by Casey Stangl
  Set by Anita Stewart
  Costumes by Linda Fisher
  Lighting by Marcus Dilliard

A Christmas Carol
Charles Dickens
  Adapted by Barbara Field
  Directed by Gary Gisselman
  Set by Neil Patel
  Costumes by Jess Goldstein
  and David Kay Mickelson
  Lighting by Marcus Dilliard
  Music by Victor Zupanc

Oedipus
Sophocles
  Adapted by Ellen McLaughlin
  Directed by Lisa Peterson
  Set by Riccardo Hernandez
  Costumes by David Zinn
  Lighting by David Akerlind
  Music by Gina Leishman

As You Like It
William Shakespeare
  Directed by Joe Dowling
  Set by James Noone
  Costumes by Helen Q. Huang
  Lighting by Matthew Reinert
  Music by Mel Marvin

She Loves Me
Book by Joe Masteroff
Music by Jerry Bock
Lyrics by Sheldon Harnick
  Based on a play by Miklos Laszlo
  Directed by John Miller-Stephany
  Set by James Youmans
  Costumes by Mathew J. LeFebvre
  Lighting by Donald Holder
  Choreography by James Sewell
  Music direction by Andrew Cooke

<u>Guthrie Lab</u>

Lady with a Lapdog
Anton Chekhov
  English translation by Julia Smeliansky
  and Ryan McKittrick
  Adapted and directed by Kama Ginkas
  Set and costumes by Sergey Barkhin
  Lighting by Michael Chybowski
  Original costumes by Tatiana Barkhina

**The Sex Habits of
American Women**
Julie Marie Myatt
  Directed by Michael Bigelow Dixon
  Set by Victor A. Becker
  Costumes by Marcia Dixcy Jory
  Lighting by Matthew Reinert

Pericles
William Shakespeare
  Adapted and directed by Joel Sass
  Set by John Clark Donahue
  Costumes by Amelia Busse Cheever
  Lighting by Marcus Dilliard

A Body of Water
Lee Blessing
  Directed by Ethan McSweeny
  Set by Michael Vaughn Sims
  Costumes by Rich Hamson
  Lighting by Matthew Reinert

<u>On Tour</u>

Dublin Theatre Festival
Death of a Salesman
Arthur Miller
  Directed by Joe Dowling

**Freezing Paradise:
An Evening with
Kevin Kling**
  Written and performed by Kevin Kling

<u>Guthrie WorldStage</u>

The Notebook and
The Proof
  De Onderneming Theater Collective,
  Antwerp, Belgium

4.48 Psychosis
  The Royal Court Theatre, England

Oedipus.
Isabell Monk O'Connor,
Peter Macon, Richard Ooms

217

2005-06 SEASON

His Girl Friday
John Guare
  Adapted by John Guare from
  The Front Page by Ben Hecht and
  Charles MacArthur and the
  Columbia Pictures film
  Directed by Joe Dowling
  Set by John Lee Beatty
  Costumes by Jess Goldstein
  Lighting by Brian MacDevitt

The Constant Wife
W. Somerset Maugham
  Directed by John Miller-Stephany
  Set by Patrick Clark
  Costumes by Mathew J. LeFebvre
  Lighting by Matthew Reinert

Intimate Apparel
Lynn Nottage
  Directed by Timothy Bond
  Set by Scott Bradley
  Costumes by Helen Q. Huang
  Lighting by Ann G. Wrightson

A Christmas Carol
Charles Dickens
  Adapted by Barbara Field
  Directed by Gary Gisselman
  Set by Neil Patel
  Costumes by Jess Goldstein
  and David Kay Mickelson
  Lighting by Marcus Dilliard
  Music by Victor Zupanc

The People's Temple
Leigh Fondakowski
with Greg Pierotti, Stephen Wangh
and Margo Hall
  Directed by Leigh Fondakowski
  Set by Sarah Lambert
  Costumes by Gabriel Berry
  Lighting by Betsy Adams

Hamlet
William Shakespeare
  Directed by Joe Dowling
  Set by Richard Hoover
  Costumes by Paul Tazewell
  Lighting by Chris Akerlind

WorldStage

Arlecchino: Servant of Two Masters
  Piccolo Teatro di Milano, Italy

Measure for Measure
  Shakespeare's Globe Theater, England

Macbeth
  Out of Joint, England

His Girl Friday.
Courtney Vance, Angela Bassett.

*O*ur theater must be a place of magic, excitement and entertainment. I have a profound belief in the power of theater to change people's lives, to influence human behavior and to gladden human souls.

Joe Dowling
Artistic Director
2006

Michelle O'Neill in *All My Sons.*

Community Leadership

Since 1963, community leaders have served as members of the Guthrie's board of directors. By volunteering their time, energy, wisdom and financial support, these dedicated men and women have strengthened the theater artistically and financially. It has been a tremendous contribution.

Those who have held the presidency and/or the chair appear in all caps.
* Denotes lifetime members.

Artistic Leadership

Sir Tyrone Guthrie *1963 – 1965*
Douglas Campbell *1966 – 1967*
Michael Langham *1971 – 1977*
Alvin Epstein *1978 – 1980*
Liviu Ciulei *1981 – 1985*
Garland Wright *1986 – 1995*
Joe Dowling *1996 –*

Executive Leadership

Oliver Rea *Administrative Director 1963*
Oliver Rea and Peter Zeisler *Managing Directors 1964 – 1965*
Peter Zeisler *Managing Director 1966 – 1969*
Donald Schoenbaum *Managing Director 1969 – 1986*
Edward A. Martenson *Executive Director 1986 – 1996*
David Hawkanson *Managing Director 1996 – 2001*
Susan Trapnell *Managing Director 2002*
Thomas C. Proehl *Managing Director 2003 –*

Rep. Ron Abrams
Mrs. John W. Adams III
Linda L. Ahlers
Mrs. Andrews Allen
Martha B. Alworth
Sarah J. Andersen
William A. Andres
ALBERT ANDREWS, JR.
DeWalt Ankeny, Jr.
Lillian D. Anthony
Jeffrey R. Arnold
* **MARTHA ATWATER**

Dale L. Bachman
KAREN BACHMAN
Ruth G. Bachman
Dr. Arthur H. Ballet
Kenneth H. Bayliss, Jr.
John B. Bean
George J. Beck, Jr.
Dr. Jacquelyn Belcher
Charles S. Bellows
Howard S. Bellows
Y. Marc Belton
Mr. and Mrs. Judson Bemis, Sr.
Judson Bemis, Jr.
DAVID A. BENNETT
Sue Bennett
Mrs. Richard Benzian
Kenneth E. Berg
E. Thomas Binger
* **JAMES H. BINGER**
Lois B. Bishop
Rolf F. Bjelland
Jane Robertson Blanch
Dr. David Bloom
David L. Boehnen
A. Rodney Boren
Marvin Borman
L. K. Boutin
Mrs. Robert E. Bowen

William M. Bracken
Mary K. Brainerd
Michael J. Brand
Gerald J. Bratter
Karl J. Breyer
Paul Bridston
Barbara B. Brown
Lillian Brown
Mrs. Julian Bruner
Worth Bruntjen
Wesley Brustad
Arthur C. Buffington
Bruce L. Burnham
Mrs. Edward Butler
Pierce Butler III
Winslow Buxton

Anne S. Cameron
Michael E. Cameron
Douglas Campbell
Joan Capen
Jean E. Carlstrom
Emerson F. Carr
John T. Chapman
Mrs. Paul Christopherson
Michael V. Ciresi
Liviu Ciulei
Edward J. Clark
Maurice Cohen
Sen. Richard Cohen
Jane M. Confer
Sigrid Connor
Jay Cowles
* **JOHN COWLES**
DAVID C. COX
Robert W. Crawford
Jack J. Crocker
Hume Cronyn
John H. Crowther
Molly Culligan

Bernice B. Dalrymple
John H. Dasburg
Patricia Davies
Fran Davis
Richard K. Davis
Northrop Dawson, Jr.
Robert J. and Joan L. Dayton
Virginia Y. Dayton
Wallace C. Dayton
Theodore Deikel
John Derus
Clifford Dinsmore
W.T. Doar, Jr.
Douglas R. Donaldson
Dr. F. Edmund Donoghue
Patrick Donovan
Peter Dorsey
Michael E. Dougherty
Joe Dowling
Rudolph Driscoll
W. John Driscoll
DONALD R. DWIGHT
Jaye F. Dyer

Ralph C. Eickhof
SUSAN E. ENGEL
Alvin Epstein
Edward N. Eschbach
Jane Evans

Patrick R. Fallon
William F. Farley
George A. Farr
George Finlay
Gary W. Flakne
Arthur S. Flemming
Nancy J. Fletcher
Richard R. Fliehr
Barbara Louise Forster
Mary Forsythe
Clarence G. Frame

Margaret Friedman
Martin Friedman
John L. Frost
Warren Frost
Marna W. Fullerton

Mrs. Stanley Gaines
Betty Ann Gardner
Sander D. Genis
WILLIAM W. GEORGE
John T. Gerlach
Joel A. Gibson
Lois V. Gildemeister
Andre Gillet
Donald R. Gillies
ARNOLD O. GINNOW
Archie Givens
JOHN R. GOETZ
Bertand Goldberg
Lillian Goldfine
Dr. Robert J. Goldish
Michael D. Goldner
David H. Goldstein
Priscilla and Erwin M. Goldstein
Harvey Golub
Mrs. Robert Gomsrud
Raymond F. Good
George K. Gosko
Dr. Kenneth L. Graham
Shelton B. Granger
Joan Freese Grant
Mrs. H. K. Gray
Bill Green

Richard Green
Richard Gregson
* **PIERSON M. GRIEVE**
C. E. Bayliss Griggs
Joseph F. Grinnell
POLLY GROSE
N. Bud Grossman
John F. Grundhofer
Esperanza
   Guerrero-Anderson
Sir Tyrone Guthrie

Susan A. Hagstrum, Ph.D.
Michael J. Hahn
SANDRA J. HALE
Betsy Atwater Hannaford
Delmar J. Hansen
Dee Dee Harris
Mrs. Thomas Hartzell
Nancy Hatch
Barbara R. Hauser
David Hawkanson
Blanche Hawkins
William A. Hawkins
Roger L. Headrick
Philip Heasley
F. Peavey Heffelfinger, Jr.
George L. Hegg
Gerry Heltzer
Mary Hendricks
Peter Hendrixson
Robert E. Hess
Phyllis S. Hetzler

George Roy Hill
Karen Himle
John G. Hoeschler
Susan Hoff
Randall Hogan
Dianne Hoge
William B. Horn
Stanley S. Hubbard
Allan J. Huber
Hella Mears Hueg
Margery G. Hughes
Cary H. Humphries
Andrew M. Hunter III
David G. Hurrell
Dr. Doris Huseboe
Alvin John Huss, Jr.
Dean E. Hutton
Liesl A. Hyde

Richard Ingman
Sally Irvine

Allen F. and Barbara Jacobson
Benjamin S. Jaffray
RON JAMES
Mrs. Richard N. Jamieson
Geraldine S. Jenkins
Stephen G. Jerritts
Dr. Carol Johnson
James A. Johnson
Gil Johnsson
David C. Johnston
Bill Johnstone
Waring Jones
Nancy Jorgeson
Wendell J. Josal
Burton Joseph
William and Suzanne Joyce
M. Joann Jundt
John C. Junek

ROGER G. KENNEDY
Jay Kiedrowski
Dr. Reatha Clark King
Robert L. King, Jr
Henry S. Kingman, Jr.
Joseph R. Kingman III
E. Robert and Margee Kinney
Peter W. Kirk
Peter R. Kitchak
Paul R. Knapp
Richard M. Kovacevich
Sister Mary Angelita Kramer
Dr. Arnold Kremen
Elisabeth M. Krueger
Anita Kunin

Mrs. David L. LaBerge
John W. Lacey

Michael Langham
George Latimer
David M. Lebedoff
Dr. Joseph Leek
Lewis W. Lehr
Kathy Lenzmeier
T.M. Levis, Jr.
Richard S. Levitt
Dorothy Levy
André Lewis
Dr. F. Bruce Lewis
Martin Lewis, Jr.
Archibald Leyasmeyer
David M. Lilly, Jr.
Diane Lilly
Patricia Lindell
Evodia Linner
Helen C. Liu
Sheila Livingston
Dee Long
Allan K. Longacre II
John S. Lucas
Mrs. Ward Lucas
George M. Lund

Harvey Mackay
Bruce K. MacLaury
David W. MacLennan
F. Bruce Madison
Thomas F. Madison
Diane Magrath
Vergil R. March
Edward A. Martenson
Ian Martin
Robert J. Marzec
Malcolm W. McDonald
Richard D. McFarland
Nadine McGuire
Susan B. McIntosh
George McIntyre
Mary McIntyre
Marjorie and Donald McNeely
Kendrick B. Melrose
Dr. R. Keith Michael
Anne W. Miller
Robert Miller
Sam Scott Miller
James H. Moar
Walter F. Mondale
C. P. (Buck) Moore
Robert E. Moore
Mrs. Malcolm Moos
Mrs. W. Dean Moran
Lucia T. Morison
Mrs. Thomas J. Morison
Christine Morrison
Mary K. Morrison
Arnold W. Morse
Lee W. Munnich, Jr.

Kingsley and Katherine Murphy
John H. Myers

George E. Nadler
Arthur H. Naftalin
Mignette Najarian
Elizabeth M. Nason
Betty Rappaport Nathanson
Vivian Jenkins Nelsen
Marilyn Nelson
Thomas P. Nelson
John J. Neumaier
Cecil E. Newman
Louise G. Otis Nichols
Charles M. Nolte

Ann M. Ober
Nathaniel Ober
Barbara D. Odegard
Dwight H. Oglesby
* Susan Mary Shuman Okie
Tamrah Schaller O'Neil
Vance K. Opperman
Mrs. John G. Ordway, Jr.
Dr. Milton Orkin
Louise Otten

Timothy J. Pabst
Sheila Paisner
Diane Palmer
Allegra and Paul Parker
M. M. Senneff Percival
Lola Perpich
Marvin J. Pertzik
Hall J. Peterson
Stephen and Ann M. Pflaum
Abigail Phillips
Edward J. Phillips
Katharine C. Pillsbury
* Sally Pillsbury
Addison Piper
Carl N. and Susan Platou
Carl R. Pohlad
William M. Pohlad
Robert M. Price, Jr.
Thomas C. Proehl

Patricia Rahders
Guido R. Rahr, Jr.
OLIVER REA
Barbara Reid
Mrs. Jeffrey Rice
Mrs. Bernard H. Ridder
Kathleen Ridder
Mrs. Edward C. Ritchell
Gordon H. Ritz
Dr. George W. Robertson
Walter G. Robinson
Harold Roitenberg

Karl F. Rolvaag
Robert A. Rosenbaum
Fred Rosenblatt
Steven J. Rosenstone
Burton Ross
Edmond R. Ruben
Robert L. Ryan

A. William Sands
STEPHEN W. SANGER
Maryan Schall
Dr. Ivan Schloff
Donald Schoenbaum
Jan Schonwetter
John Schuler
Allan L. Schuman
David J. Scott
Walter D. Scott
Alfred Sedgwick, Jr.
Boake A. Sells
James P. Shannon
Jane E. Sheer
Otto A. Silha
Bonita Sindelir
Frank L. Skillern, Jr.
Dr. Donald K. Smith
Justin Smith
Lane F. Smith
Mary H. Smith
M. Philip Snyder
Nikki Sorum
Clarence Spangle
David J. Speer
John M. Stafford
DOUGLAS M. STEENLAND
Dr. Edwin E. Stein
James P. Stephenson
John Stielow
Mary Louise Stokes
Donald R. Stone
Gerald L. Storch
Grace Strangis
Lucian Strong III
Sheldon Sturgis
Austin P. Sullivan, Jr.
Virgil Sullivan
Frank Sunberg
Robert K. Swanson
Robert Sznewjas

Joseph Tashjian
Lucie Taylor
Orley R. Taylor
Robert Tennessen
Tyrone K. Thayer
Patrick Thiele
David W. Thompson
Harv Thompson
Shelley B. Thompson

Julia C. Timm
Marcia Tingley
Thomas Tipton
E. Rodman Titcomb, Jr.
Susan Trapnell
Reed V. Tuckson, M.D.
James Turley
Emily Anne Tuttle

Rebecca L. Ueland
Harold R. Ullrich
Robert J. Ulrich
William A. Urseth

Mary C. Van Evera
Sher Vanfossan
F. Van Konynenburg
Sandra L. Vargas
* **MARY W. VAUGHAN**
Richard H. Vaughan
George J. Vavoulis
Mrs. Arnold Vogel
* **PHILIP VON BLON**

Archie D. Walker
John Warder
Toby G. Warson
George F. Waters
Steven C. Webster
Suzanne S. Weil
Al Weinhandl
* **IRVING WEISER**
Mrs. Stuart Wells, Jr.
William E. Westbrook, Jr.
Steven M. Wexler
Christopher Wheeler
Dare L. White
Frank M. Whiting
Benson K. Whitney
Frances Wilkinson
Alfred M. Wilson
Mrs. O. Meredith Wilson
Roger K. Winges
Mrs. Robert Wohlrabe
Judy D. Wood
John R. Woodruff
Garland Wright
* **MARGARET WURTELE**

F. Keen Young

Peter B. Zeisler
CHARLES A. ZELLE
LOUIS N. ZELLE
Richard Zona

Board of Directors
1963 – 2006

223

(Row 1) Sarah Agnew, Matthew Amendt, Robert O. Berdahl, Raye Birk, Jennifer Blagen, Michael Booth. (Row 2) Barbara Bryne, Virginia S. Burke, Leah Curney, Bob Davis, Laura Esping, Wayne A. Evenson. (Row 3) Nathaniel Fuller, June Gibbons, Jonas Goslow, Shawn Hamilton, Emil Herrera, Richard S. Iglewski. (Row 4) Charity Jones, Michael Kissin, Kevin Kling, Jim Lichtscheidl, Tracey Maloney, Bill McCallum. (Row 5) Ron Menzel, Kris L. Nelson, Lee Mark Nelson, Isabell Monk O'Connor, Michelle O'Neill, Richard Ooms. (Row 6) Stephen Pelinski, Randy Reyes, Stacia Rice, Mark Rosenwinkel, Doug Scholz-Carlson, Suzanne Warmanen. (Row 7) Claudia Wilkens, Reginal Marie Williams, Sally Wingert, Stephen Yoakam.

Actors
1963 Season to 2005–2006 Season

F. Murray Abraham
Elizabeth Acosta
Brent Adams
J. B. Adams
Rich Affannato
Sarah Agnew
Daniel Ahearn
Regina Ahlgren
Carlo Alban
Jay Albright
Franz C. Alderfer
Cheryl Alexander
James Alexander
Thomas Alexander
Opal Alladin
Bruce Allard
Jo Harvey Allen
Lee Allen
Penelope Allen
R. Justice Allen
Seth Allen
Anne Allgood
Michael Allinson
Warren Alm
Greg Almquist
Veronica Alvarado
Bianca Amato
Stephen Ambrose
Don Amendolia
Matthew Amendt
Maureen Anderman
Alfred M. Anderson
C. B. Anderson
D.C. Anderson
David A. Anderson
Deborah Anderson
Dwight Anderson
Erin Anderson
Eunice Anderson
Geoffrey Anderson
Richard Anderson

Sara Anderson
Barbara Andres
Jerome Anello
Miguel Angel
Ethan Angelica
Christina Apathy
Fred Applegate
Amy Aquino
Gary Armagnac
April Armstrong
Michael Arnold
Mario Arrambide
Natasha Arroyo
Helen-Jean Arthur
Lauren Asheim
Richard Ashford
Jared Aswegan
Walter Atamaniuk
Molly Atwood
Jeni Austin
Matthew Austin
Erick Avari
Peter Aylward
Arminae Azarian
Joey Babay
Nathan Babbs
Dennis Babcock
Morena Baccarin
Helen Backlin
Linda Backman
Will A. Badgett
Chuck Bailey
Hillary Bailey
Julian Bailey
Jim Baker
Mark Baker
Christina Baldwin
Paul Ballantyne
Allison Ballou
Gerry Bamman
Roger Barbieri

Charles Bari
Greg Barnell
Ken Barnett
Evalyn Baron
John Barone
Joyce Barott
Marco Barricelli
Diana Barrington
Mia Barron
Don Barshay
Megan A. Bartle
Lisbeth Bartlett
Peter Bartlett
Gary Basaraba
Angela Bassett
Ryan Michelle Bathé
Emery Battis
Brian Baumgartner
Christopher Bayes
Matthew Beach
Dameon Beasley
Jamaal Beavers
Andrea Bebel
Leigh Beery
Bernard Behrens
Christopher Bell
Michael Bell
Lou Bellamy
Terry Bellamy
Vivienne Benesch
Starla Benford
Fran Bennett
Eve Bennett-Gordon
Mark Benninghofen
Robert Benson
Robert O. Berdahl
Jolayne Berg
Judith-Marie Bergan
Andrew Bergee
Quinn Berger
Paul Berget

Samuel David Bergstrom
Shari Berkowitz
Barbara Berlovitz
Mark Berman
Ed Bernard
Maury Bernstein
Kelly Bertenshaw
Jacqueline Bertrand
Bob Beverage
Trazana Beverley
Andrea Bianchi
Ross Bickell
Dieter Bierbrauer
Theodore Bikel
Wanda Bimson
Edward Binns
Raye Birk
Olivia Birkelund
Teria Birlon
Drew Birns
David Bishop
Gerry Black
Susan Blackwell
Jennifer Blagen
Merrily Blagen
James Blendick
Edouard Blitz
Christopher Bloch
Larry Block
Peter Bloedoorn
Tom Bloom
Dan Bly
Amy Bodnar
Earl Boen
Peter Boesen, Jr.
Sandra Bogan
Bruce Bohne
Erick Bokuniewicz
Tom Bolstad
Jonathan Bolt
Eric Bondoc

Anne Bonner
Leta Bonynge
Michael Booth
Marshall Borden
Jesse Borrego
Alexandra Borrie
John Bottoms
Ron Boulden
Ronald Boulden
Elizabeth Bove
Jason Bowcutt
Melissa Bowen
Nadia Bowers
Warren C. Bowles
Julie Boyd
Michael Boyle
Brigid Brady
Raina Brady
Risa Brainin
Pierce Peter Brandt
Djola Branner
Alan Brasington
Mario Bravo
Brenda Braye
Lloyd Bremseth
Maureen Brennan
Michael Brennan
Dori Brenner
Robert Breuler
Charles Brin
Cheryl Moore Brinkley
David Anthony Brinkley
Julie Briskman
Roy Brocksmith
Jonathan Brody
Raina Brody
Ivar Brogger
Jason Ansara Brooks
Joel Brooks
Piper Brooks
Summer Tina-Marie Brooks

Blair Brown
Christine Marie Brown
Graham Brown
Richard Burton Brown
Wendy S. Brown
Myra Browning
Sterling K. Brown
Susan Browning
Adena Brumer
Cara Mia Bruncati
Trent Brunier
Brienin Bryant
Gordon Bryars
Oksana Bryn
Barbara Bryne
Mark Buchanan
Michael Buchanan
Donald Buka
Bryce Bullis
Angela Bullock
Yusef Bulos
Elizabeth Bunch
Stephen R. Buntrock
Leith Burke
Virginia S. Burke
Donny Burks
Catherine Burns
Helen Burns
Robert Burns
Larry J. Burt, II
Trey Burvant
Sherri Bustad
Gregory Butler
Michael Butler
Jennifer Butsch
David Cabot
James Cada
Adolph Caesar
James Cahill
Kevin Cahoon
Zoe Caldwell
Kristina Callahan
Dan Callaway
Bill Camp
David Campbell
Douglas Campbell
J. Kenneth Campbell
Jennifer Jordan Campbell
David Canary
Benny S. Cannon
John Cappelletti
Christopher Cara
Debra Cardona
Helen Carey
Len Cariou

Christopher Carl
Cynthia Carle
Marguerita Carlin
Johann Carlo
Alexandra C. Carlone
Laurie Carlos
Linda Carlson
Susan Dawn Carson
Alanna Carter
Cheyenne Casebier
Timothy Casey
Ann Casson
Veronica Castang
George Cattle
Joe Antony Cavise
David Cecsarini
David E. Chadderdon
David Chandler
Jeffrey Alan Chandler
Cindy Chapman
Lynn Chausow
Don Cheadle
Douglas Cheek
Kristin Chenoweth
Anne Cherne
Bruce Cherne
Hope Chernov
Michael Chernus
Yolanda Childress
Ruth Childs
Timothy Christie
Eric Christmas
Traci Christofore
Nathan Christopher
Anthony Ciaravino
Robert Cicchini
Charles Cioffi
Clarence Fountain and
  the Five Blind Boys
  of Alabama
Bryan Clark
Jason Elliott Clark
Caitlin Clarke
David Clarke
Tony Clarno
Susanna Clemn
Andrew R. Cleveland
Oliver Cliff
Jason Clusman
Jack Coan
Adrienne Cochran
Lynn Cohen
Polly Cohen
Enrico Colantoni
Gilbert Cole

Olivia Cole
Joshua Wolf Coleman
Laurel Lynn Collins
Paul Collins
Joel Colodner
Miriam Colon
Robert Colston
John Command
Carey Connell
Michael Connolly
Patricia Conolly
Frances Conroy
Jarlath Conroy
William Converse-Roberts
Jason Cooper
Maury Cooper
Bill Corbett
Nataya Cornelious
Pedro Cortes
Drew Cortese
Katherine Cortez
Clayton Corzatte
Peggy Cosgrave
Nicolas Coster
Richard Cottrell
Bridgid Coulter
Steve Coulter
Richard Council
Michael Countryman
Peggy Cowles
Richard Cox
Josie Coyoc
Jon Cranney
James Craven
Alvin Crawford
Dennis Creaghan
Saylor Creswell
Preston Crews
Jeff Cribbs
Paddy Croft
Harold Stumpy Cromer
John Cromwell
Harry Cronin
Hume Cronyn
J. Stephen Crosby
Carena Crowell
Ross David Crutchlow
Robert Cuccioli
Joseph Culliton
Torrin T. Cummings
Michael Cumpsty
Scott Cunningham
Leah Curney
Richard Curnock
Russell Curry

Zach Curtis
Robert Curtis-Brown
J. C. Cutler
Augusta Dabney
Valery Daemke
Susan Dafoe
Marvin Dahlgren
Paul Dallin
Becka Dalton
Camille D'Ambrose
Maggie D'Ambrose
Stephen D'Ambrose
Sarah Dammann
Michael Damon
Anita Dangler
Pamela Danser
Patch Darragh
Gil David
Morgan Davidsen
Richard M. Davidson
Kyle Davies
Bob Davis
Charlie Davis
Daniel Davis
Danyon Davis
Dawn Davis
Jack Davis
Janette Davis
Kevin Davis
Lance Davis
Mark Davis
Marshall L. Davis, Jr.
Mary Alette Davis
Viola Davis
Paula Dawn
Steven Dawn
Dylan Dawson
Jonathan Day
Paul de Cordova
Francois de la Giroday
Baraka de Soleil
Mark W. Deakins
Frank Deal
Charles Dean
Libby Dean
Justin Deas
Josie DeGuzman
Nicholas DeJoria
Roger DeKoven
Joe Delafield
Michele Delattre
Carmen DeLavallade
Joseph Della Sorte
Robert DeMars
Jake Dengel

William Denis
Patrick Dennison
Frank Dent
Matt Derek
Teresa DeRose
Amanda Detmer
Matthew Detmer
Susana di Palma
Josette DiCarlo
Steven Dietz
Erin Dilly
Richard Dix
Harold Dixon
Curzon Dobell
Scott Doebler
Paul Doepke
Madeleine Doherty
Jonathan Dokuchitz
Colman Domingo
Donal Donnelly
King Donovan
Emily Dooley
Sean Michael Dooley
Lura Dorbler
Robert Dorfman
Paula Dornisch
Frank Dosse
Mary Dosse
Judith Doty
Fiacre Douglas
Kathryn Dowling
Herb Downer
Sean Dowse
Patrick John Doyle
Gerald Drake
Paul Drake
Kip Driver
Denise Du Maurier
Cara Duff-MacCormick
O.L. Duke
Edna D. Duncan
Jeffrey B. Duncan
Morgan Duncan
Dale Dunham
Sally Dunn
Michael Duran
Adam Dyer
Mary Dykhouse
Mary Easter
Catherine Eaton
Vaneik Echeverria
James Eckhouse
Paul Eckstein
Christopher Edwards
George Edwards

Michael Egan
Stan Egi
Kate Eifrig
Jeffrey Eisenberg
Saidah Arrika Ekuloha
Abdul Salaam El Razzac
Hassan El-Amin
Rebecca Ellens
Scott Elliot
Patricia Elliott
Katherine Emery
Carol Emshoff
Michael Engel
Robert Engels
Priscilla Entersz
Steven Epp
Ben E. Epps
Alvin Epstein
Kia Erdmann
Tracy Erickson
Sharon Ernster
Laura Esping
Laura Esterman
Allan Estes
Elliot Eustis
Dillon Evans
Wayne A. Evenson
Patricia Everett
Geoffrey Ewing
Ron Faber
Steven Fagerberg
Don R. Fallbeck
Michael J. Farina
Derek Farnam
Felicia Farone
Michele Farr
Marshall Farrell
Rebecca Fay
Alan Feinstein
David Feldshuh
Tovah Feldshuh
Kareem Ferguson
Larry Ferguson
Katherine Ferrand
Scott Ferrara
Michael Matthew Ferrell
Tom Fervoy
Maria Feuereisen
Peter Filkins
Donald E. Fischer
Mary Beth Fisher
Matthew Fisher
John Fistos
John Patrick Fitzgibbons
Niki Flacks

Brian Flanagan
Pauline Flanagan
Ed Flanders
Kristin Flanders
David Flaten
Gus Fleming
Robert Barry Fleming
Sarah Fleming
Tony Floyd
Dion Flynn
Megan Follows
Jeremy Fonicello
Santino Fontana
Hallie Foote
Lois Foraker
Kate Forbes
Stacy Forster
Mary Fortuna
Dan Foss
Gloria Foster
Hunter Foster
Dawna Fox-Brenton
Robert Foxworth
Linda Frailich
Peter Francis-James
Richard Frank
Kenneth Frankel
Kirsten Frantzich
Gina Franz
Charles Fraser
Patricia Fraser
Ron Frazier
Dylan Frederick
Michael David Frederick
Erik Fredricksen
Sam Freed
Cassandra F. Freeman
Morgan Freeman
Mark French
Dylan Fresco
Joel Friedman
Merle Fristad
Warren Frost
Ray Fry
Kate Fuglei
Randy Fuhrman
Jonathan Fuller
Nathaniel Fuller
Dominic Fumusa
Shanara Gabrielle
Doug Gabrielli
Boyd Gaines
Frederick Gaines
Megan Gallagher
Michael Gallagher

Michael Galloway
Ann Galvin
Rita Gam
Robin Gammell
John Paul Gamoke
Geoff Garland
Katherine Garnett
Larry Gates
Christina Gatzke
Todd Gearhart
Ellen Geer
Linda Gehringer
Jim Geib
Adam Geisness
Marie Geist
Gene Gentili
Avril Gentles
Lovette George
Daniel Gerroll
Marcus Giamatti
Elena Giannetti
June Gibbons
Tom Gibis
Allison Giglio
Joseph Gillespie
Jonathan Gillman
Maxwell Glanville
Ron Glass
Thomas Glynn
Louise Goetz
Peter Michael Goetz
John Going
Russell Gold
Sheila Goldes
Steve Goldman
Danny Goldring
Mark Ira Goldstein
Maggi Good
Andrea Goodman
Bard Goodrich
Steve Goodwillie
Michael Goodwin
Philip Goodwin
Brian Goranson
Ellin Gorky
Nancy Gormley
Jonas Goslow
Robert Gossett
Annelise Christ Gould
Jason Graae
Enid Graham
Karen Graham
Ken Graham
William Graham
Kelsey Grammer

Brian A. Grandison
Barbara Granning
Gail Grate
Lucian Grathwol
Richard Gray
Marvin Grays
Fanni Green
Kenneth Green
William Greene
Bradley Greenwald
Adam Greer
Matthew Greer
Melody Greer
Casey Greig
Eric Greiling
Thomas Griffith
Thomas Grimm
William Grivna
George Grizzard
Michael Grodenchick
Bettina D. Gronning
Michael Gross
Karen Grunke
Richard Grusin
Michael Guido
Matt Guidry
Anne Gunderson
Carol Gustafson
K.C. Guy
Sean Haberle
Summer Hagen
Joseph Haj
Fiona Hale
Donna Haley
Brad Hall
Christopher Atwood Hall
George Hall
Georgine Hall
Margo Hall
Elizabeth Hallaren
Ben Halley, Jr.
William Halliday
Chad Hallonquist
Marc Halsey
Allen Hamilton
Douglas Hamilton
Melinda Page Hamilton
Shawn Hamilton
Gin Hammond
Oren Hamson
Stephen Hanan
James Handy
Arthur Hanket
Mary Hara
Brian Hargrove

Wiley Harker
Jennifer Harmon
James Harper
Steven Michael Harper
Helen Harrelson
Peter Harrer
Delphi Harrington
Harriet Harris
James Harris
James Hartman
Mike Hartman
Rosemary Hartup
Don Harvey
Michael Harvey
Ron Hasselman
Naomi Hatfield
Rana Haugen
Michael Hauser
Elaine Hausman
June Havoc
Trish Hawkins
Michael Hayden
Rob Haywood
Virginia Heathman
Paul Hecht
Cynthia Hechter
Tom Hegg
Jon Andrew Hegge
Mike Heitzig
Annette Helde
Terry Hempleman
Michael Hendricks
Steve Hendrickson
Sara Hennessy
Lance Henriksen
Maxine Herman
Peter Hermann
Sergio Hernandez
Scott Herner
Emil Herrera
John Herrera
Edward Herrmann
Jamie Hersch
John Noah Hertzler
Tom Hewitt
David Hibbard
Tana Hicken
Bryan Hicks
Munson Hicks
Richard Hicks
Allen Hidalgo
Dennis Jay Higgins
Richard Hilger
Terry Hill
Chuck Hilton

Kim Hines
Patrick Hines
Pat Hingle
Chase Hippen
Mary Hitch
Andrew Hoag
Mike Hodge
Patricia Hodges
Dennis Holland
Polly Holliday
Barbara Holmes
C. J. Holmes
Denis Holmes
Dean Holt
Ann Homan
Richard Hoover
Tim Hopper
Jay Hornbacher
James Horswill
John Horton
John Hoshko
Eric House
Bette Howard
Jordon Howard
Richard Howard
Jo Howarth
Otis Huber
Ruben Hudson
Joseph Hughes
Tara Hugo
Marceline Hugot
William Hulings
Kathleen Humphrey
Suzy Hunt
Hugh Hurd
James Hurdle
Michelle Hutchinson
Christopher Hutchison
Eric Hutson
Richard S. Iglewski
Thomas Ikeda
Dan Illian
Luke Ingles
Donna Ingram-Young
Anthony Inneo
Laura Innes
Christopher Innvar
Jim Iorio
Nate Irvin
Michael Isaacs
Susan Isenberg
Rex Isom, Jr.
Zeljko Ivanek
J. D. Steele Singers
J. J. Farley and the

Original Soul Stirrers
Robert Jackson
Todd Anthony Jackson
Tonia Jackson
Martin Jacox
Paulette James
Charles Janasz
Robert Jason
Thomas Jasorka
Joy Javits
Byron Jennings
Shanti Jensen
Keith Jochim
Amanda Johnson
Bill Johnson
J. Warren Johnson
Jody Johnson
Josie Johnson
Reginald Vel Johnson
Tammy Johnson
Justine Johnston
Charity Jones
Cheryl Tafathale Jones
Eleise Jones
James Earl Jones
Jeffrey Jones
Neal Jones
Robert Earl Jones
Seth Jones
Steven A. Jones
Ty Jones
Henry J. Jordan
Nancy L. Joseph
Shawn Judge
Gene Jundt
Leif Jurgensen
Christa Justus
Ricky Kahn
Stephen Kanee
Ellen Karas
Kathy Karas
David Karr
Vincent Kartheiser
Sevanne Kassarjian
Greg Kassmir
Art Kassul
Carole Kastigar
Cindy Katz
Joe Katz
Sasha Katz
Katie Kaufmann
Joann Kawamura
Elizabeth Keagy
Grace Keagy
Liam Kearns

Charles Keating
Stephen Keep
Nathan Keepers
Alvin J. Keith, Jr.
Eleni Kelakos
Kenneth Kelleher
Kevin James Kelly
Linda Kelsey
Martin Kelson
Roberta Kendrick
Heather Kendzierski
Dennis Kennedy
Margo Kennedy
Briana Kennedy-Coker
Karl Kenzler
Nicholas Kepros
Patrick Kerr
Philip Kerr
Ed Kershen
Sari Ketter
Anissa Keyes
Val Kilmer
Ann Kim
Jacqueline Kim
Randall Duk Kim
Matthew Kimbrough
Richard Kind
Adam King
Nelson King
Barbara Kingsley
Gary Kingsolver
Kelby Kirk
Laura Kirkeby
Hugh William Kirsch
Steven P. Kisner
Michael Kissin
Leo Kittay
Katie Kladt
Laurie Kladt
Christopher Klein
Lauren Klein
Werner Klemperer
Joseph Klimowski
Kevin Kling
Jacqueline Knapp
Marvette Knight
T.R. Knight
Alex Knold
Suzanne Koepplinger
Fred Koivumaki
Lara Kokernot
Larissa Kokernot
Joe Konicki
Sonja Kostich
Linda Kozlowski

Roger Kozol
Alissa Kramer
Heidi Kramer
Stephen Kramer
Warren Krech
Ken Krugman
Daniel Russell Kubert
Ronald Kubler
Timothy Kuhlman
Rick Kurnow
Kati Kuroda
Matthew Kwiat
Kenneth La Zebnik
Paul Laakso
Caroline Lagerfelt
Lois Laitinen
Mark Lamos
Robert Lanchester
Timothy Landfield
Karen Landry
Colin Lane
Meredith Lane
Stephen Lang
William Langan
Jodie Langel
Frank Langella
Randy Larsen
Daniel Larson
Michael Laskin
Lisa Lasley
Randy Sue Latimer
Miriam Laube
James J. Lawless
Darrie Lawrence
Gavin Lawrence
Michael Learned
Katherine Leask
Steve Lebens
Joel Lee
Linda Talcott Lee
Mark Lee
Timothy Lee
Patrick Leehan
Wendy Lehr
Russell Leib
Betty Leighton
Stephanie Lein
Jon Micheels Leiseth
Jessie Sinclair Lenat
Katherine Lenel
Zara Lenfesty
Rachel Leslie
T. Doyle Levertt
Michael Levin
Richard Levine

William Levis
Eric Levos
Hazel Lewin
John Lewin
Carol-Jean Lewis
Casey E. Lewis
Steve Lewis
Leo Leyden
Mitchell Lichtenstein
Jim Lichtscheidl
Mimi Lieber
Todd Liljenquist
Nancy Lillis
Marie Lillo
Tess Lina
Ryan Lindberg
Alan Lindblad
Delroy Lindo
James Lineberger
Rosaleen Linehan
Mary Ann Lippay
David Little
Jessica Litwak
Jose Llana
Glen Lloyd
John Bedford Lloyd
Lee Lobenhofer
Angela Lockett
Kee Lockhard
Beverly Lockhart
Kim Lockhart
Travis Lockhart
Tara Loewenstern
Cynthia Lohman
Andrew Long
Garrett Long
Richard Long
Sarah Long
Jennifer Abigail Lopez
Melinda Lopez
David Lowenstein
Gary Lowery
Tom Lubrano
Peter Lucas
Tif Luckenbill
James Ludwig
Clark Luis
Clyde Lund
Julie Lund
Chris Lundegaard
Patti LuPone
John Carroll Lynch
Meg MacCary
Heather MacDonough
John MacInnis

Joan MacIntosh
Jane MacIver
Bruce MacKay
John MacKay
Janet MacLachlan
Ann MacMillan
Peter MacNicol
Peter Macon
W.H. Macy
Donald Madden
Neil Maffin
Ken Magee
Joseph Maher
John Mahoney, III
Keith Mahoney
Ruth Maleczech
John Malloy
Larkin Malloy
Devin Malone
Charles Maloney
Tracey Maloney
Sarah J. Manci
David Manis
David Charles Mann
Emily Mann
Angela Mannella
Harold Manpin
Barbara March
Bruce Margolis
David Margulies
Terence Marinan
Vera Mariner
Lou Markert
Stephen Markle
David Marks
J.R. Marks
Ken Marks
Kevin Marron
Kaldin Marschel
Cynthia Martells
Dee Martin
J. Patrick Martin
John P. Martin
Sandra Martin
Sevanne Martin
Gary Martinez
Greg Martyn
Elizabeth Marvel
Nancy Marvy
Jack Matheson
Ann-Sara Matthews
Michael Matthys
Marcy Mattox
Roberta Maxwell
Daniel May

Deborah May
Michael Mayer
Mike Mazurki
John McAdams
Janet McCall
Bill McCallum
Kim McCallum
Sandy McCallum
Macon McCalman
Christopher McCann
Ryan McCartan
Jeff McCarthy
Laura McCarthy
Michael McCarty
Robbie McCauley
Steven McCloskey
John McCluggage
Matt McConnell
Noel McCoy
James McCreary
Galway McCullough
Daniel K. McDermott
Amy McDonald
Charlotte McDonald
Kelly McDonald
Leroy McDonald
Molly Sue McDonald
Mary McDonnell
Edwin J. McDonough
Frances McDormand
Evie McElroy
Yvonne McElroy
Paddy McEntee
Jerry McGarity
Randall McGee
Shawn McGill
Michael McGonagle
Katherine McGrath
William Biff McGuire
William Francis McGuire
William McGuire
Anthony J. McHie
Bill McIntyre
James McKeel
Richard McKenzie
Jack McLaughlin-Gray
Jason McLean
R. Bruce McLean
Pamela McMoore
Brendan McNellis
Patrick McNellis
Sean McNellis
Colin McPhillamy
Peter McRobbie
Richard McWilliams

Rod Mechem
Kathryn Meisle
Fred Melamed
Wayne Meledandri
Randle Mell
David Melmer
Katherine Meloche
Frank Melodia
Molly Meneely
Nii Adjetey Mensah
Sowah Mensah
Ron Menzel
Eda Reiss Merin
Robert John Metcalf
Edgar Meyer
Craig Michael
Ann Michels
Scott Mikita
Lilian Mikiver
Ragan Milan
Rene Milan
Eric Millegan
Betty Miller
David Miller
Reverend Earl F. Miller
Fred R. Miller
James Miller
Robert Milli
Barbara D. Mills
Alex Mingus
Laura Mirsky
Zaraawar Mistry
Elizabeth Maresal Mitchell
George Mitchell
Gregory J. Mitchell
Tony Mockus
David Monasch
James Monitor
Howard Moody
Bill Moor
Christina Moore
Christopher Liam Moore
Julianne Moore
Michael Moore
Natalie Moore
Peter Moore
Kathy Morath
Rozz Morehead
Judson Pearce Morgan
Michael Moriarty
Kiki Moritsugu
Joan Morris
Daver Morrison
Marlon Morrison
Greg Morrissey

Karen Morrow
Amy Morton
Joseph Moser
Tinia Moulder
Nancy Moyer
David Moynihan
Greg Mullavey
Todd Murken
Melissa Anne Murphy
Annie Murray
Jane Murray
Michelle Murray
P.J. Murray
George Muschamp
Rita Mustaphi
Jean-Paul Mustone
Robert Nadir
Ron Nakahara
Mariko Nakasone
Natalie Nakasone
Kathryn Nash
Lisa Naylor
Timothy Near
W. Alan Nebelthau
Ross Neil
Connie Nelson
Kris L. Nelson
Lee Mark Nelson
Novella Nelson
Ruth Nelson
Sarah Jane Nelson
Virginia Ness
Jan Neuberger
Audrey Neuman
Frederick Neumann
John Newcome
Jerry Newhouse
Andrew Hill Newman
William Newman
Paul Nickabonski
Clark Niederjohn
Kristine Nielsen
Patty Nieman
Amy Nissen
Tim Nissen
Nirupama Nityanandan
James Noah
Michael Nolan
Britta Lee Nordahl
Sarah Norman
Elizabeth Norment
David Norona
Aaron Michael Norris
Togba Norris
Kate Nowlin

Julie Ann Numbers
Seth Numrich
Sheldon Nunn
Pamela Nyberg
Gordon Oas-Heim
Mary O'Brady
Paul O'Brien
Caitlin O'Connell
Peggy O'Connell
Isabell Monk O'Connor
Jada D. Odom
Emma O'Donnell
Kevin O'Donnell
John M. O'Donoghue
Deborah Offner
Greta Oglesby
Terrence O'Hern
Robert Olinger
Rafael Oliveira
Wendy Oliver
Grace Olson
Michelle O'Neill
Richard Ooms
Alexander Orfaly
Richard Ortega
Milo O'Shea
David Ossian
Marin Osterberg
Megan Osterhaus
Gregg Ostrin
Charlie Otte
Laurence Overmire
Edwin C. Owens
Holly Palance
Sean Jeremy Palmer
Hugh Panaro
Joe Paparella
Reid Papke
Evan Pappas
Michael Parish
Stephanie Park
Craig Parker
Thomas Scott Parker
Sonja Parks
Lola Pashalinski
Robert Pastene
Bear Patin
Barbara June Patterson
Jay Patterson
Guy Paul
Joyce Paul
Erica Paulson
Virginia Payne
J. Robert Pearce
Jan Pearce

Erik Pearson
Teresa Pearson
Travis Pearson
Jonathan Peck
Jennifer Baldwin Peden
Deborah Pedersen
Maisi Pedersen
Tom Pedi
Stephen Pelinski
Jesse Penningston
Christopher Pennock
Timothy Perez
Patti Perkins
Max Perlman
Fern Persons
Brian Petchey
Franklin Peters
Lauri Peters
Ashley Marie Peterson
Deirdre Peterson
Elizabeth Peterson
Jenny Peterson
Patricia Ben Peterson
Suzanne Petri
David Philipson
Margaret Phillips
Patricia Phillips
John Pielmeier
David Hyde Pierce
Michael Pierce
Greg Pierotti
Don Pierson
Nyasha Pierson
Susan Pilar
Warren Pincus
Scott Pink
Fred Pinkard
Anne Pitoniak
Barbara Pitts
David Plant
Christopher Plummer
Alex Podulke
Jeanne Poepl
Kenneth Pogue
William Pogue
Joshua Pohja
Pamela Poitier
Joy Pommerenke
Peggy Pope
Julie Populas
Markus Potter
Arnell Powell
Michael Powell
Mike Powell
Leon Pownall

Francisco Prado
Ed Preble
Jordan Pressman
Carrie Preston
Faye M. Price
Alek Primrose
John Prosky
Robert Prosky
Jose Protko
Rajika Puri
Lester Purry
Gerald J. Quimby
Marcus Quiniones
John Rainer
David Rainey
Cliff Rakerd
T. Mychael Rambo
Maria Elena Ramirez
Richard Ramos
John Ramsey
Kevin Ramsey
Elisa Randall
Nickolas Rapacz
Gordana Rashovich
David Rasmussen
Ellen Rath
Noel Raymond
Gary Rayppy
Eileen Reagan
Nancy Reardon
Lance Reddick
Brian Reddy
Adam Redfield
Kevin Redmon
Joseph Regalbuto
Barton E. Regehr
Floyd Reichman
Barbara Reid
Dennis Reid
Paul Reighard
Odile Reine-Adelaide
Gary Reineke
Jon Reininga
Paris Remillard
Ralph Remington
Wendy Renee
Ido Reuben
Randy Reyes
William Rhys
Dena Olstad Rice
Rebecca Rice
Stacia Rice
Christopher Rich
James Richards
Lisa Richards

James Richardson
Lee Richardson
Amy Rickard
Leenya Rideout
Richard Riehle
Dudley Riggs
Eric Riley
Derdriu Ring
Ken Risch
Lia Rivamonte
Mary Rivard
Juan Rivera-LeBron
Kent Rizley
Linda Roberts
Laila Robins
Heather Robison
Kali Rocha
Kersten Rodau
Robynn Rodriguez
Reg Rogers
Ron Rogosheske
Jill Rogosheske
Patricia Roos
Wilberto Rosario
Mary Lou Rosato
Cristine Rose
Jill Rose
Irene Roseen
Ed Rosenberg
Wendy Rosenberg
Carol Rosenfeld
Clive Rosengren
Mark Rosenwinkel
Eliot Ross
Judith Ross
Alfred Rossi
Gastone Rossilli
Christina Rouner
Claude Rousseau
Mari Rovang
Martin Ruben
Amy Rudick
David Rudick
Stephen Rueff
Mercedes Ruehl
Charles Rule
Marc Rush
Ken Ruta
Nancy J. Ruyle
Steven Ryan
Thomas Jay Ryan
Steven Rydberg
Maya Saffrin
Janet Saia
Matthew Saldivar

Richard Sale
Sophia Salguero
Tracy Sallows
Andre Samples
Erik Sandberg
Socorro Santiago
Ronald Oscar Sarum
Tim Sattin
Tina Sattin
Hayden Saunier
Nick Savian
Louis Schaefer
Tara Schaefer
August Schellenberg
Jeanne M. Schiessl
Martha Schlamme
E. Richard Schlattman
Sara Schmidt
Peter Schmitz
Jana Schneider
Benjamin Schnickel
Peggy Schoditsch
Doug Scholz-Carlson
William Schoppert
Warren Schueneman
Armand Schultz
Charles Schuminski
Kurt Schweickhardt
Robert Scogin
Frank S. Scott
Monica Scott
Maurice Scroggins
Edward Seamon
Hardric Seay
Buffy Sedlachek
John Seitz
Kristin Elder Sellentine
Marquetta Senters
Michael Sevareid
Danny Sewell
Ryan Sexton
Maura Shaffer
Steve Shaffer
Omari Shakir
James Shanklin
Dan Sharkey
Barbara Sharma
Monti Sharp
Michele Shay
Paul Shenar
Bernie Sheredy
Jonathan Sherman
Willis Sherman
Armin Shimerman
Leonice Shinneman

Sandra Shipley
Sylvia Short
John Shuman
Charles A. Siebert
Margaret Silk
Leslie Silva
David Otto Simanek
Scholastica Simbi
William Simington
Gregory Simmons
Cleo Simonett
Marianne Simons
Kelli Simpkins
Parker Sipe
Rocco Sisto
Kate Skinner
Margo Skinner
Thomas Slater
Fern Sloan
Robert Sloane
William B. Smale
Andrea Smith
Ben Smith
Bo Smith
Connor Smith
Craig Smith
Fruud Smith
Gregory Stewart Smith
J. Walter Smith
Lois Smith
Priscilla Smith
Roger Guenveur Smith
Trevor Smith
J. Smith-Cameron
Arnold Soboloff
Mim Solberg
Melodie Somers
Gale Sondergaard
Robert Sonkowsky
John Soroka
Brian Sostek
Dale Soules
Daniel Southern
Robert Spanabel
Adrian Sparks
George E. Spelvin
Denny Spence
John Spencer
Cherie Sprosty
Brian Sprunck
Katherine Squire
Louella St. Ville
Lewis J. Stadlen
Richard Stafford
Alvah Stanley

Charles Stanley
Jean Stapleton
Robert Stattel
Dominique Staupe
Vincent Staupe
Christopher Stebnitz
Erik Steele
Fred Steele
Jevetta Andra Steele
Hadija Steen-Omari
Bronia Stefan
Adam Stein
David J. Steinberg
R. Stevens
Roy K. Stevens
Benjamin Stewart
Patrick Stewart
Casey Stewart-Lindley
Jerry Stiller
Henry Stram
Kelly Strange
Mary Straten
John E. Straub
Dean Stricklin
Ernest Stricklin
Henry Strozier
Will Sturdivant
Fred Stuthman
Bernadette Sullivan
Shannon Sullivan
Linda Sultze
Daniel Sunjata
Brian Sutherland
Vern Sutton
John Swanholm
Kraig Swartz
Tony Swartz
James Sweeney
Steve Sweere
Donovan Sylvest
Peter Syvertsen
Sandor Szabo
Bill Szobody
Theodore Szymanski
Kelly Taffe
Matt Talberg
Jason Tam
Jessica Tandy
Jill Tanner
Marianne Tatum
Andy Taylor
Heather Taylor
Jennifer Taylor
Kathy Taylor
Stephen Temperley

Rosalie Tenseth
Michael Tezla
Annie Thatcher
Maria Thayer
Marie-Francoise Theodore
Roy Thinnes
Deborah Thoemke
Lance Thoemke
Madlynn Thoemke
Peter Thoemke
Brenda Thomas
chandra thomas
Joe Nathan Thomas
Ray Anthony Thomas
Robin Thomas
Sheriden Thomas
Adrienne Thompson
Paul Thompson
Victoria Thompson
William W. Thompson
Peter Gregory Thomson
Jacqueline Thurik
Sharon Tibesar
Chad Tidgewell
Tim Tierney
John Tillotson
Angela Timberman
Barton Tinapp
Barbara Tirrell
Michael Tita
Lauren Tom
Peter Toran
Lorraine Toussaint
John Madden Towey
Shirin Devrim Trainer
Jan Triska
Eugene Troobnick
Christine Tschida
James Tucker
Patrick Tull
Louis Turenne
Scott Turi
Glynn Turman
Cedric Turner
Jake Turner
William Tynan
Matthew Vaky
Nathaniel Vaky
Nicholas Vaky
Carlos Alberto Valencia
Henrietta Valor
Jeffrey Van
Joan van Ark
Jill Van De Plasch
Kristin Van De Plasch

Raedell Van De Plasch
Granville Van Dusen
Peter Van Norden
Amy Van Nostrand
Amy Van Patten
Austene Van Williams
  Clark
Courtney B. Vance
Wendy vanden Heuvel
Terra Vandergaw
Noel Velez
Shirley Venard
John C. Vennema
Harley Venton
William Verderber
Kaili Vernoff
Tony Vierling
Tom Villard
Neil Vipond
Michael Vita
Peter Vitale
George Vogel
Peter Vogt
Ralph Vucci
Geoffrey Wade
Timothy Wahrer
Cliff Walinski
Andrea Kim Walker
Paul Walker
Gregory Wallace
James D. Wallace
James Wallace
Donald Wallen
Fiona Walsh
Jack Walsh
Joseph T. Walsh
Keliher Walsh
Maura Walsh
Richard Walters
Chris Ward
Suzanne Warmanen
Shannon Warne
Dennis Warning
Jennifer Warren
Thom Christopher Warren
David Warrilow
Maya Washington
Sharon Washington
Michael Watson
Danny Weathers
Margie Weaver
Brenda Wehle
Hy Weingarden
Jeff Weiss
Eric Weitz

Christopher Evan Welch
Charles Weldon
Christine Weller
Cynthia Wells
Kenneth Welsh
Dona Werner
Donald West
Monica West
Ryan West
Adam Western
Jack Wetherall
Ronnell A. Wheeler
Tony Whitbeck
Amelia White
Darryl E. White
Sophia White
Spence White
Tara White
William Whitehead
Ann Whiteside
Bradley Whitford
Jon Whittier
Margaret Whitton
Nancy Wickwire
Dianne Wiest
Jeremiah Wiggins
Alan Wilder
Wayne Wilderson
Claudia Wilkens
Arnold Wilkerson
Jeffrey Wilkins
William Byrd Wilkins
Stephen Willems
David William
Brandon Williams
James Austin Williams
Lanyard A. Williams
Regina Marie Williams
Shaun Williams
Joe Wilson, Jr.
Rainn Wilson
Sarah Grace Wilson
Tiffany Nicole Winesberry
Paul Winfield
Hy Wingate
Sally Wingert
James R. Winker
Kevin Winkler
Mel Winkler
Frederick Winship
Justin Winterhalter
Michael Winther
Sally Wissink
Meghan Wolf
John Leslie Wolfe

Andrea Wollenberg
Eunice Wong
Andrea Woods
Carla Woods
Elisha Woods
Jordan Woods
Alan Woodward
Claude Woolman
Rob Woronoff
Joyce Worsley
Aisha A. Wright
Charles Michael Wright
Ellyn Wright
Max Wright
Phyllis Wright
Wendell Wright
Todd Wronski
Mimi Wyche
Moira Wylie
Nicholas Wyman
Ray Xifo
Jeff Yagher
Stephen Yoakam
Ahanti Young
Alexandra Young
Steven B. Young
Harris Yulin
Edward Zang
Nick Zanides
Amber Joy Zemke
Stephen Zettler
Stephanie Zimbalist
Patrick Zweber

Sources and Credits

A fully footnoted copy can be accessed through the Guthrie Theater Archives (GTA). Many quotations from various Guthrie publications (GTA). Most anecdotes from interviews with the author, or submissions. Most newspaper clippings courtesy of Performing Arts Archives at the University of Minnesota Libraries, Minneapolis (PAA). Some quotes courtesy of Twin Cities Public Television (TPT). Every effort has been made to identify photos and photographers through the rather uneven Guthrie archives. We regret that, in some cases, the photographers are still unknown; forward any additions or corrections to the publisher for inclusion in later editions. 'Photo by' is abbreviated as ph b.

COVER
Building image, GTA; *The Three Sisters* ph by Marty Nordstrom.

CHAPTER 1
10-11, *Amadeus* ph b Michal Daniel, GTA; 12, *Medea* ph by Michal Daniel, GTA; 22, quote from Linda Sue Anderson; 23, *Can't Take It* ph by Donna Kelly, GTA.

SIXTIES COLLAGE
from upper left: lobbies, brochures, stage-hands, dedication, tickets, St. Paul posters, coll B. Brown; *Ui* poster, coll P Guilfoyle; committee and ticketing ph's, GTA; *Atreus* ph's b Gerald Brimacombe, GTA; outfits ph courtesy *Pioneer Press; Miser* ph b Marty Nordstrom, GTA.

SIXTIES
26, ph GTA; 27, clipping GTA; 29, ph GTA; 30, ph GTA; 30, clipping, GTA; 31, Rapson, On Stage: *25 Years at the Guthrie*, TPT; 32, Morison and Fliehr, *In Search of an Audience;* 33, clippings, coll B. Brown; 33, Mankato, Morison and Fliehr, *In Search of an Audience;* 34, ph by Marty Nordstrom, GTA; 34, tickets coll B. Brown; 35, Lady ph GTA; 35, fanfare ph courtesy *Star Tribune;* 36, Morison and Fliehr, *In Search of an Audience;* 36, brochures coll B. Brown; 37, ph by Marty Nordstrom, GTA; 38, ph by Marty Nordstrom, GTA; 40, ph from brochure, coll B. Brown; 41, ph courtesy Hennepin History Museum; 42, note coll B. Brown; 42, ph by Ron Bruncati, coll J. Bruncati; 43, clipping coll B. Brown; 43, eulogy excerpt, coll D. Babcock. **Seasons 1963-66:** ph's b Marty Nordstrom, GTA **1967-68:** ph's b Gerald Brimacombe, GTA **1969:** ph b Curt Anderson, GTA.

SEVENTIES COLLAGE
from upper left: staff ph coll L. Ambrose; Guthrie 2 ph GTA; contact coll M. Freij; staff ph coll S. Livingston; billboard ph GTA; press release, PAA; tickets coll L. Ambrose; '73, coll B. Brown; rendering coll S. Livingston; lobby ph b John L. Anderson, GTA ; class ph coll F. Bennett; stage door ph b John L. Anderson, GTA; bus ph GTA; Variety coll B. Brown; warm-up ph coll F. Bennett; football ph coll D. Babcock.

SEVENTIES
60, ph b John L. Anderson, GTA; 63, ph GTA; 64, fellows ph PAA; 64, *Mice,* ph b Act Two Photography, GTA; 65, ph's by Act Two Photography, GTA; 66, courtesy S. Wingert; 67, ph by Act Two Photography, GTA; 68, ph b Act Two Photography, GTA; 68, letter, GTA; 69, coll of M. Freij; 71, ph by Joseph Giannetti, coll D. Behl; 73, ph GTA; 75, ph b Boyd Hagen, GTA; 76, Efros ph b Boyd Hagen, GTA; 76, artisans ph coll J. Worthing; 77, ph b Boyd Hagen, GTA; 78, ph b Boyd Hagen, GTA; 79, ph b Bruce Goldstein, GTA. **Season 1970:** GTA. **1971:** ph b Donald Getsug, GTA **1972-76:** ph's b Act Two Photography, GTA **1977:** ph b Swifka, GTA **1978-79:** ph's b Boyd Hagen, GTA

EIGHTIES COLLAGE
from upper left: *Screens* phb Michal Daniel, GTA; posters GTA; costume ph coll J. Bruncati; GATE ph GTA; ticket sheet coll L. Ambrose; program GTA; symposium ph coll K. Dikken; *Earnest* ph by Joseph Giannetti, GTA; *Peer* ph by Joseph Giannetti, GTA; cost ph by Michal Daniel, coll D. Larsen; *Like It* ph b Joseph Giannetti; program GTA.

EIGHTIES
102, ph b Robert Ziegler, GTA; 103, Ciulei quote *On Stage: 25 Years at the Guthrie,* TPT; 103, Tschida *Inside Performance,* GTA; 105, Warrilow, *On Stage: 25 Years at the Guthrie,* TPT; 105, program GTA; 105, de Guzman, *Actors' Lives,* Holly Hill; 108, ph GTA; 109, ph by Kerry Dikken, coll K. Dikken; 110, GTA *Guys* and *Threepenny* ph b Joseph Giannetti; 111, ph coll B. Kingsley; 111, notebook GTA; 112, ph b Timothy Streeter, GTA; 113, ph b Kerry Dikken, coll K. Dikken; 114, ph GTA

Colonus; 115, ph b Michal Daniel, GTA; 119, ph b Michal Daniel, GTA; 120, ph GTA; 121, students ph GTA; 121, *Invalid* ph b Michal Daniel, GTA. **Seasons 1980-81** ph's b Bruce Goldstein. **1982-1988:** ph's b Joseph Giannetti. **1989:** ph by Michal Daniel.

NINETIES COLLAGE
from upper left: staff ph coll P. Guilfoyle; invitation coll B. Brown; all programs, flyers, schedules GTA; Medea ph by Michal Daniel, GTA; prop notes coll P. Guilfoyle; Garceau ph GTA; icebreaker GTA; *Twins* ph by Michal Daniel, GTA.

NINETIES
144, ph b Michal Daniel, GTA; 147, Stein, GTA; 148, Murphy, GTA; 148, letter coll J. Alspaugh; 150, ph GTA; 153, ph b Michal Daniel, GTA; 154, ph courtesy *Star Tribune;* 155, ph. Tim Rummelhoff, GTA; 157, *Christmas* ph b Michal Daniel, GTA; 157, Crow ph courtesy Star Tribune; 158, ph by Michal Daniel, GTA; 159, truck ph by Michal Daniel, GTA; 159, *Dream* ph by T. Charles Erickson, GTA. **Season 1990-99** ph's b Michal Daniel.

NEW CENTURY COLLAGE
from upper left: *Carmen* poster GTA; all programs, brochures and schedules GTA; costume page from study guide, GTA; ticket coll S. Livingston; Dowling/Miller ph b Tim Rummelhoff, GTA; *Hamlet* ph by Michal Daniel, GTA; costume ph by Michal Daniel, GTA; *Amadeus* ph b Michal Daniel, GTA.

NEW CENTURY
182, ph courtesy *Pioneer Press;* 184, plan GTA; 187, ph courtesy *Star Tribune;* 189, ph b George Byron Griffiths, GTA; 189, Amendt, GTA; 190, Cribbs, Baccarin, GTA; 190, ph by Michal Daniel, GTA; . 190-91, Miller-Stephany, Hatcher, GTA; 192, *Six* ph b Michal Daniel, GTA; 193, ph courtesy *Pioneer Press.* 194, ph b Michal Daniel, GTA; 194, Lee, GTA; 195, ph

courtesy *Star Tribune;* 196, Mee, GTA; 197, ph by T. Charles Erickson, GTA; 197, Levy, GTA; 198, *Molly,* ph by Michal Daniel, GTA; 199, *Sweeney* ph by Michal Daniel, GTA; 199, *Wintertime* ph by T. Charles Erickson, GTA; 199, *Thief* ph by Michal Daniel, GTA; 199, *Blood* ph by Michal Daniel, GTA; 200, *Pride* ph by Michal Daniel, GTA; 200, Frazzini, GTA; 200, Lane-Plescia, GTA; 201, Sordelet, GTA; 202, *Romeo* ph b Michal Daniel, GTA; 203, ph courtesy *Pioneer Press;* 204, ph b T. Charles Erickson, GTA; 205, ph GTA; 206, perf reports GTA. **Season 2000:** ph b ©Carol Rosegg. **2001-02:** ph's b T. Charles Erickson. **2003:** ph b Michal Daniel. **2004-2005:** ph's b T.Charles Erickson.

221, ph by T. Charles Erickson, GTA.

ACTOR SECTION
All photos by Mike Habermann Photography.

PHOTOGRAPHERS' INDEX

Every effort has been made to identify photos and photographers. We regret that, in some cases, the photographers are still unknown; forward any additions or corrections to the publisher for inclusion in later editions.

Act Two Photography: 64, 65, 65, 67, 68, 84-85, 86-87, 88-89, 90-91, 92-93.

Curt Anderson: 56-57.

John L. Anderson: 59 (lobby and stage door), 60.
Gerald Brimacombe: 25 (*Atreus*), 52-53, 54-55.

Ron Bruncati: 42.

Michal Daniel: 10-11, 12, 100 (*Screens*), 100 (costumes), 115, 119, 121, 140-141, 142 (*Twins*), 143 (*Medea*), 144, 153, 157, 158, 159, 160-161, 162-163, 164-165, 166-167, 168-169, 170-171, 172-173, 174-175, 176-177, 178-179, 181 (costumes), 181 (*Hamlet*), 181 (*Amadeus*), 190, 192, 194, 199, 200, 202, 214-215.

Kerry Dikken: 101 (symposium), 109, 113.

T. Charles Erickson: 159, 197, 204, 210-211, 212-213, 216-217, 218-219, 221.

Donald Getsug: 82-83.

Joseph Giannetti: 71, 100 (*Like It*), 101 (*Earnest*), 101 (*Peer*), 110, 126-127, 128-129, 130-131, 132-133, 134-135, 136-137, 138-139.

Bruce Goldstein: 79, 122-123, 124-125.

George Byron Griffiths: 189.

Mike Habermann Photography: 244 (all actors).

Boyd Hagen: 75, 76, 77, 78, 96-97, 98-99.

Donna Kelly: 23.

Marty Nordstrom: Cover (*The Three Sisters*), 24 (*Miser*), 34, 44-45, 46-47, 48-49, 50-51.

Carol Rosegg: 208-209.

Tim Rummelhoff: 155, 181 (Dowling).

Timothy Streeter: 112.

Swifka: 94-95.

Robert Ziegler: 102.

Index

Numbers in italics refer to images.

Numbers in bold refer to a page detailing a play's production information.

ST PAUL SEASON

ENRICO IV
MINNESOTA THEATRE COMPANY
CRAWFORD LIVINGSTON THEATRE
SAINT PAUL WINTER SEASON
MINNESOTA THEATRE COMPANY

MINNESOTA
THEATRE
COMPANY
WINTER SEASON

TANGO

**SHE STOOPS
TO CONQUER**

CRAWFORD
LIVINGSTON
THEATRE
SAINT PAUL

ENRICO IV
STOOPS

G

THE MINNESOTA THEATRE COMPANY
invites you to attend
A SERVICE OF DEDICATION
at the
TYRONE GUTHRIE THEATRE
Sunday, May 5, 1963 • 2:00 p.m.

OFFICIATING:
Rt. Rev. Msgr. James P. Shannon
President, College of St. Thomas

Rabbi Max A.

Rev. W

TYRONE GUTHRIE THEATRE